How to *Maximize* Your CHILD'S LEARNING ABILITY

Dr. Lauren Bradway

Barbara Albers Hill

SQUAREONE
PUBLISHERS

COVER DESIGNER: Phaedra Mastrocola
IN-HOUSE EDITOR: Joanne Abrams
TYPESETTER: Gary A. Rosenberg

Square One Publishers
115 Herricks Road
Garden City Park, New York 11040
(516) 535–2010
www.squareonepublishers.com

Library of Congress Cataloging-in-Publication Data

Bradway, Lauren Carlile.
  How to maximize your child's learning ability : a complete guide to choosing and using the best computer games, activities, learning aids, toys, and tactics for your child / Lauren Bradway, Barbara Albers Hill.
    p. cm.
  Includes bibliographical references and index.
  ISBN 0-7570-0096-7 (pbk.) 3456 9227 01/07
1. Teaching—Aids and devices—Handbooks, manuals, etc.
2. Neurolinguistic programming—United States—Handbooks, manuals, etc. 3. Learning ability—Handbooks, manuals, etc.
4. Learning disabled children—Education—United States—Handbooks, manuals, etc. I. Hill, Barbara Albers. II. Title.
LB1044.88 .B73 2004
372.133—dc21

                                        2003013554

Printed in Canada

·10   9   8   7   6   5   4   3   2   1

Contents

Acknowledgments

I am grateful to Barbara Hill, my coauthor, for the energy she brought to our project, and to Joanne Abrams, master wordsmith, who is our editor at Square One Publishers. Thanks to my good friend Darleene Harris, M.Ed., Coordinator of the Family-Centered Clinic, Child Study Center, University of Oklahoma Health Sciences Center, for generously sharing with me her expertise about learning problems in children. Two women inspired me in the writing of this book. The first is Mother Dorothy, who read aloud to me on Saturday afternoons in Moberly, Missouri, causing me to fall in love with reading. The second is my daughter, Isabel, who, from age two to twelve, willingly tried out every new toy and game I brought home from work. And I'll always be indebted to the hundreds of children, who, over the years, have shared their personal perspectives, frustrations, and insights, and in so doing, taught me about learning styles from the inside out.

Preface

This book is the result of my many years of helping children become more balanced learners and, as a result, more confident human beings. My training and clinical experiences have led me to select the best toys, games, activities, and software to use with the young clients that come to me for speech, language, and reading therapy. *How to Maximize Your Child's Learning Ability* will help you do the same for your child at home.

Within this book, I share with you the discovery that has helped me to help my clients—that pinpointing a child's personal style of learning is the first important step in helping him become a well-rounded and successful learner.

You'll find this book to be the perfect tool for identifying your learning style as well as that of your child, and for putting this new-found information to use during regular play times to head off potential classroom struggles and to lessen or eliminate any that already exist. As a result of your gentle guidance of his play times, your child will gain self-confidence and skills that will be important throughout his academic years and beyond.

My interest in children's learning styles began in the mid-1970s, and grew out of my private practice as a pediatric speech-language pathologist in Oklahoma City. While I saw some of my clients over a span of only a few months, others needed treatment for as long as ten years. My long-term observations revealed to me that learning problems emerge early and, without intervention, tend to last. Similarly, I noticed that the way in which a particular child learns—whether through his eyes, his ears, or his sense of touch—remains the same over time. Moreover, I found that by observing a young child's learning style, I could actually predict many of the academic problems he would encounter later in life. The little boy I saw at age two because he had not yet started talking, for instance, could be expected to encounter problems with reading when he got to first grade. And the five-year-old girl who had difficulty holding a crayon could be expected to return a few years later with problems in math.

That's when I started to think in terms of prevention. It occurred to me that if I could identify learning style as early as age two and three in my young clients, it might be just as easy to identify learning style in the first year of life. And if that was possible, I reasoned that the child's parents could take steps at home to actually prevent him from experiencing academic problems in the future.

To test my theory, I asked parenting-class members at the Infant Center in Oklahoma City to complete a checklist of behaviors typical of an infant, marking those items that best described their babies. (A copy of the checklist appears on page 40). I used educated guesswork to come up with my list of behaviors. It seemed likely, for instance, that a baby "Looker" would explore with his eyes and hands, enjoy toys he could manipulate, and delight in the sight of familiar faces and objects. A "Listener," I reasoned, would babble early and often, prefer toys that made noise, and respond quickly to familiar voices and to music. To be known as a "Mover," a baby would have to be physically active, achieve motor milestones somewhat ahead of schedule, and love to be held and rocked. Naturally, many babies would have characteristics from two or even three of the categories. Nevertheless, I suspected that a strong early preference would be evident.

When the parents had finished their task, I observed the babies interacting with toys and with their parents, and completed a second checklist for each one. Comparing my observations with those of the parents, I found our conclusions to be identical in almost every case. So learning style *could* be identified as early as the first year of life. This fact revealed an exciting possibility. With the knowledge of their baby's learning style, parents could begin to play in an *intentional way* with their child. By carefully selecting toys and activities, they could make use of everyday play times to reinforce natural strengths and develop weaker skills. By the time the child entered school, then, he would be a more balanced learner.

Why is it so important for a child to achieve learning style balance? Because a child left to learn through a single learning style preference will enjoy only limited achievements. Success in reading requires strong Listener skills, while a mastery of mathematics requires well-developed Looker skills. It's the lucky child who feels equally at home with all of his senses!

Fortunately, it's easy and fun to encourage new ways of perceiving and learning. For example, by making it a practice to sing, chant, and hum to a seemingly unappreciative Mover infant, you'll gradually sharpen his ability to listen. And while a baby Looker may initially be less than thrilled by extended periods of holding and rocking, persisting with these actions can increase his sensitivity to touch. In fact, once you begin to think in terms of your child's learning style, you'll automatically change the tone and style of your daily interactions with him, and find yourself choosing toys and techniques that both affirm a favored style and strengthen needed skills.

Bill and Judy Lenner, for example, used a number of the infant techniques presented in Chapter Two to encourage their eight-month-old Mover to meet their gaze when they spoke or sang to him, and to sit still long enough to enjoy a board book. The Freemans employed several of Chapter Three's recommendations for toddlers to improve their Looker daughter's vocabulary from fewer than ten words to a level that's appropriate for a two-and-a-half-year-old—and within only about six months. The Gonzalez family needed even less time, and some carefully chosen activities for preschoolers that they gleaned from Chapter Four, to help their Listener son learn to recall letters and numbers.

But what of the older child who gets top grades in language arts, but struggles endlessly with penmanship? Or the after-school soccer star who's in demand when teams are chosen in gym class, but holds a spot in his grade's lowest reading group? Can anything be done to help a child whose particular style of learning is already slowing his progress in a particular academic subject?

The answer is *yes!* Whether your child is two-and-a-half or twelve, in preschool or in junior high, the toys, activities, and techniques presented in this book can be used to help him maximize his potential. In *How to Maximize Your Child's Learning Ability,* you'll discover that although your child's learning style is an inborn and permanent feature, you can help him develop new ways of perceiving and, in so doing, round out his overall development.

Sprinkled throughout this book, you'll find Learning Style QuickChecks—similar in design to the one I developed for my Oklahoma City parenting class—tailored to age groups from babyhood through adulthood. These QuickChecks can help you identify your child's style of learning, as well as your own.

In Chapter One, you'll learn how your child's inborn learning style affects all areas of development. You'll also be alerted to red flags in a child's development—signals that what your child is experiencing is more than a learning-style problem.

Beginning with Chapter Two, you'll be taken step by step through infancy, toddlerhood, the preschool years, kindergarten, and grades one, four, and eight—key points in a child's development. In each of these chapters, you'll see the world through the eyes of three same-aged but different-style learners. For the sake of clarity, each child is presented as having one learning style, rather than the combination of styles that is often the case.

After offering the case studies, every chapter that deals with young children lists dozens of toys, games, and techniques appropriate for that particular age group. The suggestions are grouped according to the skill area you wish to improve—looking, listening, or moving. First, you'll learn how to enhance an existing skill through activities and toys that draw upon that skill. Then, you'll learn how to encourage the development of a lagging skill through activities and toys that are multisensory in nature—that involve both the sense to be developed and another sense. Those multisensory playthings and games that employ a child's preferred sense are, of course, the ones that will work best for him.

Beginning in first grade, children are expected to master reading, spelling, and math, while the ability to successfully complete class work and homework assignments becomes high priority. Chapter Six through Chapter Eight take a subject-by-subject look at the relationship of learning style to a child's school performance. Tips are provided for communicating with your child's teacher, choosing appropriate extracurricular activities, and selecting homework strategies that best suit the learning style of your child. In Chapters Seven and Eight—which discuss fourth and eighth graders, respectively—techniques are presented for improving your child's academic performance in specific subject areas, such as science, social studies, and language arts.

Because each chapter focuses on one age or grade, you'll find it easy to locate the information you're looking for. For instance, if your little learner is five years old, you can turn to Chapter Five, "Learning Styles in Kindergarten," to read about other children—Lookers, Listeners, and Movers—who are the same age as your child. These case studies, coupled with a QuickCheck designed for a five- to six-year-old, will allow you to easily determine your child's learning style. Chapter Five also offers a wealth of suggestions to enhance and develop kindergarten readiness skills, as well as a section on picking the best type of kindergarten class for each style of learner.

A special chapter, Chapter Nine, "Learning Problems and Solutions," is designed to provide guidance for a parent whose child may require assistance beyond learning-style-based techniques. This chapter examines learning differences that can turn into learning disabilities, as well as learning disabilities of other origins. Information is provided about educational and diagnostic testing, definitions of common diagnostic terms are included, and treatments and therapies are examined, with suggestions provided for parents who wish to offer their child maximum support at home.

Finally, a Recommended Reading List is included for those parents who wish further information about learning patterns in children and adults, and a Buyer's Guide directs you to distributors of those recommended toys, games, and educational materials that you may not be able to find in your local stores.

As you browse through the lists of toys, techniques, and learning strategies, please keep in mind that my suggestions for the enhancement of your child's learning skills are suggestions only! I don't for a moment intend that they serve as ironclad rules around which parents should restructure their home lives, nor do I feel that it's critical to try out each and every one. What's important is that you consider your child's and your own personalities when making toy and activity selections. Each of us is unique, after all, and an idea that you find quite appealing or that you feel would be just perfect for your little learner may be discarded just as quickly by the next parent!

Also, I encourage you not to restrict yourselves to the recommended toys and educational materials found here. Your own search of store shelves and manufacturers' websites may well turn up something you like even better.

Finally, please remember that your goal is to help your child move through his childhood and teen years as a happy, well-adjusted individual with many learning options. If your child is of school age, you can certainly look for improvement from one report card to the next. If he is younger, and so has little incentive to focus his energy on any sort of self-improvement, winning him over to a particular toy or activity may take several tries spanning several months. But whether your child is fourteen months or fourteen years of age, you're sure to achieve the best results when your times together are unhurried and relaxed and kept short enough to end on a high note.

My clinical experience has proven over and over again that what a child is like in the crib foreshadows what he'll be like in the classroom. It stands to reason, then, that the earlier parents understand their child's style of learning, the better their chance of helping him improve and broaden that style by gently shaping his home experiences. We know that early learning preferences tend to hold firm over time. Although one learning style will take the lead throughout your child's life, *How to Maximize Your Child's Learning Ability* can enable you to reinforce those talents with which your child was blessed at birth while also encouraging the skill areas that do not come as naturally. The outcome will be a nicely balanced, confident learner and a happier home life for everyone.

A Word About Gender

Your child is certainly as likely to be a boy as a girl. However, our language does not provide us with a genderless pronoun. To avoid using the awkward "he/she" or the impersonal "it" when referring to your child, while still giving equal time to both sexes, the feminine pronouns "she," "her," and "hers" have been used in odd-numbered chapters, while the male "he," "him," and "his" appear in all the rest. This decision was made in the interest of simplicity and clarity.

Introduction

I met Joey Billings near the end of his kindergarten year. This bright six-and-a-half-year-old had started the school year as an inquisitive, outgoing chatterbox, but an ensuing eight-month struggle with printing, drawing, and letter recognition had left his self-esteem badly battered. Joey had taken to calling himself "dumb-head" and "crazy," and lately had begun to invent reasons to stay home from school.

Because of his classroom difficulties, his kindergarten teacher recommended diagnostic testing and possible special class placement for first grade. Joey's mother feared that testing would confirm her son's feelings of inadequacy. She brought Joey to my office to learn what she could do to help him regain his self-confidence and end his kindergarten year on a positive note.

To determine Joey's learning style, I asked Mrs. Billings to tell me about his early development and to fill out my Learning Style QuickCheck for six-year-olds. I then did some testing, observed Joey at play, and reviewed a portfolio of his kindergarten work.

It immediately became clear that Joey was a *Listener* by learning style, with a well-developed vocabulary and excellent verbal skills. His lagging skills in the *Looker* area—specifically, in visual recall, printing, and eye-hand coordination—were what was causing him so much distress.

Throughout my sessions with Joey and his mother, I called upon my background in educational diagnosis, my familiarity with the strengths and weaknesses of Listeners, and my years of experience with children who have similar problems. Mrs. Billings, an expert source of information about her son, had already shared her personal observations with me. She was now about to take on the role of teacher, developing Joey's Looker skills for school success.

Three issues were resolved from the start. First, Joey's "home therapy" program must be fun. To build visual skills, simple mazes and snap-together blocks replaced the puzzles that Joey found so frustrating, and projects and outings were planned with his interests in mind. For example, an ant farm and trips to a planetarium and video arcade were used as enjoyable ways to focus visual attention. Game-like strategies were employed to incorporate Joey's strong verbal skills with beginning reading and writing. Joey was having difficulty recalling the shape of the letter *T*, for instance, so it was printed in green and given a name: "T is a tree." Unable to set his letters on a line when printing, Joey found that he could do so when the bottom line was colored green and he could pretend to set each letter on the "grass." Some letters, like "g," reached underground. Others, like "b," had parts that touched the sky.

Second, and equally important, was my recommendation that Joey's mother present all activities and techniques as *play*, rather than a prescription for academic success. That way, Joey would not feel pressured to "succeed."

Finally, it was vital that tactics and strategies be implemented in a minimum of time and as part of the family's daily routine. Joey's mother, like so many other parents with jobs and children, simply couldn't squeeze extended periods of one-to-one time into her day.

Just four months later, and in plenty of time for first grade, Joey's readiness skills tested on grade level. He could now remember the names of letters and print them from memory. Throughout his first grade year, Mrs. Billings continued to tailor her son's home experiences to his Listener learning style, and to her delight, his June report card praised both his strong reading skills and his positive attitude toward school!

I've met many Joeys over the years. Some have been Listeners just like him, needing to develop Looker skills for school success. Others have been Lookers, with excellent eye-hand coordination, but difficulty following directions and hearing the distinction between sounds—abilities critical when learning to read. Still others have been Movers, with great coordination, but problems with both auditory and visual recall. No matter what the lagging skills that led their parents to consult me in the first place, an understanding of their child's learning style enabled these parents to help their children in the same way Mrs. Billings helped Joey.

Therapeutic activities approached at home through inborn learning styles allow a child to have fun while bolstering a weak skill. Multisensory teaching, which is based on the same practice of appealing to two or more senses simultaneously, has long been an accepted practice in the field of education. Science kits, math manipulatives, and books on tape are just a few examples of multisensory materials for classroom use.

Because we know that certain academic subjects rely heavily on specific learning-style strengths, it is possible to predict those children who will have difficulty with particular subjects. This means that by knowing what to look for, we can actually *prevent* certain types of learning problems by tailoring a baby's or toddler's toys, outings, and even physical care to his innate learning style. By minimizing a child's academic frustration while encouraging his well-roundedness, sociability, and confidence, Mom and Dad stand to gain a better understanding of their youngster's needs and, ultimately, a happier parent-child relationship.

Joey was a client, so I had the opportunity to guide his home therapy program in person during my office sessions with him and his mother. *How to Maximize Your Child's Learning Ability*—which includes the same background information, the same Learning Style Quick-Checks, and the same explanations of toys and techniques that I use in a clinical setting—is a personal guide to creating a home therapy program for your child. Within these pages, I share with you the techniques and methods I use daily in my practice with children. You'll learn how to identify your child's learning style, and how to develop activities and interactions that encourage your youngster's less-favored skills while reinforcing those areas in which he naturally shines. With commitment and time, be it several weeks or several months, you'll begin to see the emergence of a more self-assured, balanced learner who has a greater chance for classroom success.

Read the case histories and use the QuickChecks, and you'll gain a deeper understanding of the way your child learns. Try the activities and techniques recommended for your child's age and learning style, and you'll discover that you can incorporate a multitude of learning experiences within your family's daily routine. Perhaps most important, you'll find that you can enjoy each other and have fun along the way!

CHAPTER ONE

Learning Styles and Lifestyles

When you step out the door on a spring morning, what is it about your surroundings that seems to command your attention? Do you first notice the violets blooming on the windowsill across the street and the fact that everyone suddenly seems to be wearing pastel colors? Do you sense the sun's warmth and the way the stiff breeze feels as it ruffles your hair and clothing? Or do you find yourself glancing toward the street sweeper hissing its way around the corner while you idly wonder whether your neighbor is ever going to replace that missing muffler?

It's more than coincidence that you find yourself drawn above all else to the sights, the sensations, or the sounds around you. Throughout our lives, we use all of our senses to learn, but tend to consistently favor one sense over the others. This natural preference dictates how we learn best—by looking, by listening, or by moving—as well as what we learn and how quickly we are able to learn it. Quite often, this preference also helps shape our attitude toward the whole educational process.

This chapter contains information that will familiarize you with the Lookers, Listeners, and Movers in your life. A Learning Style Quick-Check for Parents (see page 16) will enable you to identify your own learning style, and you'll discover how this style colors your daily dealings with your child, whose own learning style can either complement or clash with yours. Then, you'll be given a look at some common child-development stumbling blocks, as well as information on professionals who can help your child overcome these problems.

UNDERSTANDING THE THREE LEARNING STYLES

A substantial capacity for achievement is programmed into every one of us at birth. As adults, we'd certainly like to be able to say we've fulfilled our potential; but many of us, thinking back to past classroom struggles or disinterest in school, have good reason to suspect otherwise! Consider the valedictorian who later finds herself limited to low-profile jobs because of problems relating to clients and coworkers. Or the dynamic public speaker who gives up her dream of college teaching because of poor writing skills. Or the gifted high school athlete who is wooed to a prestigious university on scholarship only to buckle under academic pressures during her freshman year. Fortunately, today's parents can rescue their children from similar fates.

Throughout our lives, we learn by absorbing and using different bits of information from the world around us. Researchers and educators make reference to "visual," "auditory," and "kinesthetic" or "tactile" learners, depending on whether the subjects in questions most often rely on their eyes, ears, or sense of touch. However, I've found it simpler to use the terms "Lookers," "Listeners," and "Movers" to describe the way the children in my practice learn best.

While there's certainly no right or wrong way to learn, nor is there a way to handpick one's learning style, my years of working with youngsters have convinced me of the tie between well-developed Looker and Listener skills—those skills that allow us to follow directions, visualize, verbalize, remember, and reproduce material—and a child's classroom and social well-being. Without fail, stronger skills have meant happier, better-rounded children. So the matter of learning style surely warrants close attention from parents!

Is there a connection between gender and learning style? Might girls have an easier time than boys fitting into the classroom setting? It depends. You see, many girls favor the Listener style of learning, being sensitive to sounds and attentive to such social cues as speech pattern and tone of voice. They also tend to have larger vocabularies and to speak earlier than boys. It's been shown that many boys, on the other hand, have sharper visual skills, better coordination and muscle control, and a more accurate sense of space than their female counterparts. So boys are more often Lookers, who possess some of the skills that will benefit them as schoolchildren, or Movers, who won't find the going as easy.

There are certainly as many exceptions to this rule as there are female athletes and artists, or male lecturers and composers. It's also important to remember that learning patterns aren't always clearly defined and may be found in combination with a second style, as in Looker-Movers or Looker-Listeners. But you're bound to recognize a number of people you know in the following descriptions, because a great many people clearly exhibit one particular style.

What Are the Characteristics of a Looker?

Lookers are visual learners who rely on the sense of sight when absorbing information. They are naturally drawn to sights of familiar objects, and quickly pick up on and remember visual cues such as motion, color, shape, and size. Most Lookers possess excellent eye-hand coordination, and have an inborn tendency to look at something and then quickly put their hands to work to show what they've learned about it. In fact, most Lookers excel at all fine motor activities—that is, activities that involve both the eyes and the small muscles such as those found in the fingers.

Baby Lookers, for example, prefer gazing at the pictures and turning the pages of a book to actually listening to the story. Lookers in preschool and kindergarten are attracted to puzzles, building sets, the computer, cutting and pasting, and other activities that involve their eyes and hands. Drawing and printing come easily, as does the memorization of word configurations by the beginning reader. It comes as no surprise that Lookers go on to enjoy video games, the Internet, board games, art projects, crafts and models, and TV sports.

Lookers meet fine motor milestones—those aided by their superior eye-hand coordination—with ease. Because Lookers tend to ignore other types of stimulation in favor of the sights around them, however, they must work at developing their language ability, their social skills, and their full-body coordination.

What Are the Characteristics of a Listener?

Listeners are auditory learners, with a preference for sounds and words over information taken in by either sight or touch. Since stimulation to the ears translates into spoken language, Listeners tend to be early talkers and possess very elaborate vocabularies.

As babies, Listeners are easily soothed by music and familiar voices, and delight in imitating sounds. Listener toddlers and preschoolers love to sing and recite songs and rhymes, ask a seemingly endless stream of questions, and have clear, precise speech. They show an early interest in reading, and in the primary grades love to read aloud and are able to follow oral directions with ease. As you can imagine, older Listeners enjoy listening to CDs and the radio, are quick to memorize, and favor games that involve speaking aloud, like *Jeopardy* and *Balderdash*. They like to read for pleasure, and often involve their friends in making up and acting out stories.

Because Listeners concentrate so much energy on language, it's not unusual for them to lag behind their peers in areas commonly associated with sight and touch—namely, visual and motor skills.

What Are the Characteristics of a Mover?

Movers are tactile (kinesthetic) learners, preferring hands-on learning through both touch and movement. The information that Movers take in through the sense of touch translates into gross motor movement—large-muscle activity involving the arms, hands, legs, and feet.

Movers are usually restless, wiggly infants who are soothed most easily by rocking and cuddling. They are early crawlers and walkers, and during the preschool years are drawn to climbing, jumping, block building, and riding toys. Their natural coordination and excellent sense of space result in their taking more physical risks than other children.

By kindergarten, most Movers' problems with sitting still and paying attention come into play. Full-body activities in wide-open spaces are more their style! By first grade, fidgeting and distractibility have caused many Movers to fall behind in academic areas, while their seeming fearlessness and commanding physical presence have made them leaders outside the school. At the same time, the frantic pace typical of most Movers makes them impatient and easily frustrated. Their needs are immediate, and their willingness to pursue difficult tasks almost nil. Movers are also an emotional lot—as quick to anger as they are to share a laugh.

Older Movers delight and excel in sports and outdoor activities, from soccer, swimming, and martial arts to camping, biking, and animal care. But their continued focus on the physical, often to the exclusion of sight and sound stimulation, typically leads to language delays and classroom difficulties.

HOW PARENTAL LEARNING STYLE INFLUENCES A CHILD'S STYLE

What type of learner are *you*, the parent? The answer, you'll soon see, can have tremendous implications for both your child's school and social success and your own ability to encourage her along the way. To determine your personal learning style, take the Learning Style QuickCheck for Parents on page 16. You're likely to find your responses either divided somewhat equally between two of the learning styles, or heavily weighted to just one style. In either case, you'll have a clear picture of the method or methods you prefer to use to absorb information from the world around you.

The learning-style label you've just assumed will prove to be a very useful tool as you continue through the chapters ahead, for when adapting the described methods and materials to your own child in your own home, you're bound to find that understanding yourself will help you understand *her!* In my work, you see, I've found that until parents recognize their own learning style, most assume that their children take in information from their surroundings just as they, the parents, do. This assumption is fine when parent and child happen to share the same learning style, because Mom or Dad, calling on her or his own past experiences, can react to the child's efforts to socialize and learn with understanding and realistic expectations. But to encourage the well-roundedness that will pay a child such big dividends later, all of her senses must be exercised. To do this, both parents and child sometimes have to venture into sensory territory that's unfamiliar to them.

And what of the parent and child with *different* learning styles? Not surprisingly, they face more of a challenge, with the path of their interaction frequently made rocky by the simple fact that one's inborn gift may quite naturally be the other's weakest area. But, when this happens, a bit more patience and a dose of self-discipline are really all that's necessary for the two to work and play together successfully.

Picture the different experiences of a Mover mother—an avid cross-country skier—and her Listener husband—a freelance writer—as they relate to their somewhat clumsy, very sociable four-year-old daughter, who's a Listener like her father. Mom loves to encourage the girl's physical side with riding toys and sandbox play, but finds herself depending on reminders from the child herself to read her nightly bed-time story. Father and daughter, on the other hand, prefer listening to music and playing *Monopoly Junior* to the equally important T-ball games and playground trips. In their efforts to help their daughter become a balanced learner, you see, both parents must sometimes put aside their personal preferences. But to their delight, Mom and Dad each get just as many opportunities to share with their daughter the activities they find most exciting.

From the very start, it's natural for parents to unconsciously offer their children the types of stimulation they enjoy themselves. For instance, the insurance-broker mother, a Listener, fills her baby's room with rattles and bells, musical toys, and even a radio. Meanwhile, Dad, a carpenter, acts on the well-developed sense of touch he shares with other Movers as he rinses baby's sheets twice for softness, diligently fills the humidifier every night, and moves the crib away from a drafty window. And this practice doesn't end with babyhood. Parents, in fact, approach many child-rearing tasks from the vantage point of their per-sonal learning styles, with Mover Dad turning the child's nightly bath into an opportunity for a rubdown and powder massage, while Lis-tener Mom seizes the moment to talk about soap bubbles or the strange workings of the bath sponge.

And the child's reaction? She either encourages or discourages more of the same stimulation with her instinctive responses, which stem just as naturally from her own learning style as her parents' actions do from theirs. Your infant may turn toward the sound of your voice, widen her eyes at the sight of something special you've shown her, or ignore you in favor of her own body movements. Your pre-schooler may leap at the chance to play with you and maintain interest in the activity, or allow her attention to drift elsewhere. And your older child may respond to your words and overtures with eagerness and questions, or give you the unmistakable feeling that you've been tuned out! Depending on your learning style and on hers, you see, the play-things and activities you've been offering your child may be either what she naturally craves or what she instinctively ignores. But even when your attempts at interacting seem unappreciated because they don't happen to reinforce your child's inborn learning style, persistence on your part will encourage her to "stretch" in areas vital to her overall development.

Your own learning style has significance beyond the kinds of stimulation you offer your child. An awareness of it can actually help you or your spouse understand your youngster's frustrations. It's quite common for my clients' parents to admit to having faltered in the same academic or social areas as their child. "Math was my hardest subject, too," one father, a disc jockey, told me. "I could never memorize math facts. I'm embarrassed to say it, but I was still counting on my fingers in high school."

A mother of a struggling reader confided, "I could never sound out words either, so I know what my daughter is going through. Unfortunately, I'm not much help to her, because I still don't know how!"

I meet parents of preverbal two-and-a-half-year-olds who were late talkers themselves, parents of overly aggressive kindergarteners who shudder at memories of their own childhood tantrums, parents of socially reluctant preschoolers who are themselves quite timid—and the list goes on and on. Exactly how intelligence and learning styles are inherited is not clearly understood, but there is strong evidence that children often take after a parent or a parent's family in both of these areas.

Dr. Rita Dunn, director of the Center for Study of Learning and Teaching Styles at St. John's University in New York, and Dr. Kenneth Dunn, professor and chair of the Department of Educational and Community Programs at Queens College, City University of New York, have spent nearly thirty years researching learning patterns. In their work with clients, they've observed time and again that a familial connection exists between the learning style of grandparents, parents, and children.

Richard Restak, MD, neuropsychiatrist and clinical professor of neurology at George Washington University Medical Center, was one of the first researchers to observe the strong biological component in learning style. He spelled this out in his now classic book, *The Brain: The Last Frontier.* This book supports the idea of inherited learning style, concluding that the presence of pronounced styles in earliest infancy makes it possible to rule out environmental influence in favor of heredity as a cause of learning patterns.

In dozens of cases, twins and siblings reared separately have "found" each other years later. Their astounding similarities in personality, career choice, and a host of preferences in areas such as hairstyle and mode of dress make another strong case for the inheritance of sensory preference. During the course of my own practice, I've found that in over 80 percent of my cases, a child's learning style has been either identical to that of one parent, or a blend of both parents' styles. Another 10 percent of parents are quick to liken their child to a close relative. Particularly when learning disabilities are present, as can happen when learning-style preference exists in an extreme form, family patterns are so strong that genetic counseling is often recommended to prepare a learning-disabled parent for the likelihood of producing a child with a similar disability.

You can see evidence of this heredity factor every time you catch yourself thinking, "Gosh, she's exactly like her mother (or grandfather or aunt)!" following anything from a child's disastrous attempt at ice skating, to her delight in long afternoons curled up with a book, to her furious keyboard banging because her piano-playing fingers won't do her bidding. Actually, these wry observations of similarity to a family member are a lot more than casual comments. They're proof of how obvious children's learning styles can be.

So in the long run, it's possible that you and your child will interlock like puzzle pieces because you share a learning style. But it's just as likely that she'll favor the style of your spouse (or your brother or your mother), making her a very different type of learner from you. And, of course, learning styles can be expected to differ even more in adoptive, step, and foster families, where a match isn't genetically dictated at all.

Whether your child's sensory preferences are like yours or not, there's no question that they will affect every aspect of her life, from social behavior, to leisure activities, to tolerance for adversity. Even family relationships may be shaped by these preferences, as child and parent or child and sibling approach each other according to their own styles. You'll be sure of both your child's style and your own once you've completed the QuickChecks in this and other chapters. More important, you'll soon learn the steps you can take to help your child maximize her learning ability by developing *all* her learning skills.

CAN IT BE MORE THAN A LEARNING STYLE PROBLEM?

Occasionally, social and learning difficulties may persist despite a par-

Red Flags in a Child's Development

Certain conditions and behaviors that appear during the course of infancy and childhood may signal a problem that requires professional assistance. This inset outlines what you should look for and where you can turn for help. A child may shows several of the red flags listed in a particular category—language, for instance—or show only one. In either case, it's a good idea to consult the appropriate expert listed below. The inset on page 251 explains the focus and qualifications both of those professionals mentioned here and of others to whom you may be referred.

Language

In the area of language, a child should be seen by a family physician, pediatrician, or audiologist if she shows the following behavior:

- In the first year of life, she does not turn to the source of sound.
- At age one, she does not respond when her name is called.

A child should be seen by a speech-language pathologist if she shows the following behavior:

- At age two, she has not yet said her first word.
- From the time she begins to talk, she has consistently unintelligible speech.
- At age three, she has not combined words into short sentences.
- At age three, she frequently repeats words and phrases, and she seems to struggle—blinking and stammering, for example—to get the words out.
- In the first grade or later, she regularly mispronounces certain sounds.
- In the first grade or later, she has trouble with phonics and cannot blend letter sounds or sound out printed words.

Gross Motor Skills

In the gross motor area, a child should be seen by a pediatrician or family practitioner if she shows the following behavior:

- In infancy, she appears "floppy" and has unusually weak muscle tone.
- At age one, she cannot sit without support or crawl with alternating arms and legs.
- She never seemed to stabilize from the time she learned to walk, and still falls often and appears excessively awkward or clumsy.

> - She has great difficulty learning to ride a bike, skate, hit a ball, or perform other activities typical of her age group.
>
> ### Fine Motor Skills
>
> In the fine motor area, a child should be seen by a pediatrician or family practitioner if she shows the following behavior:
>
> - During the first year of life, she cannot follow moving objects with her eyes.
>
> - During the first year, she fails to make eye contact with family members.
>
> - In the preschool years, she is slow to develop such self-help skills as feeding, dressing, or hand-washing.
>
> A child should be seen by a developmental optometrist or ophthalmologist if she has the following difficulty:
>
> - During her school years, she has difficulty copying from the chalkboard, often loses her place while reading, or tires quickly from reading.

ent's best efforts to rectify them, because the problem stems not from a child's learning style, but from factors such as hearing loss, attention deficit, or poor vision. If you suspect that there's a reason other than learning style for your child's difficulty with reading or math, relating to others, articulation, or coordination, or if you sense that her problems are too severe for you to remedy, it may pay to seek advice from medical and educational professionals trained to work with these types of developmental delays. For details on what to look for and when to take this important step, please see the inset "Red Flags in a Child's Development," on page 13. For further information on learning problems, see Chapter Nine, "Learning Problems and Solutions."

WHY IDENTIFY AND MODIFY LEARNING STYLE?

What of children whose development is somewhat uneven, but within seemingly normal limits. Couldn't we just leave them alone? There's certainly nothing *wrong* with a Looker child who, left to her own devices, grows up to be a rather reticent computer whiz. Nor is it the end of the world when a high school Listener, her weaker skills similarly undeveloped, opts out of science and math courses as soon as she can, because those grades are playing havoc with her cumulative average. And it's a rare classroom that doesn't contain a few Movers, marking time as they wait for the dismissal bell that signals freedom from classroom frustrations. But life can hold so much more for these children that it doesn't seem fair to relegate them to a humdrum existence when parents can, with so little effort, round out those young lives with special activities and new approaches—all for the purpose of opening every possible door.

Some information, a bit of organization, and access to tried-and-true toys and techniques are all you need to first understand how your child learns and then maximize her ability to do so. To find out exactly how to extend your child's options for the future by adding a healthy—and mutually enjoyable—balance to her learning skills, read on!

LEARNING·STYLE QUICKCHECK FOR PARENTS

Directions: Check all statements that best describe you. Then total the checks in each column and compare column totals. You'll probably find that most of your answers fall into one or two of the three categories, indicating which of the learning styles you favor.

LOOKER	LISTENER	MOVER

1. Communication: When talking with others . . .

LOOKER	LISTENER	MOVER
❏ I watch the speaker carefully.	❏ I consider myself a good listener.	❏ I often touch the person I'm speaking to.
☑ I prefer to observe rather than talk, and tend to be quiet in a group.	☑ I love to talk.	☑ I tend to express myself nonverbally, using gestures.
❏ I speak in simple, clear language.	❏ I have a large vocabulary.	☑ Sometimes I have difficulty finding the right words to say.

2. Pastimes and Hobbies: In my leisure time . . .

LOOKER	LISTENER	MOVER
☑ I enjoy games like *Scrabble, Monopoly,* and *Pictionary.*	❏ I like verbal games like *Password.*	❏ I enjoy being active and participating in sports.
☑ I often watch movies and television.	☑ I frequently listen to CDs and read novels or poetry.	❏ I like to observe the action of ice hockey, races, rodeos, and soccer.
☑ I express myself with my hands through painting and crafts.	☑ I express myself verbally, through talking or writing to friends.	☑ I prefer the full-body expression of dancing, gymnastics, and swimming.

3. Motor Skills: How I feel about my physical self . . .

LOOKER	LISTENER	MOVER
☑ My fine motor skills are better than my gross motor skills; I'm good with my hands.	❏ I'm not well coordinated.	❏ I'm very well coordinated.
❏ I prefer spectator sports.	❏ I tend to avoid sports and outdoor activities.	☑ I enjoy outdoor activities like camping, climbing, and fishing.

4. Feelings: Emotionally . . .

LOOKER	LISTENER	MOVER
❏ I'm somewhat inhibited and do not often reveal my feelings.	❏ I readily talk about my feelings.	☑ I tend to be impatient and easily frustrated. I'm aware of my feelings, but don't necessarily label them.

❏ I'm embarrassed by others' emotional outbursts.	❏ I'm sympathetic to others' feelings and problems, and am a good listener.	☑ I'm empathetic to others' feelings. I laugh and cry easily, and frequently experience emotional highs and lows.

5. Memory: When remembering . . .

☑ I write down what I need to recall and find cue cards helpful.	❏ I say aloud what I have to remember.	☑ I recall actions easier than the spoken or written word.
☑ I easily form mental pictures.	❏ I talk to myself and can hear a voice in my mind.	❏ I do not readily form auditory or visual impressions, and have difficulty recalling facts.
☑ I often use a highlighter when going over written material.	❏ I tape-record material to help myself recall it.	☑ I "act out" to help myself remember specific information.

6. At work: On the job . . .

☑ I need lots of space and don't like to sit or stand too near others. I work best alone.	❏ I thrive on others' company, don't like to work alone, and enjoy bouncing ideas off coworkers.	☑ I like to be near others but not necessarily to talk. I enjoy working with others.
☑ I frequently use a flow chart to keep track of my projects.	☑ I talk to myself when working.	❏ I have difficulty meeting deadlines.
☑ I insist on keeping to the agenda at meetings.	☑ I enjoy business meetings, and like to talk to and hear the views of others.	❏ I avoid meetings when possible, and find it difficult to sit still and concentrate for long periods of time.

TOTALS: _____ LOOKER   _____ LISTENER   _____ MOVER

CHAPTER TWO

Learning Styles in Infancy

In the first weeks of life, babies demonstrate their Listener, Looker, and Mover tendencies through the ways they respond to the people and objects in their very new surroundings. At that time, you need not hesitate to offer the kinds of feedback your infant craves and to begin stimulating his less-preferred senses as well.

This chapter provides descriptions of three infants, each a different type of learner, and compares their development throughout the first year of life. A Learning Style QuickCheck for Infants is included to help you pinpoint *your* baby's learning style (see page 40), and ideas are presented to help you start your child on the road toward the learning-style balance that will pay big dividends later on.

A baby's first year is characterized by developmental strides unmatched in magnitude by any other period in childhood. Enjoy each and every one!

A LOOK AT THREE LEARNERS

Michael, Emily, and Aaron shared a hospital nursery and, in their sixth week of life, are physically within a half-pound and a half-inch of one another. But, as you will see, the similarities end there. Already, three distinct personalities have emerged, along with different tolerance levels, different coping mechanisms, and unique sets of likes and dislikes. All of these traits stem from the babies' inborn learning styles—that is, the way they naturally process the sensory information with which they're bombarded every waking moment. For the purpose of clarity, our case-study babies possess pure learning styles; that is, each exhibits the characteristics of only a visual, an auditory, or a kinesthetic learner. In reality, more than half of all children may display the traits of two learning styles. Let's take a look at our three learners.

Six Weeks of Age

Meet Michael. Each morning, six-week-old Michael wakes at daybreak, blinking his brown eyes against the glare of sunlight. As he becomes used to the brightness, he lies quietly, his eyes flitting around the nursery. They first fixate on the stuffed tiger that shares his bassinet, then jump to the dancing bears hanging overhead, then dart toward his patterned quilt and the puffs of blue ribbon with which his mother has adorned the bassinet cover. Soon, his eyes focus on the tiger again.

Michael continues to devour the sights around him until he spies movement in the doorway. He looks intently at the approaching figure, then fixes his gaze on a particularly pleasing sight: his mother's familiar face.

For as long as his eyes are open each day, baby Michael is busy using them to learn about his world. His visual search is constant, for he craves colors, patterns, and moving shapes in much the same way that he craves feeding or holding. This urge to use his eyes comes from within—sometimes subtly, sometimes powerfully. And from the same inner source comes a built-in safeguard against overstimulation, for when Michael has had enough, he simply shuts his eyes or turns his head. Michael, you see, is a Looker.

Meet Emily. Emily, also six weeks of age, sleeps on undisturbed by the sunrise, but snaps to attention if the phone rings, the dishwasher starts up, or the hallway clock chimes the hour. Just as Michael is enthralled by sights, Emily is drawn to sounds. She tenses in eager recognition of her parents' voices, turns her head toward the faintest noises, shows distress at sudden quiet, and drifts off to sleep to a CD of nature sounds. When her mother announces that it's feeding time, Emily becomes still and quiet as though waiting to be lifted. When her father sings or talks to her, she coos in response.

Emily's parents have taken to keeping a radio on in the house, since even the drone of a newscaster's voice seems to entertain their baby. By the same token, they've learned to minimize visits to noisy gatherings and busy public places because, unable to block out sensory information the way that Michael can, Emily is easily overstimulated. But the solution to even this problem lies in her penchant for sounds; no matter how tense she becomes, the hum of the dishwasher or exhaust fan puts Emily to sleep within seconds. And she'll stay that way, sometimes even sleeping though a feeding, as long as the "white noise" continues. Emily is, of course, a Listener.

Meet Aaron. Aaron was born at the same time as Michael and Emily, but has been rolling from front to back regularly since his eleventh day of life. Wriggly when awake, restless when asleep, Aaron can work free of the tightest of swaddling and then, surprised by the sudden freedom of his limbs and coolness on his skin, will sound a protest. His own movements often startle him. He'll jump at the sight of his own fist passing by or at the falling sensation he gets when he flips over. Yet even at his most relaxed, he's never still, with his fingers stretching, ankles flexing, and neck arching.

Aaron is highly attuned to motion of all types. In fact, he goes absolutely rigid, yelping in anguish, if he's not clutched tightly to an adult chest when carried down a flight of stairs or lowered to his changing table. Though no lullaby or mobile can help when he's upset, he relaxes instantly when picked up and held, moving into an almost trancelike state when his skin is stroked. His father's most effective colic remedy is to lie down, hugging Aaron to his chest, while taking long, exaggerated breaths that allow the baby to feel restraint yet float along with each inhalation and exhalation.

Even at this age, Aaron is fun to play with. He can already hold small toys, and he kicks strongly enough to send a beach ball rolling or a rattle jiggling. Like Emily, he has no defense against overstimulation—in fact, he creates it himself—so his parents have learned to keep him calm by rocking and walking him about between feedings and naps. Without a doubt, Aaron is a Mover.

How does *your* baby absorb information? Does he take in the most through his sense of sight, like Michael? Does he tend to rely on his ears for comfort, information, and entertainment, as Emily does? Or, like Aaron, does he favor the sense of touch when exploring his world? To find out, complete the Learning Style QuickCheck for Infants found on page 40, placing a mark next to those behaviors that best describe your baby. When finished, total each column to determine whether your child most clearly prefers looking, listening, or moving.

HOW LOOKER, LISTENER, AND MOVER INFANTS DEVELOP

As you've seen, the differences between Michael, Emily, and Aaron at six weeks of age are already striking. Each baby has his or her own set of responses to people, places, and things—responses deeply rooted in the infant's inborn learning preference. And as the following descriptions show, these differences become more marked as babies grow and change throughout their first year of life.

Three to Seven Months of Age

Michael. Looker Michael is unusually alert, constantly scanning his surroundings, wide-eyed, for something of interest on which to fix his gaze. Even when nursing, his eyes remain open, first studying his mother's face, then moving beyond. His father usually slips a toy or two into his crib at night, and the sight enthralls him for many minutes upon awakening. But Michael's eyes are soon on the move again, searching the nursery for more stimulation. If Michael happens to be on his stomach, he lifts his head and cranes his neck as if to assure himself that his favorite sights are still there. If he's on his back, he gazes in awe at his own fingers or swipes at his crib gym.

At five months, Michael can grab and hold those dangling toys; and soon after, he becomes adept at handling intricate multicolored items, passing these objects from one hand to the other, and even searching for them briefly when they disappear from view. He's fascinated by the toys bobbing in his bath water and by the neighborhood activity outside the picture window. At seven months, Michael begins to babble, but more often sits quietly in his playpen, either looking at himself in his mirror or manipulating the dials and knobs on his *Busy Box*.

Michael's parents and caregiver at day care describe him as a quiet, contented, but somewhat fearful baby. Because sights, his favorite entertainment, are always available; because he's in no great rush to verbalize or move about; and because he's so highly attuned to his surroundings that unfamiliar faces and places make him uneasy, their description is right on the mark.

Emily. In comparison with Michael, Listener Emily is not as interested in the sights around her. But even at three months, Emily spends a lot of time in sound play. She babbles, coos, clicks her tongue, buzzes her lips, and uses her voice to attract attention. Her favorite game takes place when her parents imitate the sounds she makes; in fact, she's receptive to anyone who tries this.

Sounds are still a source of comfort to Emily. She's content to sit toyless for long periods of time—as long as there's music or conversation around her. When things grow silent, she begins a verbal racket of her own as if to fill the void. She grows quiet at the sound of a familiar voice, seems to anticipate from her mother's intonation such events as bedtime or a ride in the car, and loves to be sung to.

At seven months, Emily takes as much interest in toys as Michael, though she plays with them in a different manner. While Michael likes to put his eyes and fingers to work, Emily is rewarded by the sound a toy makes when she has used it correctly. Unable to squeeze a rubber toy yet, she'll bang it on the floor to hear it squeak. She has just begun to roll over, and cannot yet sit without help.

Emily's disinterest in getting around and delight in noisy toys, babbling, and social games cause the adults in her life to describe her as a friendly, expressive, somewhat uncoordinated baby.

Aaron. At three months of age, Mover Aaron already shows his moods. He arches his back to show tension, bangs both feet to indicate playfulness, and jerks his head from side to side to show frustration. Aaron can still be soothed by his parents' cuddling, and is calmest when being walked or swung.

Aaron loves to play with his hands and feet and to explore things with his mouth. He hasn't yet begun to babble, but his rocking indicates that he'll be quick to get around in earnest. And sure enough, he sits by four and a half months, slides along on his stomach a month later, and crawls during month six, showing no qualms about venturing from his parents' side in his quests. He is unimpressed by even the most fascinating toys, using them only as a brief stopover during his travels. Unlike Emily, he tends to ignore background noises.

At seven months, and despite his parents' and caregiver's efforts to engage him in other play, Aaron seems to view adults as "vehicles"—with knees to bounce on, fingers to tickle, and arms to rock—rather than playmates. This, combined with his overall silence and the ferocity with which he practices new skills, causes his parents to describe him as a quiet and single-minded child who is perpetually in motion.

Eight to Twelve Months of Age

Michael. Michael, the Looker, quickly perfects his thumb-and-forefinger grasp, and loves to point with, poke with, and wag his index finger. He frequently amuses himself by filling and dumping containers of small objects, and will hold up his hands for pat-a-cake over and over again. Although he's wary of strangers, he delights in face-making and peek-aboo games involving his parents or caregiver.

Michael still studies the details of toys and household objects, and though he's never happy for long hearing a story while in someone's lap, he'll sit for many minutes examining books and magazines by himself.

Michael remains a quiet baby. He'll clap his hands and wave '"bye-bye," but responds to attempts to get him to babble with an engaging stare rather than words or sounds. The sight of an interesting item can entice Michael to crawl around and even to pull himself up to a standing position, but he needs adult assistance to take steps.

As he approaches his first birthday, Michael is fascinated by detail, both in real life and picture books; but so far, his speech is still gibberish. He rarely climbs or makes his way across a room unless a particularly thrilling sight awaits him; but he loves to experiment, under an adult's watchful eye, with a coin bank, crayons, and stickers. Socializing and full-body play still hold little appeal; but with toddlerhood just around the corner, Michael exhibits more than ever a Looker's superior eye-hand coordination and penchant for observation.

Emily. Noisemaking toys are Listener Emily's favorite plaything during the second half of the year. She particularly enjoys banging on her toy piano, babbling into her plastic phone, and pushing a click-clacking truck back and forth. Games involving noise delight her, as she can already duplicate barnyard calls and street sounds. And when the game ends, Emily finds a way to keep the noise coming by banging pot covers, throwing toys to the floor, or screeching just for the sheer pleasure of doing so. She also loves her nap- and bedtime stories— though, unlike Michael, she shows little interest in the accompanying picture book.

Emily is somewhat better at filtering out background noise than she used to be, and, while still wary, is not as overwhelmed when out in public. She is very entertained by music and the sounds of children's voices; in fact, she'll stop whatever she's doing to make her way toward the television each time certain familiar commercials are broadcast. Unfortunately, her sleep is still as easily disturbed as her play, so her parents have faced a box fan toward the nursery wall and run it year-round in the hopes of drowning out household noises.

At eleven months, Emily has already spoken several words and can follow verbal instructions with ease. Although she can certainly crawl, she still shows little need to get around; in fact, her caregiver can get her to stand only by placing her favorite toys atop the coffee table. Walking, it seems, will have to wait.

As she celebrates her first birthday, Emily still shows no preference for her left or right hand. She now walks alone and climbs stairs with assistance, but still reverts to a hands-and-knees scoot when she wants to get somewhere quickly. Although her limbs may be at rest, her mouth and ears almost never are. Emily fits the profile of a Listener more and more each day.

Aaron. By contrast, Mover Aaron can't seem to sit still. He stands, sidles along the furniture, and walks alone within the two-week period preceding his nine-month "birthday," relying on instincts and a certain fearlessness that Michael and Emily don't seem to possess. Of course, Aaron loves roughhousing and active play, and spends at least two hours a day moving between his ride-in coupe and his handlebar-equipped trampoline. He is most cooperative when he's on the move; in fact, his parents have taken to dressing and diapering him wherever he might be at the moment, and allowing him to wander about while eating. They've learned the hard way that changing tables and high-chairs annoy Aaron greatly.

Books and small toys are lost on this little Mover, though he does occasionally use them for target practice. And he doesn't take kindly to car rides, morning naps, shopping trips, or any other activities that force temporary confinement. When rocked in adult arms, though, worn-out Aaron sleeps like a stone.

As he approaches the twelve-month mark, Aaron is still the fussiest of the three babies, adept at full-body activity but frustrated to tears by sit-down play. He is physically demonstrative, wanting everything from hugs to back rubs to another child's toy, but he cannot yet express himself verbally. Aaron points, gestures, and grabs frantically for his needs, and is quick to anger when misunderstood.

Like other Mover babies, Aaron is also frustrated by his inability to duplicate others' actions in his play. He'd love to use a shovel in his sandbox, twist the dials to work his toy computer, or fit the plastic people into his pull-along school bus, but he still lacks the necessary eye-hand coordination. Yet even as he exits babyhood, Aaron can be calmed, as always, by a brisk ride in his stroller or on the back of a bike.

IMPROVING INTERACTIONS WITH AN INFANT

The descriptions of Michael, Emily, and Aaron clearly show just how different three babies can be. In the very first week of life, their respective learning styles marked each child as a unique individual, and these distinct personality differences held firm throughout infancy.

But no matter what learning style your infant may exhibit, early childhood experts agree that parents and caregivers are that infant's most important playthings—even during late infancy, when toys begin to claim his attention. The time you spend with your baby each day, be it two hours or twelve, will provide him with a feeling of importance, a healthy sense of routine, and, with a conscious effort, specially chosen sensory stimulation, all of which are vital to his development.

There are certain factors to consider when you're tending to or playing with a small baby—factors that, regardless of learning style, can improve your infant's receptivity and guarantee him your full attention. To help your infant derive the most benefit from your time together, you may wish to keep the following guidelines in mind.

- *Make Your Baby Comfortable.* A baby is happiest when he's recently been fed, rested, and changed, and is comfortably situated away from glaring sunlight and chilling breezes.

- *Make Eye Contact With Your Baby.* It will be easier to keep your child focused on you if you bring him to your level by placing his infant seat on the table beside you, or move to his level by arranging your activity on the floor. Gazing into your baby's eyes as much as possible and making exaggerated faces while you speak will keep your own attention from wandering, as well, and will encourage your baby to stare back.

- *Use an Appropriate Voice and Vocabulary.* Since research has shown that infants respond better to higher-pitched tones than to low tones, moving your voice up an octave will hold your baby's attention longer. In addition, he'll be better able to follow your words when you speak slowly and in simple sentences.

- *Eliminate Competition.* Even older babies are distracted by nearby commotion. Before you begin your play, it's a good idea to shut the dog in the bedroom, occupy older children elsewhere, take the phone off the hook, and move away from the window or TV.

- *Keep Your Baby Close to You.* Staying within arm's length of your baby will enable you to offer soft strokes, encouraging words, and loving smiles, even when elbow-deep in a household task.

- *Entertain Your Baby.* Surround your baby with the kinds of stimulation he seems to like best. If you're able to play with him at that moment, this will start things off on a high note. If you're busy with something else, it will help him stay happier while you finish your work.

- *Introduce Variety in Your Baby's Play.* Whether your baby is interacting with you or amusing himself, persistence in offering new types of stimulation—music and noisy toys, say, to a baby who tends to favor sights—will help him develop different ways of perceiving the world around him.

- *Know When to Quit.* Despite their curiosity, infants are often susceptible to "stimulus overload." Too much intense play, prolonged concentration, or overly varied stimulation may render your baby cranky and sleepless. You can avoid this by removing his toy or ending your play together before it begins to lose its appeal.

TECHNIQUES FOR AFFIRMING AND DEVELOPING LEARNING SKILLS

As you have seen, adult interaction plays a large part in coloring a baby's sensory experiences. By being aware of your child's learning style, by examining your own actions toward him, and by offering him playthings selected with his sensory preferences in mind, you can "spoon-feed" your baby the kinds of stimulation he adores and bolster his weaker areas, as well. Whether you're bathing, changing, feeding, playing with, relaxing with, or just working alongside your infant, both the way in which you approach him and the toys you choose can work wonders.

Each of the following sections focuses on building the skills inherent in one of the three learning styles—looking, listening, or moving. First, each section looks at the long-term benefits derived from strengthening those skills. For instance, a child with strong Looker skills often goes on to excel at spelling and writing, while a good Listener will have an easy time building his vocabulary and learning to read. Next, a list of suggestions is presented for further developing the skills of a baby with inborn strengths in that area. For example, you will learn how to enhance Mover skills in a Mover baby. Finally techniques are presented for promoting sensory awareness in those babies who favor the other learning styles, and therefore need a boost in the skill area under discussion.

Each of these activity lists is based on years of clinical experience and on toys and pastimes that my young clients have indicated were their favorites. My other criteria for an item's inclusion are that the plaything be readily available and, whenever possible, moderately priced; and that the suggested activity be either familiar to parents and caregivers, or easily learned. Most toys recommended can be purchased in your local toy store. If, however, you find that a toy isn't available in your area, the Buyer's Guide on page 263 will enable you to order it by phone or online. You may find that some of the toys I recommend for the enhancement of an inborn learning style are marked by the manufacturer as being appropriate for the next higher age group. In my practice, and with safety considerations always a factor, I have found that a child's learning strengths frequently enable him to enjoy these playthings a bit ahead of schedule.

The purpose of handpicking activities for a child, beginning in infancy, is to prevent him from settling into a comfort zone of playing only with those toys that appeal to his favored way of learning. Instead, parents and caregivers can also introduce playthings and activities that will challenge and stimulate all of the child's areas of learning: *listening, looking,* and *moving.* Thus, whenever possible, the suggested activities are multisensory in nature; that is, they activate more than one channel of learning by combining the type of stimulation to which your child needs exposure with his favored form of learning. For example, one of my favorite items for strengthening a Looker infant's Listener skills is the lift-and-look book, which allows him to involve his eyes and hands while he gets valuable listening practice. In fact, many toys and activities are useful for strengthening more than one skill. For instance, the classic *Corn Popper* by Fisher-Price appeals to Lookers, Listeners, and Movers. It can be used to either affirm a strong skill or develop a weak one. Just remember that when choosing a multisensory activity to strengthen one of your little learner's skills, the activity must involve your child's *strong* suit, as well. For example, when the goal is to develop Looker skills in a Listener infant, you must provide an activity that permits your child to *listen,* which he loves to do, at the same time that he's being exposed to something visually interesting.

Keep in mind that it's perfectly acceptable to borrow ideas from lists meant for other learners, provided you recognize that the activity may be a bit too advanced to be immediately successful, or may simply not appeal to your baby. By all means, though, be creative and flexible—and patient. You may find that the plaything your baby rejects today is simply perfect two months from now, just as you may stumble upon an idea from another learner's list that your baby will absolutely adore. The key, after all, is to have fun with your baby while he gains important skills from your play times.

Building Looker Skills

Well-developed Looker skills lead to strong powers of observation, the ability to remember what is seen, and good eye-hand coordination, all of which are needed when a child begins to read and write. No matter what your baby's learning style, he stands to gain either reinforcement or encouragement of his Looker skills from the activities you provide.

Looker infants, of course, possess the above-mentioned abilities from birth, and so will particularly enjoy their parents' attempts to focus on their favored sense. Listener infants are social creatures, and so will probably be most receptive to those Looker activities that are liberally sprinkled with conversation. Similarly, Mover infants will be most interested in sights that are somehow connected to their love of physical activity. Here are some ideas.

ENHANCING AN INFANT'S EXISTING LOOKER SKILLS

- Suspend colorful mobiles over your baby's crib. Using commercial mobiles made of interchangeable parts or homemade mobiles made of painted clothespins or paper-plate faces will enable you to change the toy from time to time. Of course, any mobile should be kept out of baby's reach, and must be removed altogether once he can stand.

- Indulge your baby's need for frequent eye contact. Meet his glance, gaze at him, and let him be the one who looks away.

- Keep the lights on in the nursery during the early weeks so that your baby can look around whenever he's awake. Once his surroundings begin to distract him and keep him from falling asleep, try a night-light instead.

- Place your baby in the center of things, where he can observe family members as they go about their daily activities.

- Using photos, make a picture book of the important people in your baby's life—parents, siblings, grandparents, and baby sitter. Put each picture in a plastic sleeve, and look often at the finished book together.

- Spend time in front of the mirror with your baby. Make faces, point to the various reflections, "play" with baby's image, and laugh together.

- Provide large colorful rings that stack from largest to smallest.

- Offer baby a first book with one colorful picture per page.

- A beginner set of blocks should be visually stimulating like *Discover and Play Color Blocks* by Baby Einstein.

- Offer a hands-on lesson in cause and effect. *Tote and Tinker Activity Center* by Sassy provides multiple opportunities for baby to push, move, spin, and pull.

- *My First Fish Bowl* by Lamaze, available through Genius Babies, is a soft-sided fabric fish bowl. Each sea creature—which can be taken out of the bowl and put back in—has its own distinct visual pattern.

ENCOURAGING THE DEVELOPMENT OF LOOKER SKILLS IN INFANTS WHO ARE LISTENERS

- Manhattan Toy's *Colorburst Baby Safe Mirror*, available through Genius Babies, attaches to the side of baby's crib and offers constant visual stimulation. Talk to your Listener while you draw his attention to the mirror.

- Remind baby to "see." Point out and name household objects, using the word "see" each time. Show exaggerated surprise or excitement, or act out the same with a stuffed animal when coming upon a special sight.

- Play "Where are your eyes?" "Where are the teddy bear's eyes?" "Where are Daddy's eyes?" etc. Cover or close your eyes each time to help baby connect the eyes with seeing.

- When your baby attempts an eye-hand activity, like stacking colored rings or fitting together pieces of a toy, provide a commentary of his actions to help keep him interested.

- Make a finger puppet by drawing a face on your index finger. Make a game of baby's following the wriggling finger with his eyes. Talk to your Listener.

- Play with a jack-in-the-box, and encourage your baby to watch for the character's reappearance.

- While driving, point out familiar or interesting sights to your baby: "See our house." Later ask him to locate them on his own. Don't hesitate to stop the car for a closer look at anything unusual.

- Play peek-a-boo with your baby, hiding your face, his face, or a toy beneath your hands or a light blanket, and then making it reappear.

■ *Learning Patterns Snap Lock Snake* by Fisher-Price offers pull-apart, snap-together links. When baby presses the snake's nose, a cheerful tune plays.

■ Provide an oversized, colorful set of beginner blocks, like *First Blocks* by International Playthings.

ENCOURAGING THE DEVELOPMENT OF LOOKER SKILLS IN INFANTS WHO ARE MOVERS

■ When holding your baby for a bottle-feeding, be sure to switch him from side to side, just as breastfed babies are moved from breast to breast. This will stimulate each of his eyes in turn.

■ Time spent crawling is important to the development of visual skills. Take care not to rush past this stage in favor of baby's standing.

■ Make continuous eye contact with your baby while you feed, diaper, bathe, hold, and talk to him.

■ Baby Movers love being on the go. You can take even a very young baby on sightseeing outings, keeping him in a backpack or your arms for maximum interaction. The sunlight and new sights will offer a variety of visual treats.

■ When baby hugs old friend *Gloworm* by Playskool, the face lights up and actually glows.

■ As baby kicks the footpad of *Brilliant Basics Kick and Drive Gym* by Fisher-Price, flashing lights and a colorful spinning roller are activated.

■ TOMY's *Lullaby Light Show*, available through Amazon, projects dancing figures on ceiling and walls to the soothing background sounds of "Brahms' Lullaby."

■ When baby presses the bee on Playskool's *Push Start Tumble Top*, balls begin to pop, spin, and swirl.

■ Movers love bath time. Take this opportunity to develop visual skills with *Scoop 'N Strain Turtle Tower* by Sassy. Colorful turtles create both stacking rings and a water toy. Each turtle can be used as a scoop to fill with water and pour.

■ Push baby in a stroller through your neighborhood. Point out objects of interest: a neighbor on his porch, a cat on the sidewalk.

Building Listener Skills

Listener skills go hand in hand with a child's growing sociability, speech and vocabulary, ability to follow directions, and interest in reading. It stands to reason that a baby whose Listener skills are encouraged will go on to have an easier time making friends and tackling schoolwork than will a child whose Listener skills are weak. All three types of learners, then, will benefit from their parents' attention to this area of development.

The baby whose Listener skills are inborn will enjoy and profit from any opportunity for communication or self-expression. Lookers and Movers, who delight in moving their hands and their whole bodies, will most readily accept those Listener activities that combine action with talking and listening. Here are some suggestions for all three types of learners.

ENHANCING AN INFANT'S EXISTING LISTENER SKILLS

■ Gently shake rattles, bells, and other noisemakers near your infant's ears.

■ Leave a radio playing softly in the nursery.

■ Play a CD or tape of lullabies, such a *A Child's World of Lullabies* by Hap Palmer, as background music to accompany any activity.

■ Offer your baby the conversation he craves. Talk to him as you tend to his needs, describing what you're doing, asking him questions, and using any sort of response as an answer.

■ Sing and chant to your baby. Even the youngest Listener will respond with excitement to familiar songs and rhymes.

■ Bring "home sounds" to your baby's attention. Explain in simple words what each whir, beep, ding, and whoosh signifies. For example, "Do you hear the timer? The clothes are dry now," or "Do you hear that noise? Now the dog food can is open."

■ Baby Smartronics' *High Flyin' Language Learner* by Fisher-Price uses an airplane theme to introduce basic vocabulary in three languages—English, French, and Spanish.

■ Put life into the stories you read to baby by giving distinctive voices to different characters and using expressive tones.

■ Play CDs that were created especially for babies, such as Hap Palmer's *BabySong*.

■ *The Babbler* by Neurosmith exposes infants to new sounds and words in Spanish, French, and Japanese.

ENCOURAGING THE DEVELOPMENT OF LISTENER SKILLS IN INFANTS WHO ARE LOOKERS

■ Provide your baby with a soft wrist rattle that he can wear on his forearm.

■ Use your hands to act out songs as you sing them aloud. For example, "The Itsy Bitsy Spider" can crawl up your baby's stomach, helping him associate the words with the action he loves. Hand gestures can also spice up many ordinary words and phrases, like "goodbye," "all gone," "hot," "cold," "big," and "little."

■ *Barnyard Bring Along* by Fisher-Price produces different barnyard noises when baby manipulates the various buttons and dials.

■ Introduce a first book that can be taken into the bath, like *Mimi's Toes* by Baby Einstein.

■ Imitating the sounds your baby makes will encourage him to make more. Draw his attention to your lips as you make the sounds. As he grows older, make a game of this, taking turns with a pretend microphone.

■ Manhattan Baby's *Gingham Garden Flower Pull Musical* is a soft padded flower in a pot that can be easily tied to most cribs. When baby pulls the ring under the pot, he is rewarded with the tune "You Are My Sunshine."

■ The *DiscoverSounds Hammer* by Little Tikes makes eight delightful sounds and lights up every time baby strikes it.

- When baby places a pan on the pretend stovetop of *DiscoverSounds Kitchen* by Little Tikes, he is treated to the sounds of boiling and frying. Other entertaining sounds include the ticking of an oven timer and the sound of a bell.

- Pretend to talk on a toy telephone, and encourage your baby to do the same. Even simple babbling, when repeated, models the give-and-take of conversation.

- When baby presses an animal character on the Baby Smartronics' *Nursery Rhymes Bus* by Fisher-Price, he gets to hear a cheerful verse.

ENCOURAGING THE DEVELOPMENT OF LISTENER SKILLS IN INFANTS WHO ARE MOVERS

- Slip a soft-covered rattle inside your baby's bedclothes, or tie a rattle to his infant seat. That way, his slightest movements will produce a pleasing sound.

- As you cuddle and rock your baby, sing in time to the chair's motion.

- "Turn on" your infant's ears several times a day. This technique involves gently massaging the outer edge of the ears, starting at the top and working down. By doing this, you will stimulate the acupuncture points and bring energy to your baby's ears.

- Provide a variety of floating, sinking, and squirting toys during bath time, and keep up a conversation as baby plays with the various toys.

- Make use of "fun" noises. Animal sounds and expressive sounds that replace words—"yuck," "uh-oh," "brrr," and the like—will be attempted by baby before the words themselves.

- Use "baby talk" and repetitive syllables to make words easier for your baby to mimic. A train can be a "choo-choo"; an ice cream bar, a "pop-pop"; shampoo, "poo," and so on.

- Baby Smartronics' *Kick and Learn Piano* by Fisher-Price rewards baby's natural kicking motion with music, sounds, and lights.

■ *LeapStart Learning Table* by Leap Frog introduces baby to numbers, colors, shapes, songs, and sounds in response to pressing knobs and spinning dials.

■ When baby reaches for and swats *Bat and Wobble Ball* by Fisher-Price, lights flash and music peals.

■ As baby pulls TOMY's *Quack Along Ducks,* available through Amazon, a mother duck and her two ducklings waddle and quack as they move across the floor.

Building Mover Skills

Although Mover skills may not be needed for success in academic subjects, children who possess a Mover's speed, agility, balance, and coordination are usually revered by their classmates, and thus gain an early social edge. Mover infants, of course, will be enthralled by any efforts to provide them with the sensory experiences they adore. Listeners, who prefer to talk rather than do, will respond best to verbal coaxing and a play-by-play description of the activity at hand. And Lookers, as always, will get the most from those Mover games and tasks to which visual stimulation has been added. The following ideas may be helpful.

ENHANCING AN INFANT'S EXISTING MOVER SKILLS

■ Breastfeed your baby, if possible. He'll adore the skin-to-skin contact.

■ Learn to do infant massage, and treat your baby to this sensory experience often.

■ Provide a lambskin mat or blanket. This will keep baby cool in summer and warm in winter, and will encourage relaxation and sleep.

■ Bathe with your infant. Holding him on your lap in the tub will maximize skin contact.

■ Offer crib dolls and stuffed animals for hugging and cuddling.

■ Attach a crib gym with suspended rings, bells, and knobs for baby to grab and kick at.

■ Provide toys your baby can push while standing, like *Corn Popper* by Fisher-Price.

■ *2-in-1 Snug 'n Secure Swing* by Little Tikes is a first swing, and accommodates babies as young as nine months for swinging indoors and out.

■ Mover babies adore outdoor play in a sandbox.

■ With *Baby Basketball* by Fisher-Price, babies can dunk three brightly colored balls through a hoop.

ENCOURAGING THE DEVELOPMENT OF MOVER SKILLS IN INFANTS WHO ARE LOOKERS

■ After carefully checking the interior of an empty appliance carton for exposed staples, put a favorite toy inside to encourage your baby to crawl in, or creep inside the box yourself and invite your baby to follow.

■ Make a game of covering baby's arms, foot, leg, or abdomen with a folded cloth diaper or a face cloth and letting him work free of it.

■ Touch your baby as often as possible—hold him, rock him, hug him, and caress him. When he's not in your arms, keep him near you in his cradle or infant seat for plenty of patting and stroking.

■ "Wear" your infant in a baby sling or front carrier. This increases skin contact between you and baby, and makes him more of a participant in your chores and activities.

■ Supply a large, lightweight, brightly colored ball for baby to roll, kick, and toss.

■ Provide a set of small sandbox tools—a rake, a ladle, a shovel, and a strainer, for instance—to encourage sand play.

■ Fill a plastic dishpan with one inch of dry cereal, and give your baby cups and spoons to use in his indoor "sandbox."

■ Make a game of pointing to an object and baby crawling to touch it—and later retrieve it.

■ *Step Start Walk 'N Ride* by Playskool is a sturdy, stable walker that helps baby learn to stand and walk. It converts to a riding toy and features hands-on activities.

■ With *Tube 'n Fish* by Sassy, Lookers pull the fish's tail and watch it scoot through the water. No batteries are required.

ENCOURAGING THE DEVELOPMENT OF MOVER SKILLS IN INFANTS WHO ARE LISTENERS

■ Allow your baby to move about without the restraint of a walker or playpen. Then verbally encourage his efforts.

■ Bring the books that Listeners love into the active play of bath time with *Squishy Fishie Fun Bath Time Book* by Lamaze, available through Genius Babies.

■ Sing while you're rocking and holding baby. The sensations of touch will soon be associated with the comforting sensations of sound.

■ Sit with your baby in a wading pool. Talk about the fun you're having, the toys you're playing with, and the feel of the water.

■ As a change of pace from the stroller, pull your baby around in a fenced wagon while describing the terrain of the backyard.

■ Supply a Bop Bag—an inexpensive inflatable toy with a character's face and weighted bottom. No matter what your baby does to the inflated bag, it will always return to an upright position.

■ Talk about your baby's actions and bring his surroundings to his attention. This will reduce his anxiety about attempting large-muscle activities.

■ Place a sofa cushion on the floor, and stay close by while your baby practices climbing up and over it.

■ *Musical Motion Ocean Gym* by Little Tikes encourages Listeners to kick by rewarding them with aquatic sounds and songs.

■ With *Music Lights and Sounds Activity Walker* by Today's Kids, animal sounds and whimsical songs reward your Listener for taking those first steps.

As you work and play with your infant, please do not limit yourself to the suggestions above. Toy store inventories change constantly, so it may well be that an item you have decided to purchase now sits alongside a similar toy that's even easier to use, or perhaps better suited to your baby. No one knows your child better than you, after all. So now that you've used the information in this chapter to determine your baby's playing and learning needs, feel free to consider both your own tastes and your baby's personality when making toy and technique selections.

Please bear in mind that visible results may be slow when you attempt to encourage an infant's weaker areas. And remember that efforts to round out your child's development contradict his inborn sensory urges. You may not see signs of improvement, or even enjoyment, on your baby's part for weeks. But gentle perseverance should eventually overcome your infant's resistance.

Remember that your goal is a happy confident learner, not an honor student. Have fun, and be sure to enjoy every endearing moment of infancy as you interact with your baby.

LEARNING STYLE QUICKCHECK FOR INFANTS, BIRTH TO TWELVE MONTHS OF AGE

Directions: Place a check next to all behaviors that are characteristic of your infant. Then total the checks in each column to determine which learning style he or she favors. You'll probably find that most of your responses are confined to one or two columns, just as in Chapter One's Learning Style QuickCheck for Parents (see page 16).

LOOKER	LISTENER	MOVER
1. Communication: When my baby wishes to express himself . . .		
❏ He points to what he wants.	❏ He babbled early and frequently.	❏ He relies on full-body responses.
❏ He responds with gestures, not words.	❏ He said his first word before age one.	❏ He is prone to tantrums.
❏ He plays very quietly.	❏ He follows directions easily.	❏ He shakes his head to indicate "No."
❏ He likes to observe events, rather than participate.	❏ He tries to imitate words spoken by others.	❏ He grabs impulsively at objects and toys.
❏ He began babbling late in his first year.	❏ He uses inflection when vocalizing.	❏ He rarely babbles at all.
2. Favorite Toys and Pastimes: When my baby plays . . .		
❏ He likes dangling toys, color, and motion.	❏ He likes rattles and noisemakers.	❏ He likes being bounced and tickled.
❏ He is visually alert.	❏ He likes rhymes, songs, and finger plays.	❏ He likes to be rocked, cuddled, and held.
❏ He enjoys a *Busy Box.*	❏ He seems to "eavesdrop" on conversations.	❏ He often kicks at his crib mobile.
❏ He looks at picture books.	❏ He babbles to his toys.	❏ He enjoys swing and bike rides.
3. Motor Skills: When my baby moves about . . .		
❏ He watches his hands while playing.	❏ He sat up after seven months of age, and was more interested in babbling.	❏ He sat without support before six months of age.
❏ He reached for objects before five months of age.	❏ He is consumed by talking, not walking.	❏ He crawled before eight months, and walked before age one.

❏ He often explores small objects with his hands.	❏ He prefers riding toys that make noise.	❏ He is in constant motion, rarely stopping to rest.
❏ He likes to pick up and place small pieces in puzzles.	❏ He uses toys mainly to create sounds.	❏ He used riding toys before ten months of age.

4. Ways to Soothe: When my baby is fussy . . .

❏ He is quieted by the sight of a familiar face.	❏ He is quieted by the sound of a familiar voice.	❏ He is quieted by being picked up.
❏ He is calmed by a favorite toy.	❏ He is calmed by music.	❏ He is calmed by being held and rocked
❏ He is easily distracted by a change of scenery.	❏ He is easily distracted by a piano or a ringing telephone.	❏ He is easily distracted by physical challenges such as stairs.

TOTALS: _____LOOKER   _____LISTENER   _____MOVER

CHAPTER THREE

Learning Styles in Toddlerhood

As young Lookers, Listeners, and Movers begin their second year, their actions make it clear that they're leaving infancy behind. During this evolution from baby to full-fledged toddler, a child's sensory preferences continue to influence both her development and her responses to the people and objects that figure into her life.

This chapter first describes three different learners in early toddlerhood, and then compares and contrasts their growth during the period from thirteen months to three years of age. A Learning Style QuickCheck for Toddlers is included to help you identify the way your own child absorbs information (see page 66), and lists of suggestions are provided to guide you in enhancing her daily explorations. This chapter also addresses the child-care issue, offering ideas for making your toddler's day-care experience an enriching one.

Toddlerhood may be notorious for its parent-child power struggles, but it brings with it just as many exciting social breakthroughs and physical achievements. As you encourage your toddler's growth, you'll take pride in her budding independence, as well.

A LOOK AT THREE LEARNERS

Although they're exactly the same age and have spent their infancy in similar family circumstances, toddlers Tina, Anthony, and Paul are amazingly dissimilar. Where one child seems to excel, another struggles, with their varying levels of development dictated by individual learning style. Given the tremendous impact of a child's inborn preference for sights, sounds, or tactile sensations, it probably won't surprise you to learn that Tina, a Looker, exhibits eye-hand coordination far beyond that of which Anthony and Paul are capable; that Listener Anthony's verbal skills are quite advanced; and that Mover Paul continues to perform the kinds of physical feats that have astounded his parents from the very first. Although many children exhibit characteristics of more than one learning style and are therefore considered Looker-Movers, or perhaps Looker-Listeners, our case-study toddlers display "pure" styles. This has been done to highlight the distinctions between the three learning preferences. Let's take a closer look at each toddler.

Thirteen Months of Age

Meet Tina. Like infant Michael in Chapter Two, thirteen-month-old Tina displays the Looker style of learning, preferring visual stimulation over any other. Always intrigued by detail, Tina has, until now, been content to sit quietly, exploring with her eyes and hands. But now that she is toddling in earnest, a new world has opened to her roving eyes and probing fingers. She has discovered buttons and dials on appliances, cabinet-door handles, window blinds, various cords and wires—provided, Tina seems to think, for her personal entertainment. Tina's desire to handle such tempting devices far outweighs any need to run, jump, or climb; in fact, her sole gross motor effort since learning to walk has been to step atop the baseboard heater in order to reach the drapery tiebacks or peer out the dining room window.

Tina loves imitative play, and tries to duplicate many of her parents' and caregiver's actions with toys. Her long-handled push toy serves as a vacuum cleaner, and her drumsticks as kitchen utensils or hand tools. Though she rarely makes a move to join in, she enjoys watching other children at play. When alone, she plays contentedly for long periods with nesting toys, a pegboard, puzzles, and other playthings that exercise her eye-hand coordination.

Tina recognizes words as symbols for objects, but rather than speak, prefers to point toward the window or the kitchen when coaxed to say "car" or "cookie." She waves good-bye and throws kisses, but sees no need to accompany these gestures with words. In fact, at thirteen months, Tina's speech—really just occasional babbling—is little different from what it was two months before. Her love for quiet play helps her retain the label of an "easy" baby; but at a month past her first birthday, there's already a noticeable gap between Looker Tina's visual and eye-hand abilities and her skills in language and full-body activity.

Meet Anthony. Listener Anthony, also thirteen months of age, shares Tina's disregard for active large-muscle play, but lacks her fine motor ability. Shape sorters, snap-together blocks, and stacking toys gather dust on the nursery shelf while Anthony changes the discs on his music-box record player, chats with his dolls, or trails after his parents, eager for conversation. He already indulges in pretense, chanting "A-B-E-B" to a cousin's alphabet-adorned book bag before donning it and announcing, "Go gool." Anthony also likes to perch on the stairs in his firefighter's hat, alternating the statement, "My fie duck" with siren sounds. He puts on his best performances for an audience.

When there's no one available to share his play, Anthony keeps the auditory stimulation coming by singing and humming, substituting babbles for any words he can't remember. In public, he approaches anyone in his path with keen anticipation of their smiling reactions to his sophisticated vocabulary. Unfortunately, Anthony's sociability now causes problems at bedtime. His radio is no longer an acceptable night substitute for Mom and Dad's company, so he calls for them many times during the night.

At thirteen months, Anthony walks with a waddling, bowlegged gait. He falls a lot, and so is still hesitant to climb stairs or cross unfamiliar or unlevel terrain. He'll sit on a riding toy if another child joins him in play, but prefers to settle himself beside the supervising parent for a "chat." Indoors and out, conversation takes precedence over physical activity for Listener Anthony.

Meet Paul. Paul, a thirteen-month-old Mover, is quite the opposite of Anthony—largely silent, but never still. He runs, jumps, hops, climbs, kicks a ball, and walks backwards with complete confidence, the faster the better. He has already swung himself atop a neighbor child's tricycle in a desperate attempt to ride along. Paul delights in all sorts of physical play—hide-and-seek, his rocking horse and riding toys, his slide, his pool, his sandbox, and the "house" his caregiver made from an appliance carton.

Paul received a toy tool kit for his first birthday and bashes delightedly with the hammer. He tends to ignore the other tools, though, having tried and discarded them in much the same manner that he tosses aside spoons and forks, crayons, and other small items that require manual dexterity. Not surprisingly, Paul is a messy eater and an aggressive, daring, somewhat destructive force while at play. Only his teddy bear sleeping companion escapes rough handling. This toy spends the night locked in Paul's arms and the day hidden beneath his blanket for safekeeping.

As he enters toddlerhood, Paul has a one-word vocabulary— "No"—and still relies on gestures and howls to convey his wants and needs. As the gap grows wider between this Mover's motor skills and language ability, it comes as no surprise that Paul's frustrations are beginning to take the form of frequent tantrums.

What type of learner is your toddler? Is she a Looker, like Tina, enthralled by visual stimulation? Or is she more attracted to sounds, like Listener Anthony, or movement and sensations, like Mover Paul? The Learning Style QuickCheck for Toddlers on page 66 will provide the answer. Simply check those traits that are characteristic of your toddler, and add the checks in each column. A glance at the totals will tell you which learning style your child favors, and help you understand her inborn strengths and weaknesses.

HOW LOOKER, LISTENER, AND MOVER TODDLERS DEVELOP

The pictures that have been painted of Tina, Anthony, and Paul clearly show the distinctions that exist between the three types of learners at the start of toddlerhood. The fact that these three children absorb information about their world through the sense dictated by their learning style has caused them to develop different skills at surprisingly different paces. You'll see from the accounts that follow that this trend will continue as Tina, Anthony, and Paul move through toddlerhood.

Sixteen Months to Two Years of Age

Tina. As Looker Tina passes the sixteen-month mark, her words begin to flow. First come easy-to-envision words, like "dog," "shoe," and "car." Soon the word "see" is added to form two-word sentences about the all-important sights in Tina's environment. Her first three-word sentence, also used frequently, reflects both Tina's liking for solitude and her ability to persevere at small-motor tasks: "No—Tina do!"

When at play, Tina continues to explore with her eyes and hands. When Tina's parents try to read to her, she insists on holding the book herself so that she can look ahead and back as she pleases. Tina loves blocks, a pull-toy duck whose wings and feet move as she does, puzzles, her toy farm, and anything with intricate parts. Her current favorite plaything is a child's jewelry box with doors, drawers, and a lid that lifts to reveal a mirror and a spinning ballerina.

Tina focuses on sights in her outdoor play. Although still uninterested in riding toys—she is more likely to turn her trike over to watch the front wheel spin—she simply adores sightseeing strolls to the local mall, to a nearby nature preserve, or just through the streets of her town. Tina plays with a ball, more to watch the colors blend as the ball rolls than for exercise; she uses a swing, but on her stomach so that she can twist around and watch the world spin by; and she plays in the sandbox, so long as there's a basketful of intriguing-looking sand toys beside her.

In a group, Tina still tends to keep to herself. She likes her own space, pulls away from being touched, and keeps her emotions so much in check that the yelling and crying of other children alarm her. (She relies on fleeting facial expressions to indicate her own surprise or displeasure.) Despite her penchant for being alone in a roomful of children, Tina is fascinated by the activities and interactions that take place within her play group. In fact, she devotes more time to observation than to actual play.

Anthony. Unlike Tina, who labors to produce words, Listener Anthony imitates everything he hears and quickly builds a grammatically correct sentence around almost every new word in his vocabulary. His sentences provide him with a strong sense of self, as in "No way, Daddy," "*I* do it fust," or "Dat *my* toy car." By eighteen months of age, Anthony possesses a huge, clear vocabulary, and uses such adult-like inflection and articulation that he is often mistaken for a much older child.

As he moves through early toddlerhood, Anthony continues to love being read to. In fact, if no one is available to oblige him, he'll sit with an unopened book in his lap, naming the various characters and their actions. Lately, he has discovered the art of storytelling, and he and his father exchange tales whenever they're traveling in the car. Aside from books, Anthony's current favorite toys are a mock pay phone, a toy cassette player, and various dolls and action figures he uses to act out daily events.

Anthony is a sedentary toddler, uneasy about climbing, swinging, or traversing the stairs. His avoidance of gross motor activity often borders on the comical, for he'll strike up conversations with or otherwise try to distract the supervising adult solely to avoid taking his turn at a game. At home, he needs help with zippers, clasps, and even the Velcro closures on his sneakers, but will dictate exactly what the assisting adult should do.

Not surprisingly, Anthony loves to socialize. He approaches both friends and strangers with greetings and questions, clearly enjoying every moment of conversational give-and-take. If Anthony's playmates can't quite keep up with his verbal ability, as often happens, he simply directs his attention towards the adults. At age two, Anthony mixes happily with the children in his play group, but quickly loses interest if an activity doesn't provide the noise or conversation he craves.

Paul. Mover Paul is constantly on the go, and shows little interest in communicating. At sixteen months, his vocabulary is limited to "Ma," "Da," and an occasional "No!" tossed over his shoulder as he whizzes by whomever calls out a greeting or request. Paul, you see, is far too busy to listen. In fact, he is more than twenty months of age before his language skills begin to emerge in the form of terse action words like "go," "run," and "hide." Paul seems to struggle with the formation of each word, opening his mouth and thinking hard before uttering a sound. Needless to say, Paul becomes quite anxious when the thought he wants to communicate is particularly important to him. Frustration and tantrums are appearing more and more frequently.

Unlike Tina, who is entertained by quiet play, and Anthony, who wanders between activities but makes important social connections along the way, Mover Paul derives little benefit from toys and indoor play. His favorite game is something his parents call "dump and toss," in which Paul empties cabinets, unloads shelves, or dumps dresser drawers. Sometimes, he flings the contents into his wagon and races around the house playing sanitation worker; but more often, he just moves on to the next room, leaving a huge mess in his wake. Paul's parents have tried in vain to discourage this practice, for Paul is very quick and methodical about his mess making and just loves the bending, twisting, and throwing involved.

Outdoors, Paul fares much better. He loves roughhousing of all sorts, as well as any activity that involves pushing, kicking, throwing, and pounding. He began pedaling a tricycle well before age two, is fearless aboard a slide or jungle gym, and has learned the rudiments of pumping his legs to keep a swing moving. Paul likes to engage the neighboring kindergartener in play by daring the boy to chase or race him. Of course, the five-year-old possesses a physical edge, and Paul, already overstimulated by the running around, winds up flinging himself on the ground and howling in frustration when he can't keep up with his friend.

When Paul socializes, he relies on action—chasing and grabbing rather than verbal interplay. He is quick to join any loud, wild activity that he didn't initiate himself, and just as quick to recruit additional playmates. Paul's characteristic exuberance turns to tears at the slightest hint of anger, and he is learning to evoke similar emotional responses from others by goading them. At two years of age, his gross motor actions and rough-and-tumble sort of socializing seem to his parents to be more characteristic of a three-year-old.

Two-and-a-Half to Three Years of Age

Tina. Looker Tina began using three- and four-word sentences before she was two years of age, but six months later, still omits some sounds and parts of speech on a regular basis. She says, "Dat paint boo" for "That paint is blue," for instance, and "Can' fine ma bankie" for "I can't find my blanket." Always on the alert for familiar sights, Tina has begun to recognize and read "Dead End" and "Stop" signs, as well as department-store and fast-food-restaurant logos. She naturally relies on visual cues like color, shape, and letter configuration to accomplish this, and is proud to show off her talents.

Tina spends much of her play time with her chalkboard, her doll house, and the collection of puzzles her mother borrows each week from a local toy library. She has discovered the joys of arts and crafts, and frequently asks to use paints, crayons, and markers. Tina has also become fascinated by board games. She likes to watch others play, and when no one is around, she sets up the playing pieces by herself and pretends she's a participant.

Tina continues to demonstrate excellent fine motor skills. She has been successful in all her early efforts with scissors, crayons, and clay. In fact, at two-and-a-half years old, she is able to draw recognizable shapes. Tina is a stickler for details when it comes to artwork. You can count on her to add chocolate chips to a modeling-dough cookie, or a tail to one of her animal creations. Tina's gross motor development continues at a much slower pace. It's not surprising that it takes some coaxing to convince her to try a full-body activity like climbing a slide or riding a tricycle. Even then, she quickly loses interest.

As she approaches her third birthday, Tina still prefers solitary play to games involving other children. She seems distressed by their noise and commotion, and is put off by impulsive hugs, hand holding, and other social overtures for which toddlers are known. However, she is beginning to enjoy the different reactions she can elicit by making a silly face or deliberately putting a puzzle piece in the wrong place. At three, Tina is still a confirmed Looker—quiet, content, strong on visual and fine motor skills, and weaker in social and gross motor areas.

Anthony. While Tina's speech is still fairly simple, Listener Anthony has become quite the conversationalist. Now that he understands the concept of tense, he peppers his speech with words like "yesterday," "tomorrow," "already," and "yet." Anthony also has an amazing memory for words. He mispronounces a few, but never fails to use them in the proper context. Anthony is also beginning to understand that letters make up words, and will shout, "N-O spells No!" or make reference to his "N-A-P nap."

At age two-and-a-half, Anthony loves pretend play. He drags his stuffed-animal friends into his playhouse several times a day and stages a three- or four-way conversation to fit the fantasy of the moment, but he's just as happy role-playing without props or companions. These days, a tape recorder is Anthony's favorite toy. He sings, chants nursery rhymes, and tells stories into the microphone, and enjoys the playback just as much as the recording session. He also spends a lot of time working with his realistic-sounding toy tools and sounding the siren on his pressure-sensitive toy ambulance.

Like Tina, Anthony would never choose gross motor play over other types of activities. When he absolutely has to indulge in full-body play, you can rely on him to talk himself through each and every step. His artwork is often creative, and almost always story-related, but primitive. As he approaches three years of age, Anthony ignores puzzles, shape sorters, and, in fact, the majority of his toys. As you can see, motor skills are not this toddler's strong suit.

Socially, however, Anthony shines. Not only does he talk and reason when it comes to his own conflicts, but he uses his conversational skills to help playmates resolve their problems, as well. Anthony is very much at ease with verbal instructions and helps his friends in this area, too. He loves the limelight, has a flair for the dramatic, and can be a bit bossy when organizing a game or assigning roles for one of his imaginary dramas. If the activity turns physical, however, Anthony's Listener-born confidence vanishes, and he quickly removes himself. Like Tina, Anthony displays the same strengths and weaknesses at age three that he did in infancy, for his language skills far surpass his motor ability.

Paul. At two-and-a-half years of age, Mover Paul's lagging verbal skills cause him increasing frustration. When he wants to convey a need, he does so in an almost frantic fashion, having learned to anticipate misunderstandings and delayed gratification. Paul's vocabulary is growing, though not nearly fast enough to keep pace with his increasingly sophisticated thoughts, and his speech is filled with the sort of verbal shortcuts you'd expect from someone a year younger. He omits words and ending sounds, saying "Scoo" for "Excuse me," and "Wan joo" for "I want juice." Because many parts of speech are ignored altogether, Paul's sentences are limited to two or three words.

As this little Mover grows, he needs more and more space to play. Enthralled, as always, by full-body activity, Paul pushes, chases, runs, climbs, and jumps at every opportunity. When the weather curtails his outdoor fun, you can find him moving furniture and piling up toys indoors as he imitates a delivery person or mechanic. Paul rarely sits down, and when he does, it's either to roll his collection of cars across a tabletop or to watch some cartoon superhero perform fascinating physical feats.

As he leaves toddlerhood behind, Mover Paul has many friends. Since he is faster than most children his age and has little patience with timidity, most of his favorite playmates are a year or two older than he. He is particularly well liked by the boys in his play group, and they follow his lead just as he follows the six-year-old next door. But for all his athleticism, Paul remains moody and emotionally needy. He will not sleep without the blanket and rag doll that have shared his bed since infancy, and he craves his parents' and teachers' patient reassurance to see him through his frequent episodes of frustration, embarrassment, and wounded feelings. Like that of his Looker and Listener counterparts, Mover Paul's uneven development continues to be dictated by learning style.

LEARNING STYLE AS A CHILD-CARE CONSIDERATION

Day-care centers, family day-care homes, baby sitters, and trusted friend or relative caregivers all figure largely in the lives of today's young children. Certainly, any working parent will review child-care options carefully. Did you know that when making such arrangements, learning style merits as much consideration as cleanliness, safety, and affordability? Understanding how your child learns best, as indicated by the Learning Style QuickCheck for Toddlers (see page 66), can help you select the child-care environment that best meets her developmental and emotional needs.

Child Care for Lookers

During toddlerhood, Lookers tend to be like Tina, our case-study child—quiet, serene, and good at entertaining themselves. To avoid your Looker's being lost amid children whose behavior commands more attention and more assistance, you might wish to seek out a child-care setup that stresses interaction with caregivers and doesn't routinely leave passive children to their own devices simply because they seem content.

Since a Looker toddler will benefit from daily exposure to activities that exercise her less-favored senses of hearing and touch, it's important that her child-care environment offer all types of music, a safe area for outdoor play, and occasional messy activities like painting and water play. To indulge her fascination with intricate toys, the opportunity to select playthings from a varied collection should also be available.

At first glance, a Looker toddler may seem ideally suited to an in-home, one-to-one baby-sitting arrangement. After all, this would place her in a quiet setting with no competition for the use of her beloved toys. However, it's important to also encourage development of her physical and social skills. For this reason, you might wish to consider a family day-care setting for your Looker if she is to be cared for outside the home. If she is to be cared for at home, enrollment in a play group would be beneficial.

Child Care for Listeners

Like Anthony, Listener toddlers are usually expressive, social, somewhat uncoordinated children who thrive on talking, singing, and playing with others. They do well in group situations and relate just as well to the adults around them as they do to other children.

Many toys are unappealing to a Listener toddler, but if you place her in daily contact with playmates who do enjoy them, you may tempt her to give them a try. It's also a good idea to match her with a child-care setup that offers numerous opportunities for indoor and outdoor physical play. Safe areas in which to throw balls, ride a tricycle, run, and climb will encourage the sort of full-body play from which she shies away. And finally, it's important that a Listener toddler feel free to express herself, with frequent permission to act silly and be loud.

If you're satisfied that the caregiver or staff that will interact with your toddler is knowledgeable, nurturing, and unflappable, a young Listener should fare quite well in either a day-care center or a family day-care home.

Child Care for Movers

Like Paul, most Mover toddlers speak very little and prefer to express themselves physically by means of impulsive hugs, joyful jumps, foot stamping, and tantrums. They're a bit haphazard when at play, hopping from one activity to another and leaving quite a mess in their wake, and they tend to require lots of emotional support. It's wise to consider a Mover's high activity level and moodiness when making her child-care arrangements.

Because a Mover's physical ability overshadows her language and fine motor skills, it is particularly important to provide her with a caregiver who freely offers affection, support, and comfort during times of frustration. A daily routine that is constant and offers plenty of time for transition between activities can give the Mover toddler a reassuring sense of control over her environment. She needs room—and freedom—to roam; exposure to both full-body play and eye-hand activities; and lots of adult patience regarding food spills, strewn toys, primitive artwork, and toilet training. An in-home baby sitter or a family day-care setup that includes four or less children would be ideal for affording the quantity and type of attention a Mover toddler needs to keep frustration at bay.

Sharing Information About Learning Style

Once you've settled your toddler in a satisfactory child-care setup, you'll no doubt establish regular communication with her caregiver. Naturally, frequent contact—whether by note, phone, scheduled conference, or a daily exchange at the door—will provide valuable information about your child's time away from you. But familiarity with a toddler's learning style will help you take these talks one step further. You see, once you determine that your toddler is indeed a Looker, Listener, or Mover, you will be able to share certain observations and suggestions that may prove vital to the child's development. If your toddler spends part of the day in someone else's care, you may find it easier to guide her toward well-rounded development if you first consider each of the following aspects of her behavior and then discuss your thoughts with her caregiver.

Behavior Patterns

How does your toddler act when you're at home with her, as opposed to when she is in someone else's care? Do all involved adults get the same impressions about her language and motor skills, her level of self-confidence, and her ability to socialize? If a toddler is at ease in her caregiver's presence, you can expect her to "be herself." Ask the caregiver to fill out the Learning Style QuickCheck for Toddlers (see page 66) to see if your results agree.

Kinds of Play

When in the care of others, does your toddler gravitate toward the same toys and activities each day? Are these toys predominantly Listener items, like musical instruments and talking toys? Does she prefer such Looker toys as puzzles and blocks? Or does she spend her time at Mover activities—speeding about on a riding toy or popping in and out of a playhouse? Your toddler probably favors the same types of toys while at home with you, and stands to benefit from exposure to playthings that will stimulate her other senses. You may wish to offer her caregiver a few suggestions from the lists at the end of this chapter.

Social Behavior

How and with whom does your toddler interact while you're away from her? Does she prefer to play alone, or does she seek the company of other children? Depending on your child's play habits, you and her caregiver may wish to encourage a bit more interaction by selecting a relatively passive playmate to join in some of her activities. Or you might see a need to expose her to the joys of solitary play, either by creating a private sitting area or by introducing a daily quiet play time.

Language

Does your toddler communicate as well with her caregiver as she does with you? Requests for "bowly" or "goosh" may be enough to send *you* heading for the refrigerator, but to avoid frustration on your child's part, it's a good idea to translate her home vocabulary for those who care for her. You might also wish to exchange information on any special tactics that seem to encourage improvements in your toddler's speech.

Motor Skills

What are your toddler's current physical capabilities? Is she more active with you than with her caregiver? Less active? Does she prefer full-body play, or would she rather work with her hands? If your child has recently shown interest in a new skill, both you and her caregiver should provide encouragement. If your child tends to avoid physical activity, you can share ideas about how to entice her to try different types of play.

TECHNIQUES FOR AFFIRMING AND DEVELOPING LEARNING SKILLS

A toddler needs no formal instruction to learn about her world. Whether she spends the day with a parent or a caregiver, she'll absorb plenty of important information through play and sensory experience. But when the adult in charge makes a toddler's learning style a factor in the selection of her toys, her activities, and her outings, the child will be gently guided toward well-rounded development, and will acquire skills that are sure to prove invaluable during her academic years and beyond.

Each of the following sections explains the importance of sharpening the skills associated with one of the three learning styles: looking, listening, or moving. You will then find lists of toy and technique suggestions, grouped according to whether the particular activity enhances already strong learning skills or develops weaker ones. The toys and techniques suggested for learning skill enhancement have been based on, say, a Looker's visual acuity or a Mover's natural coordination. The suggestions for skill development involve multisensory activity—auditory and tactile stimulation, for instance. As such, the play ideas are intended to overlap with your toddler's inborn strengths, so that she remains involved while you explore new territory together. Choose your favorite ideas and give them a try.

Building Looker Skills

The Looker skills acquired during the early years help a child to recognize, recall, and reproduce what she sees through such fine motor endeavors as drawing and painting. The toddler who lags behind in this area usually finds intricate toys, puzzles, crayons, tools, and even eating utensils to be objects of frustration. But the toddler whose eye-hand skills are affirmed or improved through specially chosen experiences approaches both these and later visual tasks with more interest, more confidence, and more success. Looker toddlers will delight in any visual stimulation adults can provide, while Listeners and Movers, whose skills in this area can use an extra boost, will do best when Looker activities are tied in with their preferred sense: hearing or touch. You may find some of these suggestions helpful.

ENHANCING A TODDLER'S EXISTING LOOKER SKILLS

- Offer a shape-sorting toy, which requires your toddler to insert a shape into a matching opening.

- Provide *Duplo* snap-together blocks by Lego.

- Make a photo album of people and objects familiar to your child, and look at it together often.

- Offer a set of different-sized toy barrels for your child to stack and fit inside one another.

- Provide a pegboard with pegs.

- Encourage your child to scribble in various art mediums—chalk, crayon, washable marker, and the like—on different colored papers.

- The DVD *Discovering Water* by Baby Einstein will delight your Looker with scenes of rivers, lakes, and rain.

- *Deluxe Alpha Desk* by Today's Kids is both a first desk and an easel, and offers a multitude of fine motor opportunities for your little Looker.

- Arrange to exchange puzzles with several friends so that your toddler always has several "fresh" ones to play with.

- Enjoy Playskool's *Mr. Potato Head* along with your child to give her practice in manipulating small pieces.

ENCOURAGING THE DEVELOPMENT OF LOOKER SKILLS IN TODDLERS WHO ARE LISTENERS

- To rest and refresh her eyes, encourage your child to "palm." Hold her hands, palms up, in front of her. Place the center of her cupped palms over her eyes to shut out all outside light. Then tell her to close her eyes while you count slowly to ten.

- Study an object together. Then hide it, close your eyes, and take turns describing the object to each other.

- Tell your child a story in the dark. This will encourage her to envision details.

■ Find a place outdoors to lie down and watch the clouds together. Talk about what you see.

■ Play store, exchanging pretend money for pretend items. Talk about each item and how much it costs.

■ Buckle your toddler into her highchair and give her a bowl of fist-sized novelty magnets to stick on the refrigerator door. Offer verbal encouragement.

■ Buy puzzles with knobbed pieces for easy insertion and removal.

■ Invest in a lift-and-look book, where one picture is hidden under another, and share it with your toddler.

■ Provide fist-sized easy-grip crayons.

■ Visit a local sporting event—a high school soccer game is fine—and tell your toddler various details to watch for.

ENCOURAGING THE DEVELOPMENT OF LOOKER SKILLS IN TODDLERS WHO ARE MOVERS

■ Encourage your toddler to pour water from a plastic pitcher into plastic cups. Movers love messy water play.

■ Show your toddler how to pump the handle of a top to make it spin.

■ Introduce *Blue Goat Bath Puppet* from Baby Einstein.

■ Roll a large lightweight ball to each other. Remind your toddler to keep her eyes on the ball.

■ Offer your child materials like glue sticks, felt scraps, washable markers, and other fist-sized items to be used for simple crafts.

■ Work together with clay and modeling dough.

■ *Magna Doodle* by Fisher-Price is an erasable magnetic drawing board that works both fingers and arms.

■ *Buzzz About Mailbox* by Little Tikes has three chutes for "mailing" letters, a letter flag, and a battable bee.

- Encourage play with two-inch collectible cars, some of which change color with variations in temperature or, with a few twists, convert into entirely different objects.

- Provide a pegboard with fist-sized pegs.

Building Listener Skills

A toddler calls upon her Listener skills when she speaks, when she plays, when she interacts with others, and when she learns from the sounds around her. Listener, Looker, and Mover toddlers can all profit from activities that call upon the sense of hearing. Listeners benefit because these experiences affirm an inborn strength; Lookers and Movers, because their ability to communicate and socialize improves along with their growing auditory skills. Just as with Looker skills, the toddler who already possesses this learning style will need no prodding to play with games and toys that stimulate her preferred sense. Lookers and Movers may need some convincing, though, and this is best accomplished by incorporating sights, motion, or touch with whatever Listener activities you present. These ideas may help.

ENHANCING A TODDLER'S EXISTING LISTENER SKILLS

- Provide a pair of sturdy headphones so that your toddler can listen to music whenever she chooses. Collect cassettes of children's music for use in the car.

- Encourage language development by asking your toddler to describe, explain, and otherwise expand on what she says.

- Speak to your toddler in fairly complex sentences, giving lots of detail. This will encourage her to do the same.

- Expand your child's vocabulary with a book like *Little Golden Picture Dictionary* (Golden Books Publishing), which has over 2,500 pictures of such uncommon words as oboe, unicycle, and yak.

- Set aside a special time of day for reading aloud. Let your toddler select a favorite book, and ask questions to help her express her feelings about it. For example, you might ask, "What did you like best about the puppy?"

■ Buy or make a tape of household sounds like the dishwasher, the dog's bark, the telephone, footsteps on the stairs, the doorbell, and the vacuum cleaner. Play the tape back, and ask your toddler to identify the various sounds.

■ Play a modified version of "Simon Says" by asking your child to follow the usual commands without visual cues from you.

■ Check your local library or "Y" for toddler story-time programs.

■ Encourage your toddler's auditory memory by turning ordinary activities—like dressing, meal preparation, and bath time—into sing-alongs.

■ Provide plenty of opportunities for your child to socialize with other children by enrolling her in a play group or by scheduling play dates with the children of friends.

ENCOURAGING THE DEVELOPMENT OF LISTENER SKILLS IN TODDLERS WHO ARE LOOKERS

■ Keep television watching to a minimum, and encourage talking, music, and reading in its place.

■ Browse through mail-order catalogues together. Your discussions about the pictured items will be great vocabulary builders.

■ Get in the habit of talking about what you're doing as you do it. For example, you might say, "Daddy is going to wash the car. First, I use the hose to put water in a bucket. Now, I need bubbles. What can I use to make bubbles?" Involve your toddler in the conversation.

■ Make a chalkboard picture according to your toddler's specifications. Ask her what she'd like you to draw, and have her dictate the size, color, shape, and location of each detail.

■ Make hand puppets for yourself and your toddler by sewing two buttons on a sock to look like eyes. Have the puppets talk to each other.

■ Create a special story corner with a beanbag chair or a soft rug, and a cart or bin for storing books. Encourage your toddler to sit with you while you tell stories and read aloud to her.

- Fisher-Price's *Toddlin Tunes Puppy* doubles as a piano and xylophone, and has a mallet shaped like a dog bone.

- Hide a treat, and give your toddler verbal instructions for finding it.

- Watch a video created especially for children, and sing songs from the video during other times of the day.

- Your Looker will enjoy manipulating Leap Frog's *Sing Along Microphone*. She can listen and learn the words to favorite songs, press the "record" button to sing along, and then press "playback" to hear her own voice.

ENCOURAGING THE DEVELOPMENT OF LISTENER SKILLS IN TODDLERS WHO ARE MOVERS

- Make a game of giving your toddler silly directions like "Put the washcloth on your head," "Stand on top of the book," or "Put this toy under the chair."

- Make it a practice to speak to your toddler slowly and in short, simple sentences.

- Pop-up, scratch-and-sniff, and lift-and-look books are perfect for active storytelling.

- Hide somewhere in the house, and make a game out of your child finding you by following the sound of your voice.

- Make it a practice to ask your child to relay messages to a grandparent, sibling, or friend.

- Richard Scarry's *Best Ever Word Book* by Golden Books allows toddlers to visualize distinctions between similar words. There's lots of action to appeal to Movers.

- When your toddler mispronounces a word, repeat and affirm your child's thought while pronouncing the word correctly. At a pond, for example, she might say, "Guh, kack kack." You can respond, "You're right! The duck says 'quack quack.'"

- Play supermarket with your toddler, using goods from the kitchen.

Take turns being the shopper and the storekeeper, and make conversation while you play each part.

■ Plan special outings to help build vocabulary. There's a lot to talk about at a grocery store, pet shop, or post office.

■ Stage a make-believe tea party. To encourage conversation, ask questions of your toddler such as "Do you want hot tea or cold tea?" or "How many cookies would you like?"

Building Mover Skills

Well-developed Mover skills give even small children the confidence they need to get the most enjoyment from group situations. The coordinated toddler usually emerges as the first, the quickest, and the best at physical activities, becoming a magnet of sorts for her playmates. As such, all toddlers, regardless of learning style, can profit from large-muscle activities. This is simple enough with Mover toddlers, who will be thrilled with any sort of body contact and gross motor play you suggest. Listeners and Lookers, though, will probably need some encouragement in the form of either conversation or visual stimulation, as the case may be. Perhaps you'll be able to use some of these suggestions.

ENHANCING A TODDLER'S EXISTING MOVER SKILLS

■ A backyard swing set offers the opportunity for frequent active play.

■ Little Tikes' *Big Building Blocks* provide giant lightweight interlocking blocks that are great for large-scale building.

■ For variety, exchange riding toys with friends' children.

■ Enroll in a parent-and-child swim class.

■ Throwing, catching, and kicking sponge *Nerf Balls* is great exercise for toddlers.

■ An afternoon at a local park will thrill your Mover. Allow her to swing and go down the slide—with you close by for safety, of course.

■ Enroll your toddler in a kiddie gymnastics program, or provide a tumbling mat at home for rolling and somersaulting practice.

■ Lakeshore's *Easy-Ride Taxi-Trike* enables your Mover to give a friend a ride. It's easy to pedal even with a passenger in the backseat.

■ Provide a child-sized broom, rake, watering can, and shovel to encourage your toddler's imitative play.

■ Make a balance beam from a two-by-four-inch board. Lay the board on the ground, and encourage your child to walk along with arms outstretched.

ENCOURAGING THE DEVELOPMENT OF MOVER SKILLS IN TODDLERS WHO ARE LOOKERS

■ Be sure to provide your toddler with plenty of holding, rocking, and stroking.

■ Practice climbing up and down stairs with your toddler, placing just one foot on each step and moving the other foot ahead to the next step. Be sure to hold her hand if she seems fearful.

■ Assign your toddler her own garden spot in which she can dig, squirt the hose, play with rocks, and pull weeds.

■ Invest in a wagon or stroller so that your toddler can give rides to her favorite doll or stuffed animal.

■ Provide an inflatable outdoor pool to promote water play. Naturally, an adult should always be in attendance.

■ A playground is the perfect place for hesitant toddlers to observe, and eventually attempt, such large-muscle feats as climbing and balancing.

■ *Cozy Coupe II* by Little Tikes is a toddler-sized car that moves via a child's footsteps rather than pedaling.

■ Provide a steel-framed riding pony for climbing, bouncing, and rocking.

■ Add a visual touch to cycling by decorating your child's tricycle with colored spoke covers, a basket, and handlebar grips with streamers.

■ With the *TotSports Bowling Set* by Little Tikes, when the see-through pins get knocked down, colorful balls jump and clatter inside.

ENCOURAGING THE DEVELOPMENT OF MOVER SKILLS IN TODDLERS WHO ARE LISTENERS

■ Create a special outdoor play area for your toddler, equipped with her own toys, to encourage active play.

■ March to music, alternating arms and legs, to improve your child's coordination.

■ Make a game of pantomiming such everyday actions as vacuuming, shaving, or opening a window, and have your toddler guess what you're doing.

■ Sing and act out the favorite, "This is the way we sweep the floor" (touch our toes, climb the stairs, etc.).

■ Provide a wheelbarrow to encourage outdoor play. Suggest that your toddler cart various items around the yard.

■ Using an appliance carton, make a playhouse, complete with doors and windows that open and shut. Encourage your toddler to crawl inside as you play "family" together.

■ Place materials of different textures in a pan, sandbox style. Rice, beans, water, and oat flakes are great fun to scoop and pour.

■ Play "marching band" with rhythm instruments like wood blocks, a drum, cymbals, or a triangle.

■ *No-Fail Grabby Balls* by Lakeshore are lightweight durable balls that are easy for little hands to grab, and ideal for bouncing, kicking, and throwing.

■ When one or two toddlers sit on Playskool's musical spinning machine, *Music & Lights Sit 'n Spin,* they are greeted with nine classic children's songs.

As you scan the above lists and your neighborhood toy store for those activities that would best suit your toddler, other skill-building ideas may strike you. I urge you to try them out! You've already identified your child's learning style, and you've also learned how to blend what she likes with what she needs. Most important, you know her temperament better than anyone, so don't be afraid to experiment with variations. After all, no single idea is right for every parent and child.

Although you may find that your toddler takes to a new toy or technique immediately, it's just as likely that she will resist or ignore a new item or activity the first few times you try it. Please don't be concerned. You can expect visible improvement of your toddler's weaker skills to take some time. Remember that your primary goal is a confident, well-rounded child. And as you gently shape your child's learning experiences, also keep sight of a second goal: an improved parent-child relationship that's shorter on frustration and longer on good old-fashioned fun!

LEARNING STYLE QUICKCHECK FOR TODDLERS, THIRTEEN MONTHS TO THREE YEARS OF AGE

Directions: Check all the statements below that are characteristic of your toddler. Then total the checks in each column and compare your totals. Typically, most of your responses will be in one or two of the categories, providing a clear picture of your toddler's preferred learning style.

LOOKER	LISTENER	MOVER
1. Communication: When my toddler wishes to express herself . . .		
❏ She has a small vocabulary.	❏ She has a large vocabulary.	❏ She often relies on nonverbal communication.
❏ She speaks in short sentences.	❏ She combines words into long sentences that are easy to understand.	❏ She speaks very little.
❏ She sometimes reverses the order of words within sentences.	❏ She talks all the time.	❏ She has to be encouraged to talk.
2. Favorite Toys and Pastimes: When my toddler plays . . .		
❏ She likes shape sorters and stacking rings.	❏ She prefers being read to.	❏ She often chooses the sandbox and other outdoor activities.
❏ She often chooses to play with blocks.	❏ She quickly learns the words to nursery rhymes and songs.	❏ She often pulls things out of drawers and off shelves.
❏ She likes crayons, paper, and paints.	❏ She likes tapes and CD's.	❏ She frequently takes toys apart.
3. Motor Skills: When my toddler moves about . . .		
❏ She likes to use her hands and fingers in play.	❏ She concentrates on language rather than full-body play.	❏ She especially likes to climb.
❏ While on a swing, she looks around the playground.	❏ Coordination is not her strong suit.	❏ She is very well coordinated.
4. Social Skills: When my toddler is around other people . . .		
❏ She often pulls away from being touched.	❏ She likes to be close, but prefers talking to touching or holding.	❏ She likes to be rocked and held, and always wants more.
❏ She tends to stand back and watch.	❏ She changes the volume of her speech according to her mood.	❏ She seeks out hugs.

5. Emotions: When it comes to my toddler's feelings . . .

❏ She is not very emotional.	❏ She expresses her feelings with dramatic flair.	❏ Her feelings are easily hurt.
❏ She seems surprised by the outbursts of other children.	❏ She uses names for feelings, such as "happy" and "sad."	❏ She is prone to frequent and surprising outbursts of joy and anger.

6. Memory: When my toddler learns . . .

❏ She remembers faces.	❏ She adds words to her vocabulary quickly.	❏ She imitates the actions she sees, such as washing the car.
❏ She remembers activities best after seeing them.	❏ She remembers a word or name after hearing it only once.	❏ She remembers activities best after doing them.

TOTALS: _____ LOOKER   _____ LISTENER   _____ MOVER

CHAPTER FOUR

Learning Styles
in the Preschool Years

B etween the ages of three and five years, a child makes tremendous strides toward independence. He still requires lots of reassurance and support from his parents, and even more frequent guidance and instruction, but what he learns during the preschool period helps a child bridge the gap between the emotional neediness of toddlerhood and the relative self-reliance he'll have to draw upon when he begins school.

Most of the experiences that bombard the preschooler during these important months are a function of his learning style. From ages three to five, a child's inborn sensory preference can cause his perceptions to be quite different from those of his peers and playmates. This is because preschool-aged Lookers, Listeners, and Movers continue to be drawn to and responsive to very different types of stimulation, even when their surroundings are the same.

This chapter introduces you to a Looker, a Listener, and Mover at the start of the preschool period. Comparisons of each learner's development from age three to age five are also provided to demonstrate the impact of learning style on a child's different skill areas.

Preschool programs and their accompanying social experiences can play a big part in a three- or four-year-old's development. This chapter explains how to make your preschooler's learning style a factor in your selection of his school, in your reinforcement of the learning he does there, and in your discussions with his teacher. The chapter concludes with lists of easy-to-implement ideas, grouped according to learning style, for building up your preschooler's weaker skills while providing him with plenty of opportunities to play at the activities he loves best. A Learning Style QuickCheck for Preschoolers is included to help you determine your child's learning-style preference (see page 91).

The child who enters the preschool phase of life may still seem very much a toddler. But by the end of this stage, both feet are firmly planted in childhood. Have fun with your preschooler as he travels the meandering path that will lead him to the social and academic challenges of kindergarten.

A LOOK AT THREE LEARNERS

Elena, Rachel, and William are all three years of age. Each of the children has caring and involved parents and a school-aged sibling. All three children are veterans of baby gym, story time programs, and adult-child activity groups, and all will attend preschool next fall. But, as you will see, similar backgrounds do not necessarily yield like children. Because our three preschoolers have different learning styles, from the very beginning, they have responded to, absorbed, and processed information from their surroundings in diverse ways and at varied speeds. While it's not uncommon to encounter children who exhibit combinations of learning styles—Looker-Listeners, for instance, or Looker-Movers—for the sake of clarity, you will see that each of our case studies demonstrates characteristics of a single learning style. Let's look at our three learners.

Three Years of Age

Meet Elena. Looker Elena is a quiet but contented child. Her speech and vocabulary are within normal range for her age, but Elena keeps to herself, just as she did throughout babyhood. Working alone, she produces tremendous quantities of artwork, which she displays all over the house. Elena can draw or paint a person, a tree, a flower, a house, and a variety of animal-type creatures, complete with detail. She also loves cutting and pasting and working with clay. However, Elena's dexterity doesn't carry over into gross motor areas. Her climbing, hopping, and other full-body efforts are still hesitant and somewhat clumsy.

Elena has recently discovered fashion dolls. She delights in matching the little outfits, and does more dressing and undressing of the dolls than actual pretend play. Elena is also a great fan of her library's children's room, which has eight computers, an enclosed magazine and puzzle area, papier-mâché replicas of various storybook characters strung from the ceiling, a puppet stage, and a rug modeled after a giant game board. Every visit she makes is a visual treat.

Just as she always has, Elena learns best by observing. She is quick to say, "Show me" or "Let me see" when she doesn't understand something, and gets many play ideas by watching other children. In a Looker's typically reserved fashion, though, Elena waits until that child is elsewhere before trying the activity herself. She can recognize and read the logos on various delivery trucks; can spot words like "library," "school," and "deli"; and can spell out her name with magnetic letters. At age three, Elena is the very picture of a preschool Looker: visually oriented, good with her hands, and somewhat below the norm in gross motor and social skills.

Meet Rachel. Rachel, a Listener, is just four days younger than Elena. She, too, avoids gross motor activities when she can, well aware that they're not her strong suit. In fact, Rachel has begun to volunteer her services as "judge" or "audience," depending on which part assures the most sedentary role. This satisfies Rachel's need to socialize without demanding too much running around on her part. Rachel's fine motor coordination is on a similar level, so she frequently asks for help with the eye-hand portion of activities, requesting, for instance, that her parents "Draw some characters for my story" or "Build a block house for my circus animals."

Rachel's verbal skills are quite advanced for a child of three. She knows scores of rhymes, chants, and jingles, and she sings—on key—to almost every activity. She can also recite her street address and phone number, as well as the names of family members. Rachel is fascinated by words; in fact, when she hears something new, she'll ask for a single repetition and then immediately assimilate it into her vocabulary.

When it comes to play, Rachel's current favorite pastimes include joke- and storytelling, playing "Mommy" or "school," and listening to all types of music. Because children her age find her somewhat bossy, and because older playmates provide conversation better suited to her sophisticated tastes, Rachel often trails after her big sister's friends. But the lagging fine and gross motor skills that are so typical of a young Listener keep Rachel from really enjoying either group's games and fun.

Meet William. Like Rachel and Elena, Mover William is three years of age. However, gross motor activities pose no problem for him. He loves to run, climb, wrestle, and play "karate." In fact, William is so given to full-body movement that he simply cannot sit still for table play or stories. Within minutes, he's rolling or crawling around on the floor, instead.

At play time, William ignores puzzles, games, and paper and crayons in favor of his fleet of construction trucks, his bicycle, and his growing collection of sports equipment. He manages to turn even his sister's playthings into Mover props: her purse becomes his mailbag; her dolls, his "bad guys"; her doll stroller, his snowplow; and so on. He is patently uninterested in drawing, bead stringing, or any other activity involving eye-hand coordination, for these pose quite a problem for him. At night, he spurns books and stories in favor of a back rub and lots of hugs.

At three years of age, William still speaks in two- and three-word sentences. He thinks hard before uttering all but the simplest words, yet still mispronounces many of them. William becomes understandably upset when he can't express himself, crying, stomping, and shrieking in frustration. Tantrums, which have been part of his behavioral repertoire for almost two years, still occur daily. The give-and-take of ordinary conversation is much too fast for William, and he loses interest almost as quickly as he tunes out instructions, lectures, and even the briefest of monologues. This little Mover will soon be entering preschool with excellent full-body coordination, but with verbal and fine motor skills that lag far behind those of many of his classmates.

Does your preschooler seem most tuned in to visual stimuli, like Looker Elena? Does he react to and learn from sounds, like Listener Rachel? Or is he most like Mover William—highly sensitive and in perpetual motion? The Learning Style QuickCheck for Preschoolers on page 91 will tell you how your child learns. Simply check off the characteristics that best describe your child, and then total each of the three columns: Looker, Listener, and Mover. The column with the most checks is the category into which your little learner fits.

HOW LOOKER, LISTENER, AND MOVER PRESCHOOLERS DEVELOP

You've seen that their diverse learning styles have led Elena, Rachel, and William to become strikingly different three-year-olds. The way these children absorb, process, and respond to environmental information is still determined by the sensory preference each possessed at birth. As you follow our three learners throughout the preschool period, you'll see that the developmental differences that exist at age three only become more marked with the passage of time.

Three-and-a-Half to Five Years of Age

Elena. As she moves through the preschool period, Looker Elena continues to express herself in short, unelaborated sentences. Even at home, she rarely volunteers information, and must be coaxed to provide details about school. Elena plays regularly with one neighboring child; when several are present, she usually retreats to the sidelines to watch for a while before deciding whether to join in their games. Elena's gross motor skills are now acceptable for her age, though she's far better at swatting or bouncing a ball than at activities requiring full-body coordination, like racing or hopping.

Since so many gross motor activities call for either socializing or getting dirty—neither of which thrills her—Elena gravitates toward art projects and solo play. She enjoys board games and puzzles, and has taken to building projects—high-rises, bridges, and castles—from a variety of blocks. Elena takes pride in her precise coloring and skillful cutting and pasting, and presents each masterpiece to her mother for display.

Elena has a carton of "favorite" picture books and has begun to sight-read words that crop up with any frequency—mom, dad, yes, no, dog, cat, and the like. She also employs her memory when reading whatever street and traffic signs she passes. Lately, Elena has become fascinated by the details on automobiles, and she can now discriminate between different makes and models by their trunk and hood ornamentation, wheel covers, or taillight configuration. In fact, one of her favorite games is to "match" passing cars to those of people she knows. "There's a car like Grandma's, only blue!" she may shout. Or "David's mom has that same car, only her lights aren't broken."

At preschool, Elena never commands the limelight. There, as at home, she is attentive but quiet, busying herself with solitary games and projects. Her sophisticated artwork stands out from that of her classmates, and she is one of the few preschoolers who can print the entire alphabet—neatly—from memory. By her fifth birthday, Elena can copy the names of all her classmates, and about a dozen other words as well. As her very rewarding preschool experience ends, Elena looks ahead to the start of kindergarten with excitement.

Rachel. Listener Rachel is as much a chatterbox as Elena is reserved. She uses elaborate sentences and multiple-syllable words, and astounds her teachers and classmates daily with such vocabulary gems as "binoculars," "wigwam," and "diagonal." When she's not taking the lead in home or school discussions, Rachel can usually be found relating every detail of a story or reciting some rhyme or song—verbatim.

It comes as no surprise that Rachel delights in group activities and considers almost everyone her friend. Because her advanced verbal skills make her a natural organizer and leader, Rachel's earlier tendency toward bossiness flourishes during her preschool years. Accustomed to assigning roles and detailing instructions, she is quick to "tell" on friends or classmates who don't follow the rules.

Rachel still shows little interest in arts and crafts or intricate toys. She cannot yet print, and when asked to draw, dashes off a simple picture and then dresses it up with an accompanying story. She seems to view painting, drawing, and cutting and pasting activities as opportunities to socialize, and is more concerned with conversation than with completing the project at hand. Rachel has come to enjoy time spent on the playground because of the opportunities for interacting with friends. As she does at home, Rachel attempts to control her group's play verbally, as in "Let's pretend we're the three bears walking back to our home, which is here, under the slide. You be the mother, you be the father, and I'll be the baby bear." If the game takes a more physical turn, with the "bears" chasing one another or careening down the slide, Rachel usually makes her way indoors—just as she does when the weather happens to turn a bit too hot, cold, damp, or windy to suit her.

At preschool, Rachel separates easily from her parents. She is helpful, personable, knowledgeable, and so eager to read that she grabs every chance to ask what labels, posters, and notes "say." Of course, Rachel consistently receives glowing reports from her teachers. Like Looker Elena, Rachel will enter kindergarten with confidence and eager anticipation born of a positive preschool experience.

William. Unlike talkative Rachel, Mover William's more rudimentary speech is labored and difficult to understand. He mispronounces sounds, misinterprets some of what is said, fails to grasp common expressions, and has trouble recalling spoken instructions or details. Even at five, William still relies on body language to communicate, grabbing, hitting, and pushing before thinking of expressing his needs in words. Still, he is a sensitive child, easily hurt himself, and alert to, if not always considerate of, the feelings of others. Just as he has since babyhood, William constantly seeks out body contact with family, friends, and teachers. In fact, he is often reprimanded for his habit of bestowing exuberant bear hugs on his peers.

William is extremely well coordinated. The training wheels on his bicycle are long gone, and he can climb a pole, kick a football, and swing a racket as well as boys two years older. Brave and daring, William takes the lead during most outdoor play, with the habitual disarray of his clothes serving as testimony to his activity level. William has become more interested in art projects of late, but likes to work "big." Easel and mural projects are much more to his liking than cutting and pasting, partly due to the fact that he has yet to designate a dominant hand. William has already abandoned any attempts at neatness; in fact, the messier the activity, the better he likes it. You can count on this little Mover to throw down his fist-clutched crayons when the finger paints appear. Few of his creations make it to the refrigerator door, though. Usually, they're dropped, torn, or forgotten.

Preschool presents a problem for William because he doesn't have the patience for the sit-down activities that accompany so much of the curriculum. Class discussions, story time, worksheets, sing-alongs, and intricate art projects exact a heavy toll on a child who would prefer to be running about. Since he lacks the visual and auditory skills needed to print a number, learn a song, or recite the alphabet, William quickly turns his attention to diversionary activities—making animal noises, throwing paper, or tickling his classmates. Not a morning has passed during which William hasn't suffered consequences for misbehavior, and his teachers have grave reservations about his preparedness for kindergarten.

LEARNING STYLE AS A PRESCHOOL CONSIDERATION

A generation ago, preschool was somewhat of a luxury. Today, most parents view it as an important step in a child's progression toward school readiness. A year or two spent in the company of qualified adults and a roomful of busy three- or four-year-olds teaches a child a great deal about separating from his parents, responding to different authority figures, focusing on the completion of tasks, and functioning as part of a group.

With luck, the preschool you select for your youngster will exercise all of his developmental areas—physical, social, emotional, and intellectual—rather than focusing on the more formal class work he'll face as a kindergartener. Since most children aren't really ready to read or write until they're past the age of five, any pre-academic work that's covered should be presented in the spirit of play. Of course, the bottom line is that preschool will have to be fun if your child is to enjoy going there.

Assuming that your community offers a choice of schools, what else should you look for? Once you've pinpointed your child's learning style with the Learning Style QuickCheck for Preschoolers (see page 91), you'll be able to make a more informed selection. These general guidelines may help you.

Preschool for Lookers

During the preschool years, the quiet, visually oriented Looker learns by first observing and then imitating what he sees. He's perfectly suited to classrooms in which there are different learning centers—science and math tables, a reading corner, a dress-up area, a block section, and the like—from which he can choose. Naturally, he'll gravitate toward puzzles, games, building sets, and other forms of solitary play every chance he gets, so it will be helpful if classes are small and there's an extra adult or two on hand to note his habits and occasionally steer him toward group activities. A preschool setting that emphasizes cooperation and offers daily exposure to music, as well as provisions for outdoor and indoor full-body play, will stimulate a Looker's less-favored senses of hearing and touch and, as a result, help him gradually strengthen his Listener and Mover skills.

Preschool for Listeners

The sociable, talkative Listener learns by putting what he hears to work. He'll flourish in any classroom with materials for dramatics—a puppet theater, a housekeeping corner, a mock store, or a make-believe post office. And for a Listener, a piano, rhythm instruments, and cassette player should be viewed as necessities rather than frills.

A Listener preschooler rarely accepts things at face value, and he'll feel most free to ask the questions, rattle off the instructions, and offer the explanations so characteristic of his learning style in a permissive classroom atmosphere, in which individuality and independence are highly regarded. Since he's likely to ignore the chalk, stamp pads, blocks, trucks, and *Tinkertoys* that are provided during free play time, the Listener will benefit from scheduled gym and crafts periods or from other teacher-directed opportunities to exercise his large and small muscles.

Preschool for Movers

The Mover preschooler learns best what he experiences with his whole body. For him, the school facilities are an important consideration, for more than anything else, the Mover needs space—floor space, a gym, and a play yard in which to roam free. He'll find only frustration with a teacher who heavily emphasizes paper-and-pencil tasks or sit-and-listen activities. More than either of the other learners, the Mover needs a setting in which different ability levels are expected, accepted, and used as a basis for personalized activities. It's wise to remember that the Mover's awareness of his lagging skills is usually keen at this age. The smaller the pupil-teacher ratio in his preschool, the more support and attention he'll receive.

Though he should feel free to be messy until his maturing fine motor abilities permit neater work, the Mover still needs encouragement in the use of his small muscles. Simple crafts that emphasize free expression rather than duplication of a teacher's prototype can gradually stretch a Mover's eye-hand capabilities, as can almost any free-time activity that's made into a game—piling checkers into a tower, for example. Moreover, the Mover stands to benefit from a classroom atmosphere in which cooperation, assistance, appropriate conversation, and other social skills are painstakingly taught and rewarded.

Sharing Information About Learning Style

Once your child is enrolled in a preschool that is well suited to his learning style, it's important to enlighten the teachers about how he best learns, plays, and socializes. From the beginning, parents can mention that their child seems to be a visual, auditory, or kinesthetic learner. The terms "Looker, "Listener," and "Mover" may crop up on their own as you and the teacher discuss the specifics of your child's learning preference. If not, you can simply describe your child's learning strengths and weaknesses, and then mention a tactic or two with which you have had success at home. For instance, you might say to the teacher, "Kerry remembers everything she sees, but she seems hesitant to talk and doesn't always pronounce words as well as other children her age. Recently, we began a word book in which we paste photographs of new vocabulary terms. Now, Kerry seems more interested in using new words when she speaks."

Conclusions about your child's learning preferences will, no doubt, be reached by the preschool staff eventually. But early communication may spare a quiet Looker child weeks of being overlooked, or prevent a Mover child from initially being coerced into sit-down activities that he's simply not equipped to handle. A child's happiness and well-rounded development are the goal, and this goal is most likely to be attained when adults share the following information.

Learning New Skills

How does your child learn best? If he's a Looker, like Elena, he will learn best when provided with demonstrations or illustrations that he can copy. If he's a Listener, like Rachel, he may need detailed spoken instructions and verbal reinforcement. A Mover, like William, generally requires the most assistance. Because of the Mover's difficulty paying attention within a group and processing information spoken across a room, teacher and child or parents and child may need to perform the new skill together.

Correcting Behavior

What approach seems best when correcting your child's behavior? Often, a warning glance is all that's required to set a Looker preschooler back on track. Listeners, of course, respond best to explanations and to such verbal validations of their own protests as, "I'm sorry you're tired. Maybe you'd like to take a rest after you pick up the toys." Movers, who thrive on action, often require redirection to some acceptable action. For example, karate kicks of a block tower can be redirected toward a Bop Bag; while the tendency to lie down *anywhere*—on a table, for instance—can be refocused to a beanbag chair. Movers also need more touching—more hugs, more lap time, more by-the-shoulders steering—than other learners.

Kinds of Play

How does your child like to play? At school, he probably gravitates toward the same types of toys and games that he chooses at home. It's also likely that these activities and playthings are a clear reflection of his learning style. Lookers, for example, often love building sets, while Movers prefer riding toys. You may wish to exchange suggestions with your child's teachers about games, activities, and techniques that have been used successfully to strengthen your child's weaker skills.

Observations About Development

Are there aspects of your child's development that warrant attention? Does he sufficiently communicate his needs? Are his fine and gross motor skills significantly behind those of his classmates? Does he have the ability to listen and pay attention for short periods of time? You might wish to exchange observations about your child's development with his teachers and compare notes periodically about his progress in these areas.

Support Services

Are speech, hearing, and vision screening available at your child's school? If so, it would be a good idea to take advantage of these services. And should further evaluation be recommended, it would be best to follow up immediately rather than delay and, thus, risk a widening of the gaps in your child's skills.

TECHNIQUES FOR AFFIRMING AND DEVELOPING LEARNING SKILLS

As the preschool-aged child becomes more independent of his parents, grows comfortable with the preschool staff, and acquaints himself with his classmates, he becomes part of a world of rapidly expanding horizons. Between time spent playing alone and time spent with parents and teachers, a child is—with luck—treated to sensory experiences that are both constant and varied. And when a preschooler's learning style becomes a consideration in the planning of his daily activities, he receives healthy measures of both the stimulation he craves and that which he needs to bring weaker skills up to par.

The sections that follow describe the benefits of developing those skills that are part of the three learning styles: looking, listening, and moving. In the case of each style, this is followed by a list of toys and techniques meant to strengthen the skills of children who show a preference for that style. Then suggestions are presented for developing a similar sensory awareness in children who possess one of the other two learning styles.

The ideas for learning-style affirmation include toys and games that challenge a learner's strengths. The suggestions for developing lagging skills have been selected because they are multisensory. That is, they employ two or more senses simultaneously—one of which, in this case, is the sense your child needs to develop. Those multisensory activities and materials that also involve your child's preferred sense are, of course, the ones that will work best for him.

As you peruse the lists, looking for ideas suited to your child, remember that *fun* should be your main criterion. Please enjoy yourselves, whether the activities you choose are for your child's use alone or for the two of you to try out as a team.

Building Looker Skills

Children rely on their Looker skills when they observe, memorize, and recreate. These are the skills that give certain children the edge when it comes to reading readiness, artwork, and paper-and-pencil tasks. While good eye-hand coordination and the willingness to persevere at a task are both skills that come naturally to the Looker child, these skills can also be encouraged in other learners when the right play experiences are provided. Of course, preschool-aged Lookers will be the most receptive to activities involving visual stimulation; after all, these children are naturally inclined to use their eyes and hands. Listeners, who much prefer socializing to solitary play, but can certainly use some fine motor development, may find their interest piqued by toys and games built around conversation. Movers, who also need help with visual and eye-hand skills, will be happiest about those Looker activities that are the least restrictive. The following ideas should help you strengthen your child's visual abilities.

ENHANCING A PRESCHOOLER'S EXISTING LOOKER SKILLS

- Provide a fishing set with a pole and line containing a magnet or hook that your child can use to catch brightly colored toy fish.

- Hasbro's classic *Tinkertoys* is a building system with colorful, diverse pieces and illustrated instructions for assembling various creations.

- The *Where's Waldo?* series of books (Candlewick Press) has Waldo and other unusual characters waiting to be found somewhere in each illustration—on a busy street, in a prehistoric scene, and so on.

- *Lincoln Logs*, a classic since 1916, allow children to build structures like a cabin and post office with wooden logs that interlock.

- Provide puzzles of increasing complexity and numbers of pieces.

- Introduce a first board game like *Hi-Ho Cherry-O* by Hasbro.

- Offer your child a collection of small objects, and make a game of sorting them according to color, shape, and size.

- A *View-Master 3D Viewer* by Fisher-Price has reels of television and movie characters appearing in 3-D. The pictures change with the flick of a lever.

- *Pixter* by Fisher-Price is a hand-held electronic toy that allows children to draw pictures, change them, and even save their creations.

- *My First LeapPad* by Leap Frog teaches the alphabet, counting, shapes, and color identification. Children touch a "magic pen" to points on the flip book to hear accompanying words.

ENCOURAGING THE DEVELOPMENT OF LOOKER SKILLS
IN PRESCHOOLERS WHO ARE LISTENERS

■ Provide different-colored and different-sized beads and cord for your child to use in creating bracelets and necklaces for herself and for family members.

■ Your Listener will enjoy learning the rules of a simple game, as well as the social interactions of playing with family and friends. Try the *Little People Matchin' With Maggie* game by Fisher-Price—a variation of the classic *Memory* game.

■ Playskool's now-classic *Mr. Potato Head* has a large plastic head with holes for the insertion of various brightly colored facial features and accessories.

■ *Tinkertoy Plastic Starter Set* by Hasbro encourages less-adept fingers to build and create.

■ Invent "pretend" scenarios to encourage visualization. Your child can be the gas station attendant, postal worker, waiter, or shop-keeper, and you can be the customer. Few props are needed as you act out your parts together.

■ Place several small toys in a bag. Ask your child to slip his hand into the bag and identify a toy by touch. Once he guesses, he can remove the toy to see if he's right.

■ Jumbo-sized crayons, which are much easier to manipulate than their standard-sized counterparts, are available in most variety and toy stores.

■ To encourage drawing, provide "fun" writing implements like glit-ter pens, scented markers, neon-colored pencils, four-color pens, and character pencil toppers.

■ Make a game of scribbling on blank paper and then examining the results for hidden "pictures." Take turns pointing out what you see in each other's creations.

■ Pore over photo albums together, recounting the stories behind your child's favorite snapshots.

ENCOURAGING THE DEVELOPMENT OF LOOKER SKILLS
IN PRESCHOOLERS WHO ARE MOVERS

■ Take your child for a walk around the block. When you return, show him how to "palm." Do this by holding his hands, palms up, in front of him. Place the center of his cupped palms over his eyes to shut out all outside light. Then tell him to close his eyes. While his eyes are closed, ask questions about what he saw in the neighborhood, such as "What color was the big moving truck?" and "Was the mail carrier wearing a hat?"

■ *Play-Doh* by Hasbro makes a variety of different play sets—like an ice cream shop and flower garden—that enable a child to press, roll, and slice colored modeling dough into diverse forms.

■ Give your Mover an opportunity to look and move simultaneously by playing the Hap Palmer video *Baby's Busy Day*. Live-action finger-snapping songs introduce colors, shapes, and number concepts.

■ Allow your child to dial numbers on the telephone pad. As you call out a number, he can push the corresponding button.

■ Provide a brush, a cup of water, and a paint-with-water book. The colors will appear as soon as water touches the page, so your youngster's finished picture will look great every time.

■ With *Magna Doodle Plus Color* by Fisher-Price, children use the spiral art wheel to create fun designs and then color them with three washable dry-erase markers.

■ Large, soft sidewalk chalk is perfect for drawing and scribbling on driveways or cement. Your child's creations will last until the next rainfall.

■ *Duplo* blocks by Lego are the big brothers of the classic Lego blocks. The pieces snap together and come in a variety of forms and sizes. Most important, they aren't so small that they will frustrate a child with an unsteady hand.

■ A chalkboard affixed to the wall at your child's height will encourage drawing, particularly when you leave him daily picture messages and prompt him to do the same for you.

■ Finger painting on large sheets of paper gets the eyes and hands working together, and allows your Mover to be as messy as he likes.

Building Listener Skills

Because socialization is so important to a preschool-aged child, Lookers, Listeners, and Movers can all benefit from building those skills that facilitate conversation and social behavior. At the same time, encouraging a child's self-expression and reliance upon auditory memory helps him vent frustrations and prepare for the academic work that awaits him in kindergarten. Offering a Listener child a toy or activity that taxes his verbal skills is a simple matter, of course. You won't find the going as easy if he's a Looker or Mover. But chances are, he'll be most receptive to Listener games and playthings that also call his favored sense into play. Here are some skill-developing suggestions for all three types of learners.

ENHANCING A PRESCHOOLER'S EXISTING LISTENER SKILLS

■ Continue the practice of regularly scheduled story times. Encourage your child to relate part of the story or fill in a blank as you tell it. For example, "When Goldilocks sat in Baby Bear's chair, _____." Pause long enough for your child to explain what happens next.

■ *Bob the Builder Walkie Talkies* by Hasbro have a 100-foot outdoor range, and a belt clip to keep hands free when not talking.

■ Attend children's concerts and storytelling festivals. The combination of music and words is very stimulating to Listeners.

■ Most public libraries schedule story hours for preschoolers. This opportunity to hear a tale and sing a few songs—all in the company of other young children—will delight Listeners.

■ Just for fun, make it a practice to make up poems and rhymes as you travel in the car or work at a task together.

■ Familiarize your preschooler with the world of poetry by borrowing and reading aloud collections from your library's children's section.

- *Deluxe Karaoke Stage Microphone*, available from JC Penney, has two detachable microphones to allow two Listeners to sing a duet!

- Teach your child how to select and borrow cassettes and CDs from the library. This will provide him with the largest and most varied selection of songs and stories possible.

- The Fisher-Price *Tuff-Stuff Tape Recorder* has a sing-along microphone and easy-to-push buttons. Your child can listen to prerecorded tapes or make tapes of his own.

- Allow your Listener to call friends on the phone and chat.

ENCOURAGING THE DEVELOPMENT OF LISTENER SKILLS IN PRESCHOOLERS WHO ARE LOOKERS

- *Listening Lotto*, distributed by Lakeshore, offers playing cards of pictures that correspond to sounds on a tape. When your child hears a baby's cry, for example, he covers the picture of the baby on his card.

- Look through magazines together, and take turns making up stories about the people in the various pictures.

- Turn the key and slide the gearshift to hear words and sounds with *See 'n Say Drive and Learn Phonics* by Fisher-Price.

- A toy cash register or ATM machine will visually appeal to your Looker while providing him with opportunities to talk with "customers."

- *What's Wrong?* by Lakeshore is a set of picture cards with such obvious mistakes as a telephone with a banana for a receiver, or a man bathing in his clothes—all sure to get a laugh from your Looker! Be certain to ask him to describe what he sees.

- Treat your child to a new vocabulary word each day. You can start by presenting, defining, and acting out the day's word, and then attach a picture of it to the refrigerator or your child's lunch bag. Be sure to use the word in conversation as many times as possible.

- *Vtech Bright Buddy Laptop*, available from JC Penney, will appeal to your Looker because it looks just like a real laptop, and teaches letters and numbers through ten different sound-enhanced activities.

■ Lookers will enjoy manipulating the plastic pieces in a jigsaw puzzle map of the United States, while you provide the names of the states and some interesting information about each one.

■ Invite your Looker to help you set the table for a tea party and enjoy some conversation.

■ Audio books permit listening and looking simultaneously. For starters, try *Green Eggs and Ham* from the Beginner Book and Cassette Library, available on Amazon.

ENCOURAGING THE DEVELOPMENT OF LISTENER SKILLS IN PRESCHOOLERS WHO ARE MOVERS

■ Join your child in pretend play with a farm, an airport, or a marina play set. Encourage him to make up a story and provide the voice of a character as you set up the scenery and play with the various pieces.

■ The *There Goes a Fire Truck* video, available on Amazon, will mesmerize your Mover with its action while he simultaneously processes verbal information.

■ Read picture books to your child about things that move—trains, planes, construction vehicles, and fire trucks. He'll love stories with built-in action.

■ Keep hats, badges, toy tools, and other dress-up accessories on hand, and encourage conversation and the assuming of various roles as you and your child stage highway repairs, a cab ride, or a visit to the doctor.

■ Childcraft's *Storytelling Sets* transform story time into a mini-theater with accompanying puppets and props.

■ When your preschooler accompanies you on an errand, occasionally allow time for him to explore, touch, and taste the things you encounter en route. The more involved he is in the outing, the more likely he'll be to respond to your questions with dialogue of his own.

■ Play "beauty shop" or "barber shop" to encourage both action and conversation.

- Play "doctor, nurse, and patient" with a toy doctor's bag and stethoscope.

- To ensure your Mover's attention, embellish nursery rhymes with movement. For example, during "Little Miss Muffet," you can encourage your child to sit, use an imaginary bowl and spoon, and then leap up in fright.

- Sit with your preschooler during a broadcast of his favorite television show. Your presence and encouragement will help to focus his attention.

Building Mover Skills

Well-developed Mover skills have little to do with a child's conversational ability, attention span, or other classroom "pluses." But by preschool age, the agile and coordinated child exudes a sense of confidence that puts him in the lead both in the gym and on the playground. It follows, then, that a body image and overall athleticism that are improved by exposure to large-muscle activities will stand every preschooler in good stead.

A child who is a Mover will, no doubt, be a willing participant in any gross motor game or technique you wish to try, simply because these activities appeal to his inborn sensory preference. In contrast, Lookers and Listeners will be navigating foreign waters each time they attempt full-body play. But you can make the going a bit easier for them by building in some of the visual and auditory stimulation they adore. You should find some of these ideas helpful in encouraging your child's Mover skills.

ENHANCING A PRESCHOOLER'S EXISTING MOVER SKILLS

- Provide your child with knee pads, a helmet, and a pair of ice, roller, or in-line skates.

- Encourage your preschooler to walk, hop, and twirl on a ground-level balance beam. A street-side curb or a two-by-four placed on the grass can serve the same purpose.

- Seek out a cargo net, knotted rope, or rope ladder for your child's climbing practice.

■ Available from JC Penney, *Hot Wheels* makes a first bike that adjusts to a child's growing body and includes training wheels.

■ Access to an outdoor swing set encourages a child to hoist himself into a swing and pump his legs to get in motion.

■ Several companies make a Bop Bag, which is a sand-weighted inflatable toy with bounce-back action. This is the perfect target for venting frustrations or just-for-the-fun-of-it rhythmic punching.

■ Tonka makes a realistic heavy-duty mixer, dump truck, and crane that are perfect for use in sand, dirt, leaves, and pebbles.

■ Provide your child with a lightweight nylon tent—or just tack an old blanket to a fence—for all kinds of outdoor play.

■ The Fisher-Price *Grow-to-Pro Basketball* adjusts from three to six feet to grow with your Mover.

■ Provide a tumbling mat and some indoor space for somersaults and back rolls.

ENCOURAGING THE DEVELOPMENT OF MOVER SKILLS IN PRESCHOOLERS WHO ARE LOOKERS

■ With its retro design and its red color, Radio Flyer's twelve-inch *Classic Red Tricycle*, available on Amazon, will appeal to your Looker's sense of style.

■ Dance and exercise with your preschooler, encouraging him to move at different energy levels to different tempos.

■ A two-sided easel, with a clipboard on one side and a chalkboard on the other, will permit your child to involve his whole body in various large-scale projects.

■ For no-miss dunking, present your child with a height-adjustable basketball net and a *Nerf Ball* basketball.

■ Offer one of the widely available games in which Velcro-covered balls are tossed at a large, colorful target. This safe variation of darts encourages throwing practice, because a "hit" is almost guaranteed.

■ Make pom-poms out of lightweight paper and encourage your child to play cheerleader, with lots of running, jumping, bending, and stretching.

■ Seek out a two-step flight of stairs on which your child can practice climbing and jumping.

■ Provide a collection of washable cars and trucks for your preschooler's indoor and outdoor use.

■ Give your child a paintbrush and a bucket of water, and ask him to "paint" the fence, the steps, or the sidewalk.

■ Play a child-sized game of ring toss or horse shoes.

ENCOURAGING THE DEVELOPMENT OF MOVER SKILLS IN PRESCHOOLERS WHO ARE LISTENERS

■ A selection of pool toys—floats, swim rings, and ride-on inflatable animals—makes water play almost irresistible.

■ Play catch with a large, soft *Nerf Ball*. Stand very close to your child as you aim the ball into his outstretched arms. As his skills improve, you'll be able to move farther apart.

■ Listeners learn to dance with *Dance Maker*, available from JC Penney. Using blinking lights to indicate the steps, the colorful electronic dance mat guides Listeners through four different dance patterns at three different speeds.

■ Introduce your child to gardening. Your Listener will enjoy learning the names of the plants, and will get practice raking, planting, and watering.

■ Create an outdoor play spot that's just for your child. Occasionally change the accompanying toys to vary his activities.

■ Enroll your child in a preschool dance class. Your Listener will enjoy making new friends.

■ A child-sized easel will allow your Listener to "play teacher" and get in some full-body movement at the same time.

■ Your preschooler can take on the role of navigator, passenger, or pilot when you provide a child-sized wagon for his outdoor use.

■ *Big Strike Bowling Set* by Little Tikes has clear plastic pins with brightly colored balls inside. They make a reinforcing clatter sound when the pins are knocked down.

■ Buy an exercise video created for preschoolers, and "work out" with your child.

When selecting activities and playthings for your preschooler, keep in mind that flexibility is important—even vital. Naturally, no two children will be ready for a given toy at exactly the same time, nor will they derive equal enjoyment from it even when its introduction is timed exactly right. A trip to the toy store may well convince you that a different toy from one I've recommended will achieve the same developmental purpose, while being much better suited to the tastes of you and your child. You are certainly the best judge of your youngster's temperament, so I urge you to trust your instincts in modifying my suggestions or in borrowing ideas from the lists compiled for other types of learners.

It's also important that you not expect overnight success in your efforts to round out your preschooler's learning skills. The fact is that many weeks may pass before you first notice that there's a new sureness to his grip, that he's becoming more observant, or that he's relying more frequently on verbal rather than bodily expressions of his wants and needs. But the changes will come in time, bringing with them a satisfying sense of achievement that will put smiles on both of your faces.

LEARNING STYLE QUICKCHECK FOR PRESCHOOLERS, THREE TO FIVE YEARS OF AGE

Directions: Review the following list of behaviors, checking off those that are characteristic of your child. Then total each column and compare your results. In most cases, you'll find your responses concentrated in one or two of the columns. The learning style listed at the top of that column is the learning style of your preschooler.

LOOKER	LISTENER	MOVER
1. Communication: When my preschooler wishes to express himself . . .		
❏ He speaks in short sentences using simple language.	☒ He talks a lot and uses complete sentences.	❏ His sentences are brief, and sometimes he searches for words.
❏ He could be considered a "quiet child."	☒ He relates stories in detail.	❏ He communicates with body movement and facial expression more than with words.
☒ He communicates through drawing and painting.	☒ He enjoys the give-and-take of conversation.	❏ He sometimes talks to inanimate objects such as his toys.
2. Favorite Toys and Pastimes: When my preschooler plays alone . . .		
❏ He likes beads, blocks, puzzles, and crayons.	☒ He makes up stories.	❏ He wants to play outside no matter what the weather.
☒ He likes watching TV and videos.	❏ He likes books, tapes, and music.	☒ He heads for tricycles and other wheeled toys.
☒ He enjoys drawing, coloring, and crafts.	☒ He likes to look at books while telling himself a story.	☒ He loves to climb.
3. Motor Skills: When my preschooler moves about . . .		
☒ He cuts, colors, and prints with ease.	☒ He prefers talking to fine or gross motor activities.	☒ He runs, jumps, and climbs with coordination.
❏ He's not an "active child," preferring sit-down activities at a table or desk.	☒ He loves to talk about the artwork he produces.	☒ He prefers active play to sit-down activities.
☒ He draws a recognizable person.	☒ He talks and instructs himself while drawing.	❏ He does not yet draw anything recognizable.
4. Social Skills: When my preschooler mixes with other children . . .		
❏ He's one of the quiet ones.	☒ He makes conversation easily.	❏ He is very sociable.

❏ He often pulls away from physical contact.	☑ He is sometimes bossy.	☑ He enjoys the company of peers.
❏ He usually observes before joining in a game.	☑ He takes charge during pretend play.	☑ He relates physically, with lots of touching.

5. Formal Group Settings: When my preschooler is at day care or school . . .

☑ He likes working on individual activities like cutting and pasting.	☑ He likes to talk in front of the group.	❏ He likes active group games.
❏ He prefers to watch others in play, rather than participate.	☑ He prefers to play in groups rather than by himself.	☑ He fidgets and squirms during sit-down activities.
❏ He needs time to feel at ease.	☑ He is attentive and follows directions well.	☑ He often indulges in distracting or attention-getting behavior.

6. Emotions: When it comes to my preschooler's feelings . . .

☑ He has trouble expressing emotions.	❏ He uses names for his feelings like "angry" and "happy."	☑ His feelings are easily hurt.
❏ Sometimes he is startled by the outbursts of others.	☑ He is vocal and dramatic.	☑ His moods are often extreme. He can be angry one moment and laughing the next.
❏ He finds conflicts fascinating to watch.	☑ He uses words to settle disputes.	☑ He craves the reassurance of hugs, smiles, and praise.

7. Memory: When my preschooler learns . . .

☑ He readily recalls what he sees.	☑ He remembers best what he hears.	☑ He imitates the actions he sees.
☑ He learns colors, numbers, and letters quickly.	☑ He memorizes songs and rhymes quickly.	☑ He remembers activities best after trying them out.
☑ He recognizes product and store logos.	☑ He loves to ask and answer questions.	☑ He is most attentive when he can play an active part in a lesson or exercise.

TOTALS: __10__ LOOKER   __12__ LISTENER   __14__ MOVER

CHAPTER FIVE

Learning Styles
in Kindergarten

The kindergarten year provides a child with gentle exposure to academic work within a play environment. Five-year-olds are not yet ready for a full-time diet of worksheets, workbooks, or chalkboard lessons. A kindergarten atmosphere of exploration, experimentation, and discovery provides the perfect transition from the freedom of preschool to the relative regimentation of the elementary grades.

Just as it has since infancy, in kindergarten, a child's inborn sensory preference determines what she notices and how she absorbs and responds to that information. Depending on learning style, you'll find that some five-year-olds are instinctively drawn to the sounds, some to the sensations, and others to the sights that surround them. This, naturally, colors what, how, and when they learn.

Chapter Five presents three different learners—a Looker, a Listener, and a Mover—at the beginning of the kindergarten year, and follows and compares their differing rates of development between ages five and six. A Learning Style QuickCheck for Kindergarteners is included to help you pinpoint your own child's sensory preference (see page 119).

This chapter also explores the effects of learning style on a child's kindergarten experience, and offers ideas on the types and durations of programs best suited to each learner. Finally, you'll find lists of toys and activities that will provide the kinds of play that your child finds most appealing while bolstering her weaker skills, as well.

Kindergarten is a time of tremendous social growth as children replace some of their attachment to Mom or Dad with close friendships and pupil-teacher relationships. At school, kindergarteners become part of a world designed especially for them—a world that encourages, informs, and teaches them to cope with the structure and teacher expectations they will face in grade school. Make the most of the kindergarten experience, for though it spans only ten months, your child is likely to seem far wiser at its conclusion!

A LOOK AT THREE LEARNERS

Nicole, Brendan, and Robby turned five years old during the summer that preceded kindergarten. The children live in similar neighborhoods, have several friends who reside within walking distance of their homes, and have toddler siblings. Each attended preschool last year and enjoyed various community children's programs, as well. Despite our case studies' common backgrounds, however, you'd have to look hard to find three children who are less alike!

You see, Nicole, Brendan, and Robby were born with different sensory preferences; that is, each child instinctively responds to a different element—be it sight, sound, or motion—within the same environment. Take the three to a horse farm, for example, and you'll soon find Robby astride a fence, flicking imaginary reins; Brendan executing near-perfect snorts and whinnies; and Nicole staring intently at everyone and everything that crosses her path.

Five years of this sort of inborn response have caused the three children to develop an array of learning skills at vastly different paces. Of course, many children are combination learners and display the traits of two, or even three styles. For clarity, however, our case-study children have only one style each. Let's take a look at our three learners, and examine the role that sensory preference plays in each child's adjustment to kindergarten.

Five Years of Age

Meet Nicole. Nicole is a Looker—a quiet, solemn child who is given more to observation than conversation. When she does speak, her sentences are simple and direct, with little inflection and few accompanying gestures. Nicole rarely exhibits excitement, fury, or other mood extremes. More often, milder emotions are displayed with widened eyes, a furrowed brow, or the set of her jaw.

At play time, Nicole can usually be found drawing and coloring, poring over picture books, or making an elaborate creation from snap-together blocks. Generally she prefers to play by herself, but occasionally she joins a friend for a card or board game. *Go Fish* and *Chutes and Ladders* are among her favorites, and she insists on playing by the rules. If her playmate gets the giggles and starts to make her playing piece hop around, or if she suggests that two-of-a-kind is better than four-of-a-kind, Nicole walks away in a huff. Her need for order carries over to her appearance, as well: Nicole is extremely fussy about her clothing, her hair, her room, and her workspace.

Nicole is not a risk taker, nor is she particularly quick or agile, so she rarely seeks an active role in outdoor play. Her excellent eye-hand coordination enables her to excel at T-ball, but she is frustrated by most of her other gross motor performances. As a Looker, she gets much more enjoyment from watching other children run, climb, and play ball than from trying to join in their games. Nicole is a standout at fine motor activities; however. She can print the entire alphabet from memory, and she produces artwork that is remarkably neat and detailed. She has the skill and patience to play marbles and pick-up sticks, and she assembles jigsaw puzzles as quickly as some adults.

Nicole has been in kindergarten for only three weeks, but she has adjusted beautifully. Her classroom, adorned with papier-mâché animals and decorations of every kind, is a nonstop visual treat. And there are shelves of games and puzzles, as well as a crafts center to which Nicole makes a beeline at every opportunity. As a pupil, she is reserved but very agreeable. She rarely volunteers answers or information, but she cooperates when called upon. Though Nicole enjoys watching her classmates at work and play, she is still somewhat daunted by the sea of new faces and the level of activity in the room. When the bustle and confusion become overwhelming, Nicole usually makes her way to the teacher's side, where she watches and waits until things quiet down again.

Nicole's social and gross motor skills could be stronger, but she is likely to succeed in kindergarten on the strength of her Looker abilities alone. Her self-control, visual acuity, and sense of order will stand her in good stead in any classroom.

Meet Brendan. Listener Brendan is as effusive as Nicole is reserved. He expresses his feelings easily, using the same adult-like speech he has relied upon since toddlerhood, and understands slang and colloquial phrases that go over the heads of most of his classmates. When the teacher calls out, "Hold your horses!" on the playground, Brendan is one of the few to stop dead in their tracks. Most of the others crane their necks in search of four-legged animals. Brendan uses sentence context to determine the meaning of an unfamiliar word; seconds later, he can usually spout a precise definition of his own making. He is somewhat haphazard about his appearance and his work and play areas, but there is always a reason for the disorder: "These trucks *have* to stay on the floor, because it's rush hour and traffic isn't moving."

Needless to say, Brendan makes friends easily. He loves to lead activities, assign roles, and set rules. On the playground, you'll often find him speaking for the quieter children and giving orders to anyone who'll allow it, for few of his peers can match his verbal skills. Brendan needs encouragement to use playground equipment for its intended purpose; for example, he'd rather use the monkey bars as his store or castle than for climbing. You see, gross motor play doesn't provide the same opportunity as pretense for Brendan's beloved socializing. When no playmates are available, he usually heads for the television or his collection of CDs.

Brendan's fine motor skills are about average for a five-year-old. He likes arts and crafts and table work, but more for the chance to sit with his friends than for the production of a particular masterpiece. He has difficulty printing letters and numbers from memory; his efforts at writing his name are usually accompanied by mumbled self-reminders, like "B—make a stick, and then a loop and another loop." Letter sounds, however, pose no problem; Brendan can sound out many three- and four-letter words.

At school, Brendan's favorite activity is Rug Time, during which the class sits together at the teacher's feet for a lesson, a story, or a song—often led by Brendan. He loves the limelight, and proudly displays his understanding of weather, time of day, and the calendar. During free time, Brendan is quick to persuade classmates to share the various play centers with him, for he loves their company. Brendan's penchant for sounds means that he can be easily distracted from work and play. A passing lawn mower, corridor noises, or the sounds of another class on the playground all cause his attention to wander from what he's doing. But Brendan follows directions so well he can get back on track quickly.

Overall, Brendan's visual and gross motor abilities are acceptable, but nowhere near the level of his Listener skills. However, his superior language ability and outgoing personality will be all he needs to make his kindergarten year a positive experience.

Meet Robby. Robby, a Mover, is having a much tougher time adjusting to the relative confines of his new classroom. His rudimentary speech is difficult to understand, and he is quick to tune out the conversation of others. Since Robby discovered that silly behavior wins the laughter of his classmates, poking and making faces have become much more fun than whatever class activity is on hand. Robby doesn't always respond when called upon for he often becomes so involved in creating distractions that he doesn't hear his teacher's voice. The most effective way to get him back on track is to steer him, physically, with a gentle grip on his shoulders.

Indoors or out, Robby plays long and hard, stopping only when exhaustion reduces him to tears. His dangling shirttails, untied shoes, and torn pants are testimony to his activity level. His favorite games have lots of action and few rules; tag, hide-and-seek, and foot races are daily "musts." Robby can always find companions on the playground, but since he is faster and more coordinated than most, they eventually tire of losing and wander away. Robby is hurt and angered by their departure, but he doesn't possess the social skills that could keep his playmates from leaving.

Robby's efforts at printing his name are hurried and primitive. Most of his letters are off the line, and some are reversed. He is often confused by the names and order of alphabet letters; the fact that they make sounds baffles him completely.

Since sitting still is a problem for him, Robby has little interest in artwork. He can think of a dozen reasons for leaving his seat—a sudden thirst, a broken pencil, the need to use the bathroom, and the desire for a closer look at a delivery truck parked outside the window are just a few on his list. When he has exhausted these excuses, Robby will crawl around on the floor in search of dropped crayons, shoelaces to yank, or ankles to tweak. With all of these distractions, it comes as no surprise that Robby rarely finishes a project.

Robby feels confined when he is steered toward his classroom's science center, library corner, or puzzle table, and wanders away at every opportunity. He's the first in line, however, for any gross motor activity—exercise time, for example, or the job of "paper passer." He also lives for the time his class spends outdoors or in the gym. Unfortunately, Robby's lack of self-control and short attention span have already made him a frequent visitor to the classroom's time-out chair. It's unlikely that his kindergarten year will provide him with benefits like those enjoyed by Nicole and Brendan.

How does your kindergartener learn? She may rely on visual stimulation, like Looker Nicole. She may be very verbal and drawn to sounds and language, like Listener Brendan. Or she may be like Mover Robby—a physical child who is highly attuned to motion and touch. A Learning Style QuickCheck for Kindergarteners has been provided on page 119 to help you decide. Simply review the behaviors in each of the QuickCheck's three columns, marking each that seems to describe your child. Since most of your responses will be concentrated in one or two categories, the column totals will provide a clear indication of learning style.

HOW LOOKER, LISTENER, AND MOVER KINDERGARTENERS DEVELOP

Nicole, Brendan, and Robby are at very different points of development simply because each child learns in a manner unlike the others'. The children's ability to follow directions, remain attentive, and recall what they've seen and heard are all functions of their diverse learning styles—styles that cause them to cope differently with the kindergarten experience. As we continue our learners' stories and follow their progress throughout the school year, you will see that the differences in Nicole's, Brendan's, and Robby's development continue to color each child's learning and behavior.

Five-and-a-Half to Six Years of Age

Nicole. Nicole has become a bit more sociable during the course of the school year. She is still reassured by first watching a game or activity before actually participating, but now joins in more readily than in the past. Nicole has become friendly with two of her classmates and, outside of group activities, doesn't seem to feel a need to mix with the rest of the children. She remains an observer on the playground, since most outdoor activities are too rough or too dirty for her liking. When she tires of watching, you can count on Nicole to head toward whichever activity requires the most eye-hand coordination. Ring toss is a frequent choice.

Nicole's fine motor skills are quite advanced. She was the first of her friends to learn to button, lace, zip, and tie, and she continues to produce the precise work her teacher has come to expect. Her efforts at printing the alphabet are frequently displayed as models for the other children, and her artwork is easy to recognize due to her use of outlining, shading, and brilliant colors. Nicole is equally neat about her appearance, and thrives on the order and routine of a typical school day.

Reserved and polite, Nicole remains a child of few words. Her sentences lack verbal detail, but she pronounces almost every word correctly because of her long-time habit of observing other speakers. Nicole's teacher encourages the use of inventive, or phonetic, spelling in the creation of one- or two-line stories. But since Nicole relies on memorization rather than a sounding-out approach to reading, and is bothered by the misspellings that seem to leap at her from her paper, most of her efforts contain just a few correctly spelled words. The accompanying illustration makes up for any missing details.

Just as she "sees" words in her mind before reading or writing them, Nicole uses visual strategies to learn other things. She learned her telephone number by carrying it for a couple of days on a slip of paper; she can tell left from right because her right arm faces the teacher's desk when her class rises for the Pledge of Allegiance each day. Nicole is adept at pre-math activities like counting, sorting, and categorizing, because each requires the visual and fine motor skills that come to her so naturally. Though she has trouble listening for long periods of time—she tends to daydream, then leap back to attention when she sees her classmates moving on to a new activity—her kindergarten year has served to reinforce the skills and behavior that made her such a willing student in the first place.

Brendan. Kindergarten is also a positive experience for Listener Brendan; in fact, the daily group activities and instant availability of playmates serve as the perfect showcase for his verbal skills. Brendan is equally comfortable interacting with children and adults. He continues to take the lead during discussions and storytelling, voicing his opinions with confidence and using multiple words that leave his classmates open-mouthed and envious.

Whether working or playing, Brendan has come to enjoy fine motor activities. His printing and artistic efforts are still quite ordinary, but he recognizes that most projects and games afford additional opportunities to socialize. Even when the teacher calls conversation to a halt, Brendan guides himself through the task at hand with whispered instructions, just as he has since toddlerhood. Saying things like, "Q is like O, but has a little squiggle on the bottom," helps keep his attention focused on his work.

Because Brendan has yet to develop confidence in his gross motor skills, he shies away from playground equipment and rough-and-tumble games. At recess, you're more likely to find him giggling with his friends than running races. Not surprisingly, Brendan readily joins any games that involve conversation, often with the girls. He loves to play "Mother, May I?" and "Bluebird, Bluebird."

In the classroom, Brendan is adept at following even three-part instructions. He can count to one hundred with accuracy, and can recite the days of the week, the months of the year, and the four seasons. His printing is laborious and his efforts at spelling poor, but Brendan's teacher encourages his love of communicating with friends through notes. A favorite activity is a weekly program during which two other kindergarten classes join with Brendan's for songs and stories. During free play time, Brendan heads for the listening center, where headphones, books, cassettes, and CDs are available; or the drama center, which contains furniture, dress-up clothes, and various adult-like props for pretend play.

Occasionally, Brendan must be reprimanded for calling out answers, eavesdropping on other children, and chatting during quiet time. Background noise and the conversation of others continue to act as a magnet for Brendan's attention. As a result, during independent work time, his pencil-and-paper efforts are interrupted with some frequency. A few words from the teacher or his own recollection of her earlier instructions is all it takes to get Brendan back on track. Overall, this little Listener is an asset to his class; and, like Nicole, he finds kindergarten exciting. Brendan can't wait for first grade, when he can make even more friends.

Robby. Mover Robby's efforts at communicating have not greatly improved during his kindergarten year, and this is a source of embarrassment whenever other children correct his grammar and pronunciation. When Robby protested, "He taked free crowns!" after a classmate helped himself to some extra Crayolas, his remark met with a humiliating chorus of "It's *crayons*, not *crowns!* In light of Robby's slow progress in language areas, his teacher has referred him to a speech-language pathologist for evaluation.

Robby is always in a hurry, and has little patience for seat work. His efforts at drawing and printing his name are awkward and rather sloppy, peppered with letter reversals and unrecognizable forms. He has better luck controlling chunky pencils and crayons than ordinary slim ones, but his overzealous cross-outs and erasures, combined with his habit of wandering away from the table, practically guarantee a ripped or unfinished product. Robby hasn't yet learned to read numbers or letters, because he simply cannot remember what each looks like. The fact that letters have accompanying "sounds" remains a mystery to him.

Robby continues to thrive on movement. He is devastated each time he learns that it's not a gym day and whenever rain threatens his class's outdoor play. As always, he loves to run and chase; for this, he is still held in high regard—on the playground, at least—by most of his male classmates. During this year, however, some of the gentler children began to shun him as their earlier awe turned to impatience with his inability to sit still and pay attention. Many of Robby's peers are now also annoyed by his tapping, wiggling, poking, and noisemaking—habits that cause their teacher to take time out for a reprimand from almost every activity.

Robby has made little social or academic progress during his kindergarten year, and is becoming somewhat hardened to the disapproval of his teacher and classmates. His parents are rightfully concerned about his ability to handle a longer day of school in first grade.

LEARNING STYLE AS A CONSIDERATION IN KINDERGARTEN

Despite the vast range of toddler and preschool programs and the importance placed on school readiness by today's parents—most of whom are preschool veterans themselves—organized kindergarten remains optional in some states of the union. Nevertheless, if for no reason other than the accompanying social benefits, the vast majority of five-year-olds attend some sort of formal school program. The following will help you select the type of kindergarten class—and the type of teacher—that would be best for your little learner.

Choosing the Best Kindergarten Class for Your Child

Depending on where you live, the kindergarten possibilities available to your child may range from just one within your public school system to dozens, including church and temple programs, boarding schools, academic preparatory schools, specialized kindergartens for the gifted or challenged, home schooling, and programs that advocate a particular teaching method. Needless to say, children's kindergarten experiences can differ greatly according to the school in which they are enrolled. Even within a single town, school hours, facilities and supplies, regulations, parental involvement, teacher credentials, and methodology are often far from uniform.

If you have the luxury of considering more than one program for your child, remember that the teacher's learning style can have a tremendous influence on classroom arrangement, the design and presentation of lessons and activities, and the teacher's interaction with pupils. As is the case with parent and child, a teacher's learning style can either complement that of the child or create the potential for friction. For this reason, it often pays to visit prospective classrooms to learn whatever you can about the practices of their teachers.

To illustrate this point, try to imagine your five-year-old learner under the tutelage of each of the three teachers profiled below. Their credentials may well be identical, but you're likely to feel that one teacher would be a much better fit for your child than the others.

Mrs. Combs, a Looker. Mrs. Combs runs a structured, orderly kindergarten. She keeps a large illustrated list of classroom rules posted by her desk, and reviews the list with her class at least twice a week. She writes the daily schedule on a nearby white board next to a colorful chart listing the names of the week's classroom helpers.

Mrs. Combs feels that it's important for children to have their own space at school, so she assigns a labeled coat hook and shelf area to each student and adheres to the traditional use of desks. At music and story time, her pupils sit on carpet squares arranged in two concentric circles. During group lessons, a rectangle of red tape that adorns the floor near the bulletin board enables the children to sit in an orderly fashion.

Most kindergarten teachers employ the concept of morning Circle Time. Mrs. Combs uses Circle Time to fill in the weather chart and calendar, present flannel-board stories, and show finished samples of projects or crafts the class will be doing that day. Visually oriented, Mrs. Combs has a magnificent classroom, with coordinated decorations covering every available space. She makes frequent use of videos, worksheets, and art supplies of every kind. Her classroom has two computers; to help her pupils memorize the keyboard, Mrs. Combs provides each child with a paper copy for his or her desk. The class is often encouraged to dictate sentences and stories, which Mrs. Combs copies onto huge sheets of lined easel paper and uses for read-aloud practice.

Naturally, Mrs. Combs makes neatness a priority. She praises her children for coloring within the lines, for printing with precision, and for helping keep the classroom clean. The best of her students' work is displayed around the room, and seasonal projects adorn hallway bulletin boards. Her penchant for orderliness extends beyond the classroom, as well. The children line up, boy-girl-boy-girl, when moving from place to place within the building, and are encouraged to walk to the right of a certain silver line that runs the length of the hallway. Mrs. Combs is a highly organized and thorough teacher. But it's easy to see that Mover children, in particular, would have a difficult time adhering to some of her teaching methods, expectations, and classroom policies.

Ms. Perez, a Listener. At first glance, Ms. Perez's classroom seems busier and noisier than that of Mrs. Combs. Ms. Perez feels that working at round tables, rather than a line of desks, will encourage conversation and cooperative behavior among her students. Ms. Perez likes to teach the class as a group; when it's time for such a lesson, the children cluster together on the rug at her feet. Like Mrs. Combs, Ms. Perez has a list of class rules. Rather than displaying them on a chart, however, she has worked them into a song that the children sing almost every day. Ms. Perez is also less formal about class jobs, for she prefers that all her students share daily responsibility for a tidy classroom.

Ms. Perez uses Circle Time to read aloud and teach songs to her pupils. An accomplished storyteller, she uses her voice, her dramatic flair, and even some amateur guitar strumming to spin amazing tales that rivet her young students to their places. Ms. Perez looks for feedback and encourages discussion, but she teaches the children to take turns, and asks for "active listening" when someone else has the floor.

Ms. Perez makes frequent use of oral directions, first making sure she has her class's attention and then requesting that the children repeat her instructions. She asks a lot of questions during the course of the day, and when forming small groups to work on projects, she pairs the most sociable children with the most quiet to help the latter "open up." Ms. Perez shows her Listener tendencies through the kinds of activities she schedules. Show and Tell, Sharing Time, and circle games like "Telephone" are all part of her routine. She often uses songs and role-playing to introduce new concepts and reinforce old ones.

Ms. Perez uses a phonics approach to reading: she trains her students to listen for and remember the various letter sounds, and employs games and songs to make the job easier. Wishing to encourage the children's writing efforts in every possible way, Ms. Perez has taught them to use inventive spelling—the writing of words as they sound—and leaves pencils, markers, and paper in many places around the room. One of the highlights of the kindergarten year is her class play, a much-rehearsed effort that is short on costumes and scenery, but long on dramatics. This allows each student a moment in the spotlight. Ms. Perez is a highly creative teacher, but her theatrics and emphasis on self-expression might well be troubling to Looker or Mover kindergarteners.

Mr. Warner, a Mover. Mr. Warner's classroom has little in common with that of Mrs. Combs or Ms. Perez. Mr. Warner's students have no assigned work spaces; instead, they are encouraged to perform tasks and tackle various activities wherever they feel most comfortable. If a child feels like stretching out on the floor to read, fine. If someone else decides to carry his tray of clay from the art table to the windowsill, that's acceptable as well. Needless to say, the appearance of Mr. Warner's room ranges from messy to downright chaotic, but he doesn't mind a bit. His own Mover tendencies ensure permission to roam.

Mr. Warner's daily Circle Times are brief, and usually employ movement and music. He starts with an "electric hello," during which each child in turn faces his neighbor for a greeting and handshake. Mr. Warner then gives a quick summary of the day's events and leads some bending and stretching exercises before sending the children on to other activities. Often, Circle Time is the only portion of the day the class spends as a group; Mr. Warner encourages individual work and the self-selection of games, toys, and projects. While the children roam freely among the classroom's learning centers, Mr. Warner himself moves from pupil to pupil, lending a hand or teaching a skill as necessary.

This kindergarten class takes as many field trips as the teacher can organize. During weeks when nothing special is scheduled, Mr. Warner leads an adventure in the schoolyard or an excursion to the farthest reaches of the building. Mr. Warner's students are among the youngest in the school, but they're the first to point out the basement entrance, the freight elevator, and the gymnasium's supply room.

Mr. Warner places less emphasis on reading and math readiness than on building his pupils' self-esteem. Children who treat each other well are roundly applauded, and the teacher is quick to offer a thumbs-up or high-five to students who reach a personal goal. Mr. Warner employs lots of multisensory and manipulative materials. To teach the alphabet, for example, he uses letters cut from sandpaper or letter-shaped cookies baked by the class. As might be expected, Mr. Warner is quick to veer from his intended daily program to take advantage of a special event. He might suggest soap-flake snowmen on a snowy day, or initiate a crawling race to help celebrate the birth of a baby sister or brother.

Mr. Warner's kindergarten is certainly the least restrictive of the three, and makes the most allowances for a Mover's sensitivity and need to wander. But it's quite likely that the lack of structure would frustrate a Looker child, just as the infrequent social opportunities would unsettle a Listener.

Clearly, a teacher's learning style colors his or her classroom setup and teaching practices. Depending on the style possessed by a particular kindergarten pupil, the same classroom can be either an ideal learning environment or a place of frustration. If you have no choice regarding your child's kindergarten placement, you can still share your knowledge of her strengths and weaknesses with the teacher, while using home time to reinforce the material presented at school. You can also remain alert for signs of discontent or frustration on your child's part, so that you and her teacher can cooperate in a search for solutions. When there are several kindergarten options available, however, it would be wise to let your child's learning style guide your final decision.

Kindergarten for Lookers

Looker children thrive in a classroom that offers lots of the hands-on materials that tap their visual and eye-hand skills. Puzzles, kits, craft supplies, small blocks, and board games are all favorites of the Looker. In fact, these children enjoy success in nearly every school setting because they are self-directed, attentive pupils who enjoy working alone. Neither the academic demands imposed by private schools nor the full-day schedule followed by many kindergartens across the country pose a problem for the Looker child. Naturally, most Looker children are happiest with a teacher who is a Looker as well, for they may be made uncomfortable by the emphasis that Listener teachers place on verbal activities or by the lack of structure found in a Mover's classroom.

Kindergarten for Listeners

Listener five-year-olds also do well in almost any kindergarten setting, because they possess the auditory skills needed to follow directions, communicate easily, and master beginning reading skills with ease. A full-length school day rarely proves too taxing for a Listener; instead, it affords extra time for the socializing she loves. Like Lookers, Listener children can usually meet private schools' academic and behavioral expectations. Listener and Mover teachers are both good choices for a Listener kindergartener, who might be somewhat put off by a Looker teacher's emphasis on neatness, visual tasks, and routine.

Kindergarten for Movers

A Mover kindergartener needs a teacher who can tolerate her high activity level and inability to stay with a task for more than a brief period. A teacher who is herself a Mover would be the ideal choice, simply because the teaching methods of both Lookers and Listeners so often require a level of organization and attentiveness that is beyond the Mover child. A Mover might also do well in a private kindergarten that provides one-to-one or small-group instruction of new concepts. She would probably not fare as well in an academically oriented program. Since the Mover's slowly developing visual and auditory skills make reading and writing quite frustrating, disruptive or withdrawn behavior might be the result. Half-day kindergarten programs are a good option for the busy Mover. When this is not an option, some parents choose to delay their Mover's kindergarten entrance until age six to allow visual and auditory skills more time to develop.

Working With Your Child's Teacher

No matter what type of learner your kindergartener is, you can help prepare your child for the increased academic demands and longer school day of first grade by keeping alert to her progress in the various skill areas. This is best accomplished by posing direct questions to the kindergarten staff and then acting on whichever of the teacher's recommendations seems appropriate. If your child is struggling with a concept or skill, you'll find that remedial help is often available through the school. If not, you can ask for referrals to appropriate community resources. (See Chapter Nine, "Learning Problems and Solutions," for more information on learning problems.) The following questions should reveal a wealth of important information about your child's kindergarten progress.

- Is my child making steady progress, or has she reached a plateau in a particular area?

- How are my child's social skills? Has she formed friendships? Does she share, cooperate, participate, and ask for help when she needs it?

- Does my child pay attention during group lessons?

- Can my child start a project and see it through to completion?

- Does my child show any signs of vision, hearing, speech, or attention problems?

- Are my child's reading and math readiness skills sufficient for success in first grade? If not, how can these skills be improved?

- What are the teacher's recommendations for at-home reinforcement of specific learning skills?

It's important to remember that each learning style has built-in strengths and weaknesses. Listeners, for example, usually learn to read with ease, but may struggle a bit with math activities. While Movers tend to lag behind in academic areas, they possess a physical confidence often lacking in Lookers and Listeners. It's wise to keep your expectations realistic while encouraging your kindergartener to be proud of her accomplishments.

TECHNIQUES FOR AFFIRMING AND DEVELOPING LEARNING SKILLS

You've seen that inborn learning patterns influence what, how, and how quickly a five-year-old learns. Without gentle intervention, the inequalities that exist among a child's skill levels at the beginning of her kindergarten year will, in all likelihood, still be present in June. However, if learning style is made a factor in the selection and presentation of a child's toys and experiences outside of school, you can encourage a balanced learner. Auditory skills can be sharpened, visual strategies taught, and motor skills improved via carefully selected activities.

In the three sections that follow, you'll learn the importance of a child's developing Looker, Listener, and Mover skills. You'll also find lists of ideas for drawing out these skills in your child, regardless of her preferred learning style.

I urge you to introduce these activities in the spirit of recreation, for your kindergartener will, no doubt, feel taxed by her hours of formal schooling. The following ideas should please both of you in that they combine skill building with fun.

Building Looker Skills

The kindergartener with well-developed Looker skills is usually a model pupil—quiet, observant, orderly, and patient. Adept with her hands and possessing a sharp visual memory, a Looker often reads and writes well ahead of schedule.

Improving visual skills in a kindergartener will result in a corresponding improvement in schoolwork. You'll want to build on your Looker's natural born strength. And if your child is a Listener or Mover, you'll want her to have the advantage of strong visual skills.

ENHANCING A KINDERGARTENER'S EXISTING LOOKER SKILLS

- Provide an ever-changing array of puzzles by borrowing from the library and trading with friends. Also encourage your child to mount a picture on cardboard and cut it into pieces to make a homemade jigsaw puzzle.

- Milton Bradley's *Pictionary Junior*, available from Hasbro, uses children's own drawings as clues to words and phrases.

- Provide a set of parquetry blocks or a magnetic mosaic set for creating pictures.

- Your kindergarten-aged Looker is ready to move up to a real computer. She'll no doubt enjoy age-appropriate software like *JumpStart Advanced Kindergarten*, available on Amazon.

- Prang's *96 Color Tuck Box* of crayons, available on Yahoo, contains many unusual shades that will delight your Looker. Fluorescent yellow, limestone gray, and melon are just a few.

- With *Lite-Brite* by Hasbro, your child can insert colored plastic pegs into a picture outline that is mounted above a small bulb, making the entire picture light up.

- Parker Brothers' *Boggle Junior*, available through Hasbro, has labeled picture cards, under which a child reproduces the same word using letter cubes. A timer adds an element of challenge.

- Milton Bradley's *Perfection*, available through Hasbro, is a timed puzzle. A child sets the timer and then hurries to insert an array of shapes and forms into the proper places before time runs out and the pieces pop back out.

- Mona Brookes' book *Drawing With Children* (J.P. Tarcher) teaches children to perceive and draw objects as combinations of five basic shapes.

■ *Domino Rally Spider Kick Out* by Pressman Toy involves the construction of a domino run, complete with stairs, curves, and various "trick" devices. The beginner set is perfect for five-year-old eyes and hands.

ENCOURAGING THE DEVELOPMENT OF LOOKER SKILLS IN KINDERGARTENERS WHO ARE LISTENERS

■ Begin a simple scrapbook about a subject that interests your child. She can start by collecting, cutting, and pasting photographs and large-type words on sheets of colored paper. The pages can be bound together with ribbon or yarn.

■ Check toy and school-supply stores for connect-the-dot workbooks. Once your child has drawn the lines needed to complete the picture, she'll have something new to color.

■ Rent children's videos. Listeners love interesting characters and story lines.

■ During a quiet moment, do a visualization together. You can say, "Let's close our eyes and pretend we're in your room. Can you see your bed? What color is your bedspread? What are the pictures on your wall?"

■ Make it a practice for family members to share last night's dreams over breakfast.

■ Buy a kaleidoscope. You and your child can take turns hunting for different shapes and patterns, and describing what you see.

■ The *PowerTouch Learning System* by Fisher-Price allows children to experience a book by lightly touching the words or pictures on a page. A Listener is rewarded with the spoken word.

■ Provide coloring books with a theme that will appeal to your Listener, such as nursery rhymes or an engaging story.

■ To encourage the use of scissors, draw a heavy black shape—a square, rectangle, or oval—around more-complicated forms that would frustrate your child. Encourage her to cut along the simple outlines you have drawn.

■ *LeapPad Learning System* by Leap Frog helps children develop key reading and math readiness skills, and combines auditory and visual stimulation.

ENCOURAGING THE DEVELOPMENT OF LOOKER SKILLS IN KINDERGARTENERS WHO ARE MOVERS

■ Milton Bradley's *Don't Spill the Beans!*, available through Hasbro, requires no reading. Children try to strategically place beans in a pot without tipping it over.

■ Buy a paddle to which a ball has been attached by a long rubber string. This toy is an old-fashioned way to challenge a child's eye-hand coordination.

■ Take a pair of binoculars to a sporting event, and encourage your child to use them to view the game and her surroundings.

■ Rent videos that Movers love, such as superhero cartoons and action stories.

■ Provide an inexpensive camera so that your child can photograph the important people in her life and start her own photo album.

■ Play simple card games with your child like the ever-popular "Go Fish," "Crazy Eights," and "Old Maid."

■ School-supply stores carry workbooks of simple mazes, which you can make more interesting with action—"Let's race this pencil around the track without crashing into any walls."

■ Childcraft offers a host of tactile counters that will appeal to Movers. Beginning math skills are taught via plastic tiles, beads, and bears.

■ The game *Cariboo* by Cranium teaches number-, letter-, and shape-matching skills. The variety of tactile experiences available on the treasure hunt will thrill your Mover.

■ Milton Bradley's *Connect Four*, available through Hasbro, is a vertical tick-tack-toe. Children drop a checker down a slot on an upright grid. The first player to line up four checkers in any direction wins.

Building Listener Skills

Listener skills help a five-year-old follow directions, remain attentive, comprehend the basics of phonics, and foster friendships through conversation. Therefore, every kindergartener stands to gain from activities that stimulate her language skills.

Listener children will require no convincing to play with toys and games that appeal to their favored way of learning. Improving the Listener skills of Lookers and Movers can be most easily achieved by pairing Listener activities with the child's favored type of stimulation. For example, the game "Simon Says" combines listening with moving. Here are some suggestions to help you build your child's listener skills.

ENHANCING A KINDERGARTENER'S EXISTING LISTENER SKILLS

■ Make up an auditory memory game in which each player repeats and embellishes the words of the previous player. Try something like, "I'm going on vacation, and in my suitcase, I'm going to pack _____," or "I'm ordering a pizza with _____." As each player adds a suggestion, the responses grow longer.

■ *JumpStart Spanish* by Knowledge Adventure, available on Amazon, is software that teaches numbers and counting, colors, days of the week, and telling time in Spanish. An animated rabbit serves as guide, and music further enlivens the experience.

■ Your Listener will be delighted with a book of tongue twisters.

■ Select books to read aloud that are a bit beyond your child's age level. This will introduce new concepts, causing her to think in new ways.

■ While you watch from nearby, allow your child to place her own order at a store counter or to purchase her own movie ticket.

■ Treat your child to vocabulary words from a foreign language. Berlitz Kids' *Spanish Language Pack,* available through Amazon, contains an audiocassette, storybook, and word picture dictionary.

- Encourage your child to write letters using inventive spelling—words spelled as they sound—accompanied by her own illustrations. Help her mail the letters, and ask a few family members and friends to write back.

- Offer some examples of rhyming words. Then say a word and ask your child to think of a rhyme as quickly as she can. Then switch roles.

- Listeners love books of poems and rhymes.

- Provide a first set of phonics books, like *Books by Bob,* available at www.booksbybob.com. These simple and inviting beginning readers were developed and designed by parents.

ENCOURAGING THE DEVELOPMENT OF LISTENER SKILLS IN KINDERGARTENERS WHO ARE LOOKERS

- Encourage your child to answer the telephone at home. You may wish to practice various greetings and responses beforehand on a toy telephone.

- When you're working or playing side by side, make a game out of naming words and their opposites—black/white or over/under—for instance.

- When reading a story together, point to the pictures and ask your child to help tell the story. You can prompt her by inserting transitional phrases like, "The next thing that happened was _____" or "At last _____."

- Make a "Word Book" with your child by cutting out pictures of unusual or favorite items and pasting them into a scrapbook.

- Rebus stories have tiny pictures within the text, each of which stands for a word in the story. Enchantedlearning.com will provide a huge selection of rebus stories and rhymes—many with animation—for a small yearly fee.

- Make a game of identifying a thing by its sound alone—a jackhammer on the street or a nearby woodpecker.

■ Play "What Am I?" with your child, asking her to identify an object from the image created by your words. You might say, "I'm round and fairly flat, with a handle and a cover. I'm silver, and I get very hot. Can you guess what I am? I'm a frying pan!"

■ Choose fantasy stories with elves, fairies, and other magical characters to read to your Looker. These characters will come alive in her imagination.

■ *Phonics Tiles* by Neurosmith help children discover the relationship between letters and the sounds they make.

■ Software that provides lots of interesting visuals is a good vehicle for teaching beginning reading skills to Lookers. The Learning Company's *Reader Rabbit Preschool,* available through Broderbund, is a good choice.

ENCOURAGING THE DEVELOPMENT OF LISTENER SKILLS IN KINDERGARTENERS WHO ARE MOVERS

■ When traveling by car or taking a walk, encourage your child to count aloud as high as she can go.

■ Provide a set of toy walkie-talkies, and exchange messages with your child from different parts of the house.

■ Ask your child to dial the local Time and Temperature numbers, and have her repeat to you the information she receives.

■ Choose action stories to read to your Mover about adventures, sports figures, and "bad guys."

■ For listening practice, play "Simon Says." Movers especially will enjoy obeying Simon's various commands: "Touch your toes," "Jump up and down," "Turn around three times," etc.

■ When you say any word that's new to your little Mover, define it in the same sentence, as in, "Those twinkling lights are blinking on and off."

■ Provide a tape player and an action story on cassette. Earphones will help your child focus her attention.

- A set of toy dishes and utensils will encourage your child to verbalize the roles of baker, chef, or storekeeper.

- Children roll, turn, and spin the *Jumbo Music Ball* by Neurosmith. It's a child-sized ball that teaches colors, shapes, and letter and sound recognition.

- Summit Financial Group's *Cash Register With Scanner,* available through Amazon, combines auditory and visual stimulation with action. The display changes and the machine beeps when an item is scanned.

Building Mover Skills

While Looker and Listener skills come into play in the classroom, Mover skills enable a child to shine in other areas important to her social well-being. Kindergarteners who display a Mover's coordination, agility, and speed are gym-class, backyard, and playing-field standouts who enjoy the admiration of peers.

Movers, certainly, will greet with delight any parental attempts to increase opportunities to be active. By working in an auditory or visual element, you'll see improvement in the gross motor skills of Listeners and Lookers. The following ideas will help you encourage Mover skills in your five-year-old learner.

ENHANCING A KINDERGARTENER'S EXISTING MOVER SKILLS

- The *Radio Flyer #88 Racer Pedal Car,* available on Yahoo, has real tires, a clutch, and a working hand brake, and is guaranteed to provide an exciting ride.

- Kick, pass, and throw a child-sized football or soccer ball.

- Provide a child-sized hammer and saw and plenty of supervision!

- Purchase a pair of child-sized in-line skates, and accompany your child down the street or to the local rink.

- If your Mover's abilities allow, take the training wheels off her first bike.

- Enroll your child in a swimming program at your local "Y."

■ Provide your child with her first organized sports experience by signing her up for a community soccer or T-ball team—whichever she prefers.

■ You probably can't keep your Mover off a skateboard, so insist that she wears a helmet, elbow pads, and kneepads.

■ Take your child to an ice rink for skating lessons.

■ The *Radio Flyer #38 Classic Red Scooter,* available on Yahoo, has a fun "retro" style.

ENCOURAGING THE DEVELOPMENT OF MOVER SKILLS IN KINDERGARTENERS WHO ARE LOOKERS

■ Encourage outdoor play by offering sprinklers and water guns in the summer.

■ In winter months, provide a sled and a child-sized snow shovel.

■ Introduce your child to miniature golf. The eye-hand skill required will appeal to your Looker.

■ Enroll your child in a gymnastics class or beginner swim class, making sure that the teacher has a gentle approach and does not encourage competition.

■ Draw a hopscotch board on your sidewalk, and teach your child to play.

■ Introduce your child to pinball at a local arcade.

■ Teach your child to use a jump rope and a Hula-Hoop.

■ Kid Starts' *Silly Stilts,* available from JC Penney, are heavy-duty steel poles with plastic "feet" and kid-resistant footpads.

■ Pack some flashlights in a backpack and accompany your child on an after-dark adventure. You can catch fireflies, stargaze, and chase each other's shadows en route.

■ The *Nerf Ball* foam basketball is safe and fun, and there's even a suction-cup net available for indoor play.

ENCOURAGING THE DEVELOPMENT OF MOVER SKILLS IN KINDERGARTENERS WHO ARE LISTENERS

■ Have a parade by marching and playing rhythm-band instruments.

■ Play a game of charades, using exaggerated body movements to depict words, animals, and occupations.

■ Take a hike together or jog around the block. Talk about what you saw when you get home.

■ Check with your local bowling alley to see whether it provides "bumpers"—guards that deflect the ball from the gutter. If so, take your child bowling!

■ Turn a nursery rhyme or familiar story into a mini-drama, and act it out with your child. Demonstrate that gestures can be used to communicate ideas in place of words.

■ Take your child to a park or playground frequently. This will delight her social side while encouraging gross motor play.

■ Ask your child to help you with dusting or yard work. Keep a conversation going as you work.

■ Suggest slow-moving games, like backyard croquet, or games that require as much luck as skill, like dropping pennies into a jar at the bottom of a water-filled bucket.

■ Listeners like jump rope games with accompanying songs and rhymes. "Teddy bear, teddy bear, turn around . . ." is one example.

■ Hedstrom's *Mini Trampoline*, available through JC Penney, offers a slip-resistant mesh mat for jumping fun. The corner handle helps stabilize young athletes.

As you scan the above lists of toys and activities, remember that they are intended only as guidelines to help you round out your kindergartener's learning skills. If a suggested toy happens to be something that you can recall disliking as a child, or if the presence of an exploring baby in the house makes you extra cautious about toy purchases, feel free to pass certain items by. Similarly, if an activity from a skill-enhancement list aimed at other learners seems ideal for your child, don't hesitate to give it a try. Certainly, your discretion and knowledge of your child's tastes should be a factor in the toy-selection process. It's not necessary, nor is it advisable, to bombard her with every suggested idea.

Be aware that you may not see an immediate improvement in your child's learning skills. In fact, depending on her personality, learning style, and initial skill level, it may take many weeks to effect a noticeable difference. But regardless of whether improvement takes twelve days or twelve weeks, offering the right activities and playthings will bring balance to your kindergartener's development. And her self-esteem will be boosted in the bargain.

LEARNING STYLE QUICKCHECK FOR KINDERGARTENERS, FIVE TO SIX YEARS OF AGE

Directions: Check each of the statements below that best describes your child. Then total each of the three columns and compare results. You'll probably find your responses concentrated in one or two columns, clearly indicating the learning style of your kindergartener.

LOOKER	LISTENER	MOVER
1. Communication: When my kindergartener wishes to express herself . . .		
❏ She uses simple language.	☒ Her speech is adult-like.	❏ Some of her spoken words are difficult to understand
❏ She mispronounces a few words and sounds.	☒ Her sentences are structurally correct, and her pronunciation is nearly perfect.	❏ She speaks in short, grammatically incorrect sentences or phrases.
❏ She omits adverbs and prepositions.	☒ She tells elaborate stories.	☒ She acts out what she can't quite explain with words.
2. Favorite Toys and Pastimes: When my kindergartener plays alone . . .		
❏ She likes puzzles and board games.	❏ She likes tapes and CDs.	❏ She likes to play outdoors.
☒ She likes watching TV and videos.	☒ She looks through favorite books, reading some words.	❏ She enjoys swinging, sliding, and climbing.
☒ She enjoys computers and calculators.	☒ She likes fantasy play.	☒ She likes the neighborhood playground—especially the jungle gym.
❏ When playing with blocks, she builds low and long structures.	❏ When playing with blocks, she makes a house for dolls or action figures.	☒ When playing with blocks, she builds high structures that are likely to topple over.
3. Fine Motor Skills: When my kindergartener uses her hands . . .		
☒ She prints neatly.	☒ Her printing is acceptable.	❏ Her pencil grip is awkward.
❏ She cuts, colors, and pastes with ease.	☒ She talks to herself while working.	☒ She reverses some letters and numbers.
❏ She produces neat, attractive artwork.	☒ She makes up stories to accompany her artwork, which is acceptable.	❏ Her artwork is messy.
4. Gross Motor Skills: When my kindergartener moves about . . .		
❏ She prefers table games over outside play.	❏ She does more talking than actual playing when spending time with others.	☒ Her play involves large spaces on the playground.

| ❏ She chooses games that require eye-hand coordination, such as badminton. | ❏ She chooses games like "Simon Says," which involves verbal interaction. | ☑ She likes games such as "Tag." |
| ❏ She likes games with rules. | ❏ She talks herself through activities. | ☑ She is very well coordinated. |

5. Social Skills: When my kindergartener mixes with other children . . .

❏ In a group, she tends to be a loner.	❏ She thrives on her friendships.	❏ She is sociable, though not very verbal.
❏ She watches to see what's expected of her before taking part.	❏ She gets into trouble for too much talking during class time.	☑ She gets intro trouble for poking and hitting during class time.
❏ She warms up slowly to new people and situations.	❏ She often answers for others and tends to be bossy.	☑ She likes to roughhouse.

6. Emotions: When it comes to my kindergartener's feelings . . .

| ☑ Her facial expressions reveal her feelings. | ❏ She talks freely about her feelings. | ☑ Her feelings are easily hurt. |
| ❏ She may seem puzzled by the outbursts of others. | ❏ She confronts others with her feelings. | ☑ She reacts with anger rather than regret when disciplined. |

7. Memory: When my kindergartener learns . . .

| ☑ She recalls what she has seen. | ☑ She learns by listening to instructions. | ❏ She has difficulty focusing her attention to learn new things. |
| ☑ She produces numbers and letters from memory. | ☑ She knows the sounds made by alphabet letters. | ❏ She has not yet made the connection that letters make sounds. |

8. At School: When my kindergartener is in the classroom . . .

❏ She dresses neatly and likes to stay clean.	☑ Her appearance is neither messy nor overly neat.	❏ She seems unconcerned with her appearance and may look bedraggled.
❏ She keeps her work area very neat.	☑ She has to be told to clean up her work area.	❏ She works amid a mess, cluttering her workspace within minutes.
☑ She's beginning to show an interest in math.	☑ She's beginning to show an interest in reading.	☑ She prefers playground time to desk work.
❏ She rarely volunteers information, but responds when asked a question.	❏ She leads most class discussions and reports misbehavior to the teacher.	☑ The teacher must ask several questions to draw out information.

TOTALS: ____ LOOKER   ____ LISTENER   ____ MOVER

CHAPTER SIX

Learning Styles
in First Grade

No matter what type of preschool or kindergarten experience a six-year-old may have under his belt, first grade represents a radical change. Spending over thirty hours a week away from home is a novel experience in itself, even before academics and separate teachers for art, music, and physical education are added to the picture. First graders must assume a degree of responsibility for their behavior, possessions, movement about the school building, and completion of tasks that, until now, rested more upon the shoulders of their teachers.

Some first graders are better equipped to cope with this new responsibility than others. You see, organizational, academic, and social skills—all of which result from years of learning and playing according to inborn sensory preferences—differ greatly among six- and seven-year-olds. Children who have been visually oriented since birth, for example, usually learn beginning reading and writing skills with ease. Yet these Lookers' conversational skills may not approach those of a child naturally attuned to the auditory, and Lookers also lack the superior coordination of a child who favors touch and movement.

Chapter Six illustrates exactly how learning style colors the first-grade experience by following the development of three children—a Looker, a Listener, and a Mover—throughout the course of their school year. A Learning Style QuickCheck for First Graders is included to help you identify the way your own child absorbs information (see page 153).

This chapter also takes a subject-by-subject look at the relationship of learning style to first-grade school performance, and suggests ways to effectively communicate with your child's teacher. Tips are included to help you select extracurricular activities with an eye to learning-style enhancement, and strategies are presented to help your child apply his preferred way of learning to the mastery of reading, writing, spelling, and math. Finally, you'll find lists of toys and techniques specifically chosen to encourage your child's interests and strengths, while improving those weaker skills that are part and parcel of his learning style.

Whatever a child's first-grade experience may be, his time at home is an important aspect of the "big picture." For some, home provides relief from a stressful academic pace or a level of socialization that is at once fascinating and overwhelming. For others, it may be a place that's too quiet or offers limited opportunities to burn off energy. Making your child's at-home learning a low-pressure, made-to-order, fun experience while allowing plenty of unstructured time, will enable him to be most receptive to your skill-enhancement efforts and help you both get the greatest benefit from the time you spend together. Enjoy!

A LOOK AT THREE LEARNERS

Christopher, Angela, and Thomas have just begun first grade. The three children are veterans of the same preschool and kindergarten classes and happen to be almost exactly the same age; each child turned six in July. Despite these similarities and other likenesses stemming from their home environments, the children entered first grade with three distinctly different sets of expectations and readiness skills. It is their inborn learning styles that have made the difference. Christopher, you see, is naturally drawn to the visual aspects of his surroundings; Angela responds to language and sounds; and Thomas responds to motion and touch. Not every child exhibits the traits of a single learning style in this manner. Looker-Mover and Looker-Listener combinations, for example, are quite common. However, for the sake of clarity and to highlight the characteristics of each type of learner, our case-study children will each display a "pure" style. Let's take a look at our three learners as they begin their adjustment to the first grade.

Six Years of Age

Meet Christopher. Looker Christopher has a highly developed sense of order. Before he leaves for school each day, he checks his room to make sure that his toys and possessions have been neatly put away. When he arrives at school, he goes straight to his desk to organize its contents. Christopher is equally fussy about his personal appearance. He selects his outfits carefully and becomes quite upset if his clothing gets wrinkled or soiled.

Christopher is a loner. Reserved by nature, he does not make friends easily. He is happiest playing by himself because doing so frees him from the strain of socializing. Christopher enjoys the role of observer. He is fascinated by the interactions and play of other children, but remains on the sidelines as though unsure of how to join in their games.

Christopher's gross motor skills are about average for his age. But rather than engage in full-body play, he is certain to find and devote his attention to some visual aspect of the activity at hand. When he's at the shore, he shuns the water, preferring instead to write in the sand. When he goes bowling, he shows more interest in the automatic scoring device than in taking his turn. At the park, he sits motionless on a swing, eyes darting back and forth so as not to miss anything. Wherever there's noise, activity, and the potential for messiness, you'll find a daunted Christopher watching intently from a safe distance.

Christopher's fine motor skills are excellent. He loves to draw and write, for he finds his sophisticated finished products very gratifying. Not surprisingly, Christopher's superior eye-hand coordination makes him a whiz at video games and the computer. He is also adept at mazes, connect-the-dot pictures, and pencil-and-paper games of every kind. Christopher also adores picture books, as he has since babyhood, and greatly enjoys card and board games. Building sets, TV game shows, and children's magazines take up the remainder of Christopher's play time.

At the start of first grade, Christopher has quite a large "sight" vocabulary—that is, he can recognize many words from memory. He doesn't hesitate to guess at unfamiliar words, but is rarely correct unless the words appear in the context of a sentence. Christopher can add and subtract up to ten with accuracy by envisioning a line of sequential numbers and moving an imaginary counter ahead or back as needed. He is also quick to grasp new concepts because he is able to commit to memory everything he is shown.

Christopher's adjustment to first grade has so far been a bit slow. He has trouble listening for long periods of time, but even when his attention wanders, his good behavior and respectfulness continue. Although at first Christopher was tense and silent much of the time, he is now beginning to feel more at home with his new teacher and classmates, and, as a result, more tolerant of group activities. Certainly, some of his skills are stronger than others. Still, Christopher stands to gain a great deal from first grade on the strength of his visual orientation alone.

Meet Angela. Listener Angela's work and play areas are as cluttered as Christopher's are tidy. To her, the game at hand is much more important than the surroundings in which it takes place; and besides, her pretense requires a myriad of props and players, be they real or stuffed. Children gravitate toward Angela, for they admire her self-assurance and the ease with which she talks to older children and adults. Angela turns her own adoring gaze toward the friends of her ten-year-old sister. Because she copies their clothing and hairstyles and mimics their speech, Angela has become somewhat of a trendsetter among the first-grade set.

Angela's sophisticated vocabulary and confident demeanor make her a natural at masterminding role-playing games. She loves this sort of play, and the fact that she usually reserves the role of Queen, Boss, President, or Leader for herself adds to her enjoyment. When she's alone, Angela gravitates toward the TV, the tape player, and a toy microphone.

Angela's fine motor skills—cutting, coloring, and printing—are acceptable for her age. At school, she often heads for the crafts corner during free time, not necessarily to work but because there's always a group gathered there with whom she can try out her play ideas. Her own artistic efforts are not particularly detailed or imaginative, but she's good at instructing other children. Things are not much different outdoors, for there, again, Angela views play time more as a means to socialize than as exercise.

Angela is very much at home in first grade. Reading poses no problem at all, because her Listener's knowledge of the different letter sounds enables her to sound out even multiple-syllable words. Math comes just as easily because of her immediate recall of addition and subtraction facts. The teacher encourages Angela's outspokenness about her opinions and feelings, but has to reprimand her almost daily for general talkativeness and a tendency to speak for everyone in her class. Angela's auditory recall enables her to follow even the most complicated of directions, but it comes as no surprise that social Angela becomes quickly bored both with seat work and with individual projects. Nevertheless, Listener Angela is so rewarded by her everyday academic success and built-in circle of friends that she can't wait to get to school in the morning.

Meet Thomas. First grade is not as much fun for Mover Thomas. In fact, it's something of an ordeal. This active, sensitive six-year-old chafes at the constraints of classroom life and is repeatedly frustrated when his efforts to "buck the system"—by falling back on the full-body activity he loves—meet with failure.

Thomas tends to mumble when he speaks, mispronouncing words and using short, poorly sequenced sentences. When he has an urgent need to communicate an idea, you can count on Thomas to express himself physically rather than verbally. The impulse to push, grab, hug, and wrestle strikes him long before he thinks of talking things out. Naturally, many of Thomas's classmates keep their distance for fear of becoming one of his targets. The other children are, in fact, slightly horrified by Thomas's shenanigans and the frequency with which he is scolded by the teacher.

Things are different at home and outdoors, for where there are obstacles to scale and balls to throw and kick, agile Thomas emerges as a leader. He has a group of pals who meet each day on the playground for races or a game of tag. And the neighborhood boys flock to Thomas's backyard, because when school is out, that's where you'll always find him, climbing trees, tackling a buddy, or playing policeman. Most of the boys' parents, unsure of how to deal with Thomas's frequent tears and wild behavior, discourage his presence at their homes.

Thomas has trouble with printing. He holds the pencil incorrectly and presses so hard that he snaps not just the point but often the pencil itself. Many of his letters are reversed, and none is properly shaped or sized. Art projects, free-time activities, and any class work that requires sitting still are nonstop struggles for Thomas, for he has trouble staying with any task that doesn't allow him to move about. So far, Thomas has enjoyed only two class activities—the creation of a "Things With Wheels" mural, which focused on a favorite topic of his and allowed him to roam while working, and the class's train trip to a duck pond several towns away.

Thomas cannot yet read. He recognizes his name and that of his brother, but because he does not remember alphabet letters and their sounds, he can neither recall nor sound out any other words that he encounters. He manages simple addition by counting on his fingers, but he can't envision number groupings the way Christopher can, and is completely baffled by word problems.

Thomas is well aware of his academic shortcomings, but is powerless to change his activity level and attention span. In school, he requires a place to work where he won't create too many distractions for others, a place to calm down when he becomes upset, and lots of support and encouragement in the form of pats, hugs, and handshakes. First grade promises to be quite a challenge for Thomas.

What kind of learner is your first grader? Is he a Looker, attracted to color, movement, and shapes, as Christopher is? Is he more like Listener Angela, highly attuned to sounds and language? Or is he drawn to sensations and motion, like Mover Thomas? The Learning Style QuickCheck for First Graders on page 153 will give you the answer. Just review the traits in each of the three columns, checking those that are characteristic of your first grader. After you total the checks in each column, you'll have a clear picture of your child's sensory preference.

HOW LOOKER, LISTENER, AND MOVER FIRST GRADERS DEVELOP

At age six, our three children's strengths and weaknesses are obvious. As we follow our learners through their first-grade year, you will see that without intervention, each of them will succeed in those subject areas that "fit" with his or her learning preference. And by the same token, the children's struggles will persist—and, in fact, increase—in subjects that call for skills they do not naturally possess. Let's see how Christopher, Angela, and Thomas fare as they move through the first grade.

Seven Years of Age

Christopher. Throughout the school year, Christopher continues to prefer his own company to group play. He has one special friend with whom he plays during free time, but if that child is absent or tries to vary their games by introducing a new rule or a third child, Chris wanders off in search of a solo activity. When spoken to, Christopher expresses himself clearly but simply. But despite his reticence, Christopher is roundly admired for his prowess at computer and video games—prowess assured by his superior eye-hand coordination. Chris's parents encourage his creativity. They have enrolled him in a drawing class, and they make sure that he has plenty of craft supplies to keep him busy at home. And, of course, Christopher remains interested in books, magazines, board games, and computer games.

This spring, at his parents' urging, Christopher joined a T-ball team. He is certainly no star in the making—in fact, he hates getting sweat and dust on his uniform and is almost always "out at first"—but Chris adores playing the role of statistician when it's his turn on the bench. With T-ball, just as in other areas of his life, Christopher is concerned foremost with following the rules of the game.

Christopher's progress in reading has been slower since spring. Without the sounding-out skills needed to master phonics, he cannot decipher the two- and three-syllable words that have begun to crop up in classroom literature. Chris still relies on visual memory when the text is simple, and this same ability comes into play when he enjoys comics and the puzzle and hidden-message books his teacher provides for free-time use.

Christopher is enjoying great success with math. He adds and subtracts quickly and accurately, because he can envision groups of numbers in his mind. He has immediate recall of the names and meanings of the symbols for addition (+), subtraction (−), and equals (=), and has quickly grasped the idea behind geometric shapes, graphs, and measurements. He is adept at completing the worksheets that confound so many of his classmates, and he delights in his teacher's visual feedback in the form of stars, stickers, and written words of praise.

Christopher is still an observer. He is particularly attuned to the misbehavior of others, and has taken to biting his nails during tense moments. Chris becomes impatient with long listening tasks, and has trouble absorbing complicated verbal instructions. When Christopher is taught, he requires a demonstration instead of spoken directions.

At year's end, Christopher's teacher notes that he sometimes seems to tune her out with either a blank stare or closed eyes. (Actually, he is hard at work forming mental images.) She mentions that he is a perfectionist and should be less critical of himself and more assertive about his ideas, rather than parroting what he deems to be a "proper" opinion. It's apparent that Looker Christopher will need help with his social and auditory skills to ensure his becoming a happy, confident second grader.

Angela. As Listener Angela moves through first grade, she becomes more sociable than ever. She has play dates quite frequently—in fact, she hates to play alone—and attends a constant round of birthday parties and sleepovers. She makes and receives phone calls quite regularly, and impatiently counts the days between Brownie troop and church school meetings. Angela continues to be talkative to a fault, for her impulsive chattiness often disturbs the teacher's lesson or her classmates' work. Nevertheless, she expresses herself beautifully, voicing sophisticated opinions in precise adult-like language.

Angela's fine motor skills have changed little since September. Her printing and artwork are acceptable, nothing more. She still reverses an occasional letter, and seems unaware of misspellings in her written work. She is enrolled in a crafts class, but attends only when her friends do, because her real interest lies in socializing. If she had her way, she'd schedule a play date every day. Outdoors, Angela likes activities that she can share with her friends, like skating, bicycling, and jump rope games. She signed up for a soccer team earlier in the year, but was bored by practice sessions and found the pace of the games so difficult to keep up with that she eventually quit the team.

When reading, Angela's sounding-out skills keep her at the top of her class. She is particularly good at reading aloud. As the books become more difficult, though, Angela is losing her place on the page with increasing frequency. She has similar trouble following the lines of problems printed on math worksheets, though she rarely makes an error when the class practices addition and subtraction facts aloud or solves word problems within a group.

Angela asks a lot of questions and makes occasional inappropriate comments in class. She is still distracted by noise and talking, and has difficulty focusing on visual tasks for more than a few minutes at a time. Angela's teacher suggests that the child learn to be more organized, and mentions that Angela's schoolwork would improve if she expended less energy on socialization and more on her written work. It appears that Angela, like Christopher, could profit from some skill development before tackling second grade.

Thomas. As the school year progresses, Mover Thomas becomes somewhat more communicative. He is still difficult to understand, but his sentences are longer and he uses his hands to help convey difficult messages. Nonetheless, Thomas is not very articulate. Rather than grope for an elusive word, he refers to objects in general terms, like "that thing over there," or "The whatchamacallit."

Thomas has become a tease. He seems to have a sixth sense that enables him to zero in on a child's sore spots. He enjoys wrinkling the paper of a neighboring neatnik or placing his chair a scant inch away from that of a child who needs lots of space to feel comfortable. When Thomas's classmates are working, he often intrudes with a bear hug, a poke, or a tug of the hair.

Thomas shows great pride in his accomplishments on those occasions when he completes an assignment, but becomes frustrated and angry when he can't sustain such a work pace. These days, Thomas's printing is more legible, but he is a long way from keeping his letters within the lines, and he still reverses many letters when printing from memory. Few of Thomas's written words are spelled correctly, for he hasn't yet grasped the phonetic skills necessary to make an educated guess. Not surprisingly, Thomas still reads on a level appropriate for a kindergartener. Even at the school year's end, he has a very small sight vocabulary, and tends to lose his place on pages with more than one line of text. Lately, he has taken to trailing his finger along the pages to follow each sentence word by word.

Thomas uses his fingers in math, as well. In an effort to reinforce the concepts of addition and subtraction, his teacher has provided a number line and buckets of teddy bear counters in the back of the room. While these are helpful to Thomas when counting, they provide a new distraction and a built-in excuse to walk around instead of working at his seat.

As he approaches seven years of age, Thomas loves skateboarding, karate, and soccer, though he frequently ignores the rules inherent in the latter two. He signs up for a team sport every season and is usually the undisputed star of any team. However, his coaches will all attest to the fact that during practices and games, Thomas is always getting into trouble of some sort. He simply cannot tolerate waiting.

Thomas has begun to visit the school's speech-language pathologist for help with articulation. He has little difficulty with the thirty-minute sessions, mainly because he is the only student present, and the therapist's unwavering attention helps him concentrate on his work. In class, he finishes his work only when the teacher stands beside his desk to keep him on the task. Thomas loves physical education, art class, and the hands-on projects his class does during science lessons. He loathes the sitting still and listening required by music class. Thomas's teacher is rightfully concerned about his inability to adhere to rules, keep track of belongings and assignments, and remember the sequence of months-old routines. Much of Thomas's behavior and many of his skills are more typical of a four-year-old, and his teacher makes an end-of-year recommendation that he be evaluated for possible learning disabilities and placement in a transition class before advancing to second grade. (For an in-depth look at learning problems like those that Thomas is experiencing, refer to Chapter Nine, "Learning Problems and Solutions.")

THE RELATIONSHIP OF LEARNING STYLE TO A FIRST GRADER'S SCHOOL PERFORMANCE

The academic and fine arts material covered during the primary grades can be divided into Looker and Listener subjects. For the most part, only physical education specifically targets a child's Mover skills. Because different senses and learning skills are called into play during class time, each lesson's appeal to a child is largely dependent on his inborn learning preference. The discussions that follow separate first-grade Looker subjects from Listener subjects, and describe the auditory and visual components of each area of study. Sample first- and last-quarter report cards are also provided to illustrate the different types of success experienced by Lookers, Listeners, and Movers.

Looker Subjects

Considering the many visual aids used in academic work, it's easy to see why Looker skills are so necessary for classroom success. Spelling, for instance, is primarily a visual exercise. At first, most Listener children are good spellers. This is because they rely on their ability to sound out words, and so can easily reproduce the simple one-syllable words found on early first-grade spelling tests. But because the English language is awash with exceptions to the rules of phonics, it is the Looker, able to envision a word's spelling in his mind's eye, who remains a good speller through the grades.

Handwriting is also a subject at which Lookers excel. For beginning writers in particular, good visual memory is needed to recall letter and number shapes before putting pencil to paper. Well-developed eye-hand coordination is also necessary to reproduce the letters and numbers exactly as recalled. These skills also serve Looker children during art class. When designing and creating a project, Lookers are able to envision a finished product before putting their deft hands and fingers to work to give life to their plan.

Math also can be considered a Looker subject. Children who have the ability to visualize can easily recall symbols used in addition and subtraction (+, −, and =), and utilize them as visual cues to the operation being performed. Lookers can make immediate sense of graphs, and can call to mind pictures of number values—two stacks of six blocks each, for example, when adding six plus six. Children with strong Looker skills can also easily visualize various geometric shapes and form mental images of the actions involved in story problems: "Jim had six apples and gave two of them to Meg. How many does Jim have left?"

Listener Subjects

Of all the subjects that require Listener skills, perhaps reading is the most essential. The mastery of reading requires that a child be able to sequence and blend sounds to form words. Even when reading silently, a child "hears" each word in his mind. The earliest readers are usually Lookers, who recognize printed words via visual recall. Looker children, however, eventually fall behind their classmates as their reading material becomes progressively more difficult. As sight readers, they can pronounce only those words they have seen before. They lack the Listener skills needed to sound out unfamiliar letter combinations.

Primary music class is also a Listener subject. Usually, the teacher begins by telling the story behind a new piece of music. Children are then expected to listen to instrumental compositions and memorize lyrics and tempos that become longer and increasingly complex as the school year progresses. Children with below-average auditory skills are hard-pressed to listen and vocalize in this manner. In fact, even Listeners may have trouble with either music reading or tone recognition, as each skill originates in a different brain hemisphere, and the two hemispheres are not always equally developed.

Math, or a good portion of it, comes easily to the Listener child. His well-developed auditory memory and quick grasp of language concepts enable him to process the information contained in story problems. The Listener also relies on immediate recall of math-related words such as "quarter," "circle," and "o'clock"; easily memorizes the basic rules of addition and subtraction; and readily comprehends the terms "more," "less," "plus," "minus," and "equals."

Typical Report Cards for Lookers, Listeners, and Movers

Now that we've examined the skills called into play by each first grade subject, it would be helpful to return to each of our three learners and objectively assess his or her academic performance. Let's imagine for a moment that Christopher, Angela, and Thomas are classmates. The types of first-grade report cards each learner can expect at the end of the first and final marking periods are detailed below. If you imagine further that each grade of "E" means "Excellent," "AA" means "Above Average," "A" means "Average," and "I" means "Improvement Needed," you'll get a clear picture of the learning skill differences among the three children. In Christopher's and Angela's report cards, you'll see evidence of academic plateaus—the leveling off of progress in certain subject areas.

FIRST-GRADE REPORT CARDS FOR LOOKER CHRISTOPHER

First-Quarter Report		*End-of-Year Report*	
Reading	E	Reading	A
Spelling	E	Spelling	E
Math	E	Math	E
Handwriting	E	Handwriting	E
Art	E	Art	E
Music	AA	Music	A
Physical Education	A	Physical Education	A
Conduct	E	Conduct	E

Quiet, intense Christopher displays his first-quarter report card with pride, for here is visible proof of his academic ability and self-control. Music and physical education are the only two subjects in which he is not at the top of the class. Later in the year, Christopher is disappointed to find that his reading grade has dropped from "Excellent" to just "Average," but sounding-out skills are being called into play more and more during reading class, and phonics does not come easily to a Looker. Christopher's music grade also falls, reflecting his boredom and frustration with that class's increasingly complex auditory slant.

FIRST-GRADE REPORT CARDS FOR LISTENER ANGELA

First-Quarter Report		*End-of-Year Report*	
Reading	AA	Reading	E
Spelling	E	Spelling	A
Math	E	Math	E
Handwriting	A	Handwriting	A
Art	A	Art	A
Music	E	Music	E
Physical Education	A	Physical Education	A
Conduct	AA	Conduct	A

Angela's report cards are quite typical of a first-grade Listener. Her work in math and music is consistently good, and her reading skills improve throughout the year as phonics begins to play a larger role. On the other hand, she becomes weaker in spelling as the words she encounters defy the rules of phonics upon which she has always relied. Angela's "Average" grades in art, physical education, and handwriting reflect her average motor skills. Because her sociability and chattiness occasionally approach a disruptive level, her conduct grade drops to "Average" by year's end.

FIRST-GRADE REPORT CARDS FOR MOVER THOMAS

First-Quarter Report		*End-of-Year Report*	
Reading	A	Reading	I
Spelling	I	Spelling	I
Math	A	Math	I
Handwriting	A	Handwriting	I
Art	A	Art	A

Music	A	Music	I
Physical Education	E	Physical Education	E
Conduct	I	Conduct	I

Thomas's report cards tell the whole story. His performance in physical education is always outstanding; his conduct, always a problem. Thomas's academic skills are already a bit below the norm at the time of the first-quarter report, but his teachers choose to be positive and assign him "Average" grades in reading, math, handwriting, art, and music. By the end of the school year, however, Thomas has made so little progress that the gap between his abilities and those of his classmates has widened, and an "Improvement Needed" grade is the only recourse. In art, where Thomas is freer to move about the room, he enjoys some success despite his weak fine motor skills; thus, his maintenance of an "Average" grade in that subject.

WORKING WITH YOUR CHILD'S TEACHER

In this chapter, we've seen three first-grade classmates who are very different learners. Christopher learns best by visual means, and despite his determination and penchant for organization, still needs help with certain aspects of his schoolwork. Angela, who is most responsive to sound and language, is also a good student. However, she has an entirely different set of academic skills, some of which also need improvement. Thomas, who is an active learner, requires a great deal of extra help with almost all schoolwork.

Whatever your child's learning skills and problems may be, you will be able to offer the most emotional support and practical assistance if you remain informed about his life at school. Biannual conferences and quarterly report cards can, of course, be enlightening. However, they don't always provide enough information on a sufficiently frequent basis to keep parents abreast of peer problems, changes in work habits, or a particular unit of study that just won't "sink in." Depending on the teacher's communication style and the size of the class, additional contact with him or her can take the form of behavior checklists, regularly scheduled notes, or brief lunch-hour phone calls. To avoid overlooking important points, make it a practice to prepare yourself by jotting down notes ahead of time. You can encourage a sense of participation and responsibility in your child by sharing his teacher's input with him.

Regardless of the way you communicate with your child's teacher, it's important to create an atmosphere of give-and-take in which each of you apprises the other of important information about your child's academic and social well-being. The list below suggests facts that you might wish to share with your child's teacher. Following this are eight key questions to ask of your child's teacher.

Eight Facts to Reveal to Your Child's Teacher

- *Your child's degree of personal organization.* The teacher should be made aware of the fact that your child has a strong need for order and routine; that he functions best in an open, cluttered workspace; or that he requires ongoing assistance with the organization of materials.

- *Your child's mastery of basic facts.* If your child struggles with addition or subtraction, or if he has special strategies that he uses to memorize subject material, advise his teacher.

- *The hiring of a tutor.* Let the teacher know if you've employed a tutor to provide your child with extra help. Chances are, the teacher and tutor will want to keep their approaches and expectations uniform. It's equally important to advise the teacher if *you* have been providing this sort of help to your child on a regular basis.

- *Health-related information.* The school nurse will undoubtedly have your child's health records on file, but the teacher should also be made aware of allergies or other medical conditions for which medication is being taken on an ongoing basis. Also include any pertinent information about hearing, vision, or attention problems.

- *Past evaluations and screenings.* If your child's past school performance resulted in educational or psychological testing, his teacher should be informed of the test dates and outcomes. The teacher will no doubt be aware of any diagnosed disabilities. However, he or she should also know about testing that resulted in a no-change recommendation.

- *At-home situations.* You'll be doing your child a favor by apprising the teacher of the existence of any upheaval at home, such as an illness, injury, or substance-abuse problem of a family member. Major changes such as these can greatly affect a child's ability to function in the classroom.

- *A second language.* If another language is spoken in your home as either a primary or a secondary means of communication among family members, your child's teacher should know about it. This will help the teacher understand any discomfort your child might exhibit when faced with slang expressions or complex oral directions.

- *Prior recommendations.* It's important to relay to your child's teacher the suggestions made by previous teachers and professionals. By candidly asking for preferential seating, leniency with regard to timed assignments, help from a peer tutor, reduced workloads, or a quiet place for your child to "decompress," you may spare your child months of frustration.

Eight Questions to Ask Your Child's Teacher

- *Is your child's homework completed and turned in on time?* If not, find out what the classroom procedure is for noting assignments and packing materials to take home. Ask how you and your child can work together to eliminate homework problems.

- *Does your child complete the bulk of his class work?* If not, what factors seem to stand in his way? Ask if a seating change would help, or if it is possible to temporarily modify your child's workload so that he can experience classroom success and thereby develop a more positive attitude toward his schoolwork.

- *Does your child pay attention in class?* If there's a problem in this area, what does the teacher think is the cause? Ask how he or she helps your child stay focused, and describe strategies that you have employed successfully at home to keep your child's attention on the task at hand.

- *What are your child's current reading and math levels?* Even if your child has not taken standardized reading and math tests, the teacher should be able to estimate reading and math levels based on classroom performance. Ask whether the teacher believes that your child's progress accurately reflects his abilities.

- *Does the teacher recommend any sort of professional intervention?* Based on your child's classroom performance, does the teacher think that a tutor, a psychological evaluation, or educational achievement testing is warranted? If so, ask the teacher to explain the reasons for such a recommendation.

- *On what level does your child participate in class discussions?* Does your child volunteer information, or does he offer answers only when called upon? Can he verbalize satisfactorily when he has an idea to express? Is he a good listener when others have the floor? If not, ask the teacher what could be done to help the situation.

- *How does your child get along socially?* Ask the teacher who your child's friends are, and if there is anyone who might make a particularly good weekend or after-school playmate. Find out whether your child is at the center of things, on the fringes, or more of a loner, and discuss your child's feelings about this standing. Also ask how your child treats his classmates.

- *What can you do at home to help your child?* Your child's teacher may have specific ideas about emotional or academic support that could hasten your child's growth or remedy an existing problem. Indicate your willingness to work together with the teacher for the benefit of your child.

LEARNING STYLE AND EXTRACURRICULAR ACTIVITIES

As important as homework is, it should take up only a portion of a child's after-school time. Extracurricular activities and informal play times are also important to first graders. Whereas homework develops study skills and reinforces material taught in school, sports, clubs, and at-home amusements encourage a child's social development and allow him to pursue interests at whatever pace, in whatever form, and to whatever degree he chooses. It is this freedom of choice that delights most children. After the regimentation of the school day and the routine of homework, several hours of free time are quite a luxury!

Young children are usually drawn to after-school activities because their friends are involved or because the club or sport holds visual appeal. Most would-be ballerinas entertain visions of themselves in sequined tutus, just as the majority of first-year Little Leaguers wait breathlessly for their team shirts and caps. Scout uniforms and karate garb hold a similar attraction.

Chances are, your child will eventually lose interest in activities that don't appeal strongly to his favored sense. Looker Christopher, for instance, would probably delight in an art class, but might give up fairly quickly on ice skating. Brownies would be a good fit for Listener Angela, and a tumbling class would be well suited to Mover Thomas, but both children would no doubt abandon piano lessons. However, even when the club or sport to which your first grader aspires seems an odd choice because of his particular learning style, there's no harm in allowing your child to experiment—time and budget permitting, of course. All types of extracurricular pursuits will help your child develop interests as well as social skills. Even quickly forsaken activities serve a purpose, in that they make a child aware of those pursuits which bring out his best.

No matter how sports-minded or socially inclined your first grader might be, it's never a good idea to allow an overscheduling of his free time with club meetings, classes, and team sports. Family-oriented activities—chosen for their broader appeal, for the purpose of exercise, or just to get parent and child out of the house for an afternoon—are equally important. Bike rides, picnics, drives, visits to friends, and outings to museums or historical sites all give families the chance to talk, to laugh, and to focus on one another away from household distractions and the demands of meetings and practices. Time alone is important to your child, as well. A first grader needs ample opportunity to read, watch television, hang out with friends, daydream, and play with siblings.

Remember, though: It's not unusual for a first grader to cheerfully leave the planning of his extracurricular activities to a parent. To be sure, some children voice a strong wish to learn karate, for example, or to become a Boy Scout. But an equal number of children give their free time little thought and, left to their own devices, would happily spend it playing inside the house. Fortunately, most six- and seven-year-olds are still quite amenable to a parent's ideas, and still young enough to benefit not just from those activities that appeal to their sensory preference, but also from those that challenge their weaker areas. So if your first grader is in need of some extracurricular direction, you will be able to gently coax him toward a balance of activities—some, perhaps with which he'll feel immediately comfortable, and one or two that will help him strengthen a less-developed skill. The following suggestions, grouped according to the sensory area, should prove helpful.

Visual Activities for First Graders

An ideal first-grade visual activity provides the chance to first observe and then memorize or imitate, often by coordinating the use of eyes and hands. The following list may contain the perfect idea for your child.

- Badminton or ping-pong
- Computer-related activities
- Crafts
- Drawing or painting
- Models or building sets
- Museum educational programs
- Piano, recorder, clarinet, or other musical instruments
- Stamp, sports card, or coin collecting
- Typing

Auditory and Language Activities for First Graders

In order to appeal to the auditory and language skill areas, an activity should provide a child with the opportunity to socialize, lead a group, listen and learn, or display verbal talents. Here are some Listener activities that are perfect for a first grader.

- Backyard shows and plays
- Brownies, Cub Scouts, or 4-H Club
- Day camp or recreation program
- Chorus or choir
- Drama class
- Library story time
- Religious instruction

Gross Motor Activities for First Graders

A perfect gross motor activity for first graders is one that has few rules to get in the way of the action, involves touch or motion, encourages the use of a child's large muscles, or enables the child to spend time outdoors. Here are a few suggestions.

- Aerobics or fitness class
- Bicycling
- Hiking and camping
- Horseback riding
- Ice skating

- Nature program
- Skiing or snowboarding
- Swimming
- Tap or jazz dancing
- Tumbling

When exploring extracurricular options with your first grader, please bear in mind that every child, regardless of learning style, needs physical activity for reasons of fitness and general good health. It isn't necessary that your child's physical exercise take the form of a competitive sport or a highly structured class, either of which might make some first graders uncomfortable. But it is important to expose your child to one or two gross motor activities that suit him, whether they take the form of organized games or noncompetitive, individual pursuits.

HOMEWORK STRATEGIES FOR LOOKERS, LISTENERS, AND MOVERS

From infancy through the kindergarten year, the purpose of identifying a child's learning style is to provide him with a more balanced approach to learning by developing all skills, including those of Listeners, Lookers, and Movers. During the first grade year, a parent's task changes somewhat, as it now becomes important for children to master specific academic information. You can help your first grader accomplish this by teaching him to apply his natural learning skills to the areas of reading, writing, spelling, and math.

The first-grade year is the perfect time to explain to your child what a learning style is, how he learns best, and how he can use his strong suit to master new material. The learning strategies parents employ will, of course, differ according to whether a child is by nature a Looker, a Listener, or a Mover. Here are some at-home tactics that will make learning and homework more appealing to your first grader.

Strategies for Lookers

A Looker child requires a neat, organized workspace, with materials in plain sight. Provide colorful, neatly labeled trays and bins to store pencils, crayons, paper, and other supplies. Post a chart showing your child's various school subjects, and ask him to note each completed assignment. Use a variety of stickers, stars, and happy faces as rewards for staying with taxing language arts assignments.

Teach your child some visual strategies to help him remember letter sounds. Color-code vowels to help him distinguish short and long vowel sounds. For example, short *a*'s can be colored *orange;* long *a*'s, *blue;* short *e*'s, *red;* and long *e*'s, *green.*

Encourage your Looker to draw pictures of any troubling math problems. Groups of balls or blocks, for instance, can be used to represent the numbers he wishes to add or subtract. You can provide highlighter pens, and suggest that your child use them to color important words or names in his reading (excluding textbooks, of course). Finally, the classic flash card is an excellent learning tool for Lookers, who excel at memorization. Try buying different-colored index cards for use as cues for various subjects.

Strategies for Listeners

A Listener child seldom needs reminders to do his homework. Academic work comes so easily to him that many of his assignments seem like fun, rather than a chore. Although he may not need much encouragement at the outset, the Listener thrives on verbal reinforcement of a job well done. It's a good idea to be generous with phrases like "Good job!" and "What beautiful work!" On those occasions when a Listener's attention strays from a long writing assignment or a mostly visual task such as solving rows of math problems, you may wish to offer an appealing incentive: "You can call Shawn after you've practiced your spelling words," or "Finish this page, and then you can choose a game for us to play."

It's helpful for a Listener child to learn to talk himself through difficult tasks. Remind your first grader to do this when he prints. For the letter *q*, for example, he can say, "Go around to the left, close the circle, go straight down, and put on a tail." The same strategy comes in handy when tackling other fine motor tasks, like shoe tying and belt buckling, as well as during gross motor activities. For instance, a hesitant gymnast might reassure himself with, "Bend over, tuck the head, and roll," when learning to somersault.

Finally, encourage your Listener to use a tape recorder. When he is faced with remembering something new, like math facts or the words to a song, he can record the information and play the tape back again and again, until he has it memorized.

Strategies for Movers

Mover children need the most support when it comes to academics. It's a good idea to keep the Mover's homework periods short, ending on a positive note whenever possible. Your physical presence will help keep him focused on his task, as will the elimination of household noise and other distractions. Turn off the television, unplug the phone, put the cat in another room, and occupy younger children elsewhere when it's homework time.

Your Mover will need help staying organized. No doubt, he tends to misplace things, so provide a backpack in which he can carry homework notes, his lunch, and library books. Designate a special coat hook as the place his bag is to be hung at home. If you arrange several trays or wire baskets on his desk or the kitchen counter, your child can separate math, spelling, and workbook papers. When you explain the instructions for a particular assignment, ask for a repetition before your child goes to work.

Hugs, back pats, and high-fives motivate a Mover child. You can also offer such appealing incentives as walking the dog, playing outdoors, or helping make pizza when his homework is done. Since Movers often respond well to food rewards, periodic offerings of cheese, nuts, popcorn, or a frozen juice bar will make homework time more palatable.

It's a good idea to provide the first-grade Mover with an erasable white board for printing practice. This way, he can practice his letter shapes without the added pressure of conforming to lines and margins. Suggest that he lie on his bed, the rug, or a beanbag chair while reading. This will allow him to stretch and squirm to his heart's content. Try to add action to whatever your child is trying to learn. Write addition facts on cards, for example, and have your child jump over each card as he says it aloud. Or tape his spelling words to a wall in a darkened room, and have him move a flashlight from word to word, reading as he goes. As you can see, knowledge of your child's learning style provides an excellent perspective for working with him at home. The right environment and appropriate homework strategies can make a big difference in your first grader's receptivity to new material. Read on for more specific tactics.

TECHNIQUES FOR AFFIRMING AND DEVELOPING LEARNING SKILLS

By following the progress of Christopher, Angela, and Thomas, we've seen how different learning skills result in different academic strengths and weaknesses. We've also looked at ways in which various learning strategies can be used to help a child apply his inborn strengths to the mastery of new material.

The following sections, each devoted to one of the three learning styles, highlight the need to develop those skills that are inborn in some children but have to be cultivated in others. Each section contains lists of toys, techniques, and learning aids. By selecting the ones that seem most suitable and most fun for your child, you'll add an interesting new dimension to the time your first grader spends at home, and will most certainly help him meet the challenges of the school environment.

Building Looker Skills

Looker skills enable a child to observe his surroundings, remember what he sees, visualize concepts, and coordinate his eyes with his hands. Therefore, you can expect a first grader with below-average Looker skills to have difficulty with reading and writing, addition and subtraction, story problems, and artwork—all of which require skills that he does not naturally possess.

No matter what his ability level, however, a first grader's Looker skills can be enhanced or improved through the use of specially chosen playthings and activities. Children who are Lookers by nature will welcome their parents' efforts to provide more of the visual experiences they adore. Listeners and Movers may need a bit more convincing in the form of activities that overlap with their favored stimuli, be that auditory or tactile. Whatever your first grader's inborn style, the following ideas will help you develop his Looker skills—and have fun in the process.

ENHANCING A FIRST GRADER'S EXISTING LOOKER SKILLS

■ *Home Depot's Tool Box Set*, available through Amazon, is just made for a Looker. These high-quality implements bridge the gap between toys and real adult tools. Safety glasses are included.

■ Study maps with your child. He will enjoy this graphic bird's-eye view of his town, city, or state.

■ Lookers enjoy assembling model cars and planes from kits.

■ A backyard telescope will thrill your Looker.

■ Provide a jigsaw puzzle of a favorite subject.

■ Plan a trip to a planetarium or observatory.

■ Lookers enjoy all types of video games.

■ Knowledge Adventure's *Jumpstart Typing*, a software program available through Amazon, teaches children typing accuracy and speed via thirty arcade-style lessons.

■ Toshi Takahama's book *Quick and Easy Origami* (Japan Publications) includes sheets of brightly colored origami paper and instructions for twenty-eight different paper-folding projects.

■ *Stanley's Sticker Stories*, a software program from Riverdeep, allows a child to create his own animated storybook while building reading and writing skills.

ENCOURAGING THE DEVELOPMENT OF LOOKER SKILLS IN FIRST GRADERS WHO ARE LISTENERS

■ Treat your child to a visit to an art gallery. Talk about the characteristics of different pieces of art, and allow him plenty of time to return to those works that he finds most appealing.

■ Assemble an easy jigsaw puzzle with your child. Encourage him to match the pieces using the picture, rather than the various shapes, as clues.

■ Teach your child to focus on visual detail by providing binoculars for outdoor use or a toy microscope for use indoors.

- To encourage your child to try his hand at drawing, share Highlights for Children's *Rebus Treasury II* (Boyds Mills Press). Then suggest that he create a rebus story of his own.

- Read your child a story in a darkened room and ask him to picture the action. You can help by posing questions to stimulate visual imagery like, "What is Cinderella wearing to the ball?" and "What does her carriage look like?"

- Bill Costella's book *Cartooning With Math* (Thinkorporated) provides simple step-by-step instructions that enable children to draw cartoon characters while practicing pattern recognition and math.

- *Scrabble Junior* by Hasbro offers a beginner version of the game. Players work to match letters on tiles to letters printed on the board.

- Teach your child to play Milton Bradley's *Battleship,* available through Hasbro. This game encourages visual imagery and improves number and letter recognition.

- *JumpStart Advanced First Grade,* available through Amazon, combines auditory and visual stimulation to master first grade curriculum.

- Your Listener will enjoy the stories and songs about people around the world while improving his computer skills with *Travel the World With Timmy,* a software program by Riverdeep.

ENCOURAGING THE DEVELOPMENT OF LOOKER SKILLS IN FIRST GRADERS WHO ARE MOVERS

- Play a game of jacks. Teach your child to bounce the ball and scoop first one, then two, then three jacks before catching the ball in the same hand.

- Encourage your child's artistic expression with a plentiful selection of materials—markers, glitter, paint pens, and neon-colored paper.

- Hide a small treasure in your house or yard. Then draw a treasure map with visual clues your child can use to find the hiding spot.

- Label home furnishings—*bed, lamp,* and *table,* for instance—with cards that spell out the objects' names.

■ Seek out a hands-on science museum or an adult museum with a children's section, and take your child there for a multisensory treat.

■ Teach your child to play checkers or Chinese checkers.

■ Playing *Bingo* will improve your child's letter and number recognition.

■ Milton Bradley's *Memory Disney Edition*, available through Hasbro, is a picture-matching game that will help your child recall what he has seen.

■ Draw pictures in the squares of a calendar to signal important events—birthdays, the first snow, and school trips, for instance—and hang the calendar in your child's room.

■ The software program *Leap Frog Math* by Saddleback teaches computer and math skills. Your Mover will enjoy watching a frog hop to the correct answer, with frog races along the way.

Building Listener Skills

The ability to converse, express oneself, and socialize is invaluable to students of any age, but particularly important during the primary grades, when a child's self-confidence and attitude toward school are still being shaped. And, of course, Listener skills are also needed for reading, music, and certain aspects of math. Whether your first grader is a Looker, a Listener, or a Mover, he stands to benefit from the development of keen auditory and language skills.

As always, Listeners themselves will be most receptive to any Listener experience a parent provides. But even a Looker or Mover can improve his verbal and auditory skills by using toys and techniques that employ both his inborn learning skills and the skill you are hoping to spark. Here are some suggestions to get you started.

ENHANCING A FIRST GRADER'S EXISTING LISTENER SKILLS

■ With *Password* by Endless Games, one player tries to get the second player to guess a certain word by offering synonyms and other one-word clues.

■ Get in the habit of reading the "About the Author" information provided in most books. This may help your child view the story in a new light and stimulate his interest in the process of writing.

■ Suggest that your child start a diary or journal in which he can make notes about special events in his life. Encourage the use of inventive spelling—spelling words the way they sound—so that your child can experiment with more difficult terms.

■ Talk about any news stories that you feel are appropriate for a first grader. Show your child the headlines and newspaper photos that relate to each story.

■ Read poetry to your child, and encourage him to write simple poems of his own. Help him out by suggesting possible themes.

■ Dr. Seuss's *El Gato en el Sombrero/The Cat in the Hat* (Random House Español) is a bilingual edition of a favorite children's book, with both English and Spanish text on each page.

■ Get your child a library card of his own. Familiarize him with the layout of your local library so that he'll feel comfortable selecting books from different sections.

■ *DK Merriam-Webster Children's Dictionary* (DK Publishing) is a 912-page illustrated dictionary which is so up-to-date that it includes the term "e-mail."

■ Subscribe to a children's magazine like *Nickelodeon,* an interactive and informative humor magazine for children.

■ Read poems together from *The Random House Book of Poetry for Children,* a modern classic that gives children a taste of the best poetry written over the last several decades.

ENCOURAGING THE DEVELOPMENT OF LISTENER SKILLS IN FIRST GRADERS WHO ARE LOOKERS

■ Encourage your child to place phone calls to relatives and friends.

■ When you read together, read two books: one that your child will enjoy listening to, and a simpler one that he can read to you.

■ Choose a "word of the day," and spell it out on the refrigerator with magnetic letters. Explain what the word means and use it in conversation.

- Suggest that your child write his own storybook. Spend time with him talking about the story, encourage him to add illustrations, and bind the finished product with ribbon or yarn.

- *National Geographic Kids* magazine will appeal to your Looker because it focuses on hands-on learning, wildlife, and science.

- *JumpStart Spanish* software, available on Amazon, is a fun way to introduce a second language. Children learn common vocabulary words by picking up friends on the way to a fiesta.

- To improve your child's auditory memory, play Milton Bradley's *Simon,* available through Hasbro. This game, which comes in both pocket- and full-sized versions, requires players to remember sound and light patterns of varying lengths and speeds.

- Ask your child to draw a picture of something he likes—Grandma's house, a baseball diamond, or a favorite animal, for instance—and help him make up a story about his drawing.

- Build your child's vocabulary via a picture dictionary. *DK Merriam-Webster Children's Dictionary* (DK Publishing) offers your child a visual approach to spelling, vocabulary, and grammar. Illustrations hold young readers' attention while providing them with a wealth of information.

- Available on Amazon, *JumpStart Advanced First Grade* is kid-friendly software designed to teach reading, spelling, math, music, and science skills through both entertaining visuals and auditory stimulation.

ENCOURAGING THE DEVELOPMENT OF LISTENER SKILLS IN FIRST GRADERS WHO ARE MOVERS

- Encourage conversation by having your Mover invite a friend to stay for lunch or sleep overnight.

- Browse through the week's TV listings for a show on a topic that would interest a Mover, such as dinosaurs or hurricanes. Watch the program together, and then discuss what you're seen.

■ Provide a child-sized stage microphone with a battery-powered amplifier. Encourage your child to use it to tell a joke, sing, or make announcements.

■ Subscribe to a children's magazine like *Sports Illustrated for Kids*. This magazine contains interviews with sports heroes, hilarious comics, and awesome action photos. Read the stories aloud to your child, and use the pictures to stimulate questions.

■ Post a magnetic "letter of the week" on the refrigerator. Surround the letter with pictures of things that begin with that letter sound.

■ Encourage your child to use the pictures in a familiar book as clues to the action as he retells the story in his own words.

■ Provide a first set of phonics books, like *Books by Bob,* available at www.booksbybob.com. These simple and inviting beginning readers were developed and designed by parents.

■ Bake letter-shaped cookies, and use them to spell out words. Letter, number, and symbol shapes—dollar signs and question marks, for instance—can be found in the *Roshco 100-Piece Plastic Cookie Cutter Set,* available through Amazon.

■ Go for a walk with your child and use the time to practice rhyming words and naming words with opposite meanings.

■ The software program *Amusement Park Phonics and Reading* by Saddleback helps children practice letter sounds and reading comprehension through action-packed amusement park rides.

Building Mover Skills

Your child may not call upon his Mover skills when he reads, writes, or memorizes math facts, but that doesn't mean that Mover skills should be ignored. A child who possesses a Mover's speed and coordination also possesses a sense of self-confidence that will stand him in good stead in all his endeavors. It pays, then, to develop your child's gross motor skills, regardless of his natural learning preference.

Children who are Movers by nature can never get enough tactile stimulation, and so will delight in any gross motor activity you plan. Listeners and Lookers, who are less certain of their own agility and much less enamored of full-body play, will be most amenable to Mover activities that also draw upon their favored skills, whether visual or auditory. A Listener, for example, might enjoy a game of "Red Rover" much more than a foot race, while a Looker might prefer a bicycle ride through the park. The following ideas will help you build your first grader's Mover skills.

ENHANCING A FIRST GRADER'S EXISTING MOVER SKILLS

- Your Mover will love a basketball net mounted on the garage.

- Introduce your child to the thrill of horseback riding.

- String up a net or rope in your backyard, and use it for a game of badminton or beach-ball volleyball.

- Enroll your child in a martial arts class.

- Involve your child in an organized sport of his choosing, like softball, baseball, or soccer.

- Introduce your child to skiing or ice skating.

- Find the nearest amusement park that features bumper cars, and treat your child to a ride.

- Sign your child up for Cub Scouts, Blue Birds, Brownies, or a 4-H Club. Offer to help out at meetings.

- Invest in a bicycle rack that mounts on your car. Transport your bicycles to a novel location for rides through new and different surroundings.

- If your Mover is a good swimmer, he may enjoy the competition of a swim meet.

ENCOURAGING THE DEVELOPMENT OF MOVER SKILLS IN FIRST GRADERS WHO ARE LOOKERS

- On a breezy day, teach your child how to fly a kite.

- Pitch a tent—or design a makeshift one from blankets—and camp out with your child.

- Take your child out for a game of miniature golf.

- Plan a family hike, even if it's through city streets. Pack a blanket and bag lunch for a picnic.

- Contact your child's teacher for information about local hands-on science museums.

- Take your child to a local video arcade and introduce him to a few of the games. (To avoid crowds of older children, be there when the arcade opens.)

- Investigate new and different playgrounds where your child can play. Check parks, schoolyards, and neighboring towns to see what's available.

- Bird watching is a great ways to entice your Looker outside.

- A backyard telescope will make the outdoors far more attractive to your Looker.

- Your Looker will no doubt enjoy the eye-hand skills required in Ping-Pong.

ENCOURAGING THE DEVELOPMENT OF MOVER SKILLS IN FIRST GRADERS WHO ARE LISTENERS

- Plan mini-adventures with your child, such as trips to a beach, an arts festival, a greenhouse, or a marina.

- Enlist your child's help with the planting and tending of a flower or vegetable garden. Designate one section in which he can experiment.

- Your Listener will enjoy inviting friends to join him at a neighborhood playground.

- Call a local college or art center to find out about acting classes for children.

- Milton Bradley's *Twister*, available through Hasbro, has a spinner that determines where players must position their hands and feet on a large mat. The game progresses until one player loses his balance.

■ Suggest that your child invite friends over for kickball or another team sport.

■ Some informal dancing will no doubt prove to be fun for a Listener and a couple of friends.

■ Your Listener should enjoy shouting out the cheers of your local team—and will get some exercise in the process.

■ Encourage a bike ride with a friend.

■ A mini-trampoline offers a noncompetitive way to get a workout.

As you review the suggestions provided above, you'll no doubt think of other skill-building activities for your child's play times. My lists are intended to serve only as guidelines. Some of your own ideas may be better suited to your schedule; your tolerance for noise, clutter, and activity; and your child's own tastes. Feel free to experiment!

Please be patient as you watch for results. Your child's current skill levels were six to seven years in the making, and improvement may take weeks or months. Meanwhile, your efforts will no doubt grant your child a bit more of your attention, allowing him to derive maximum enjoyment—and plenty of learning-skill enhancement—from the time he spends at home.

LEARNING STYLE QUICKCHECK FOR FIRST GRADERS, SIX TO SEVEN YEARS OF AGE

Directions: Check each of the statements below that best describes your child. Then total the check marks in each column and compare results. You're likely to find your responses concentrated in one or two columns. This is a clear indication of your first grader's learning style.

LOOKER	LISTENER	MOVER
1. Communication: When my first grader wishes to express himself . . .		
☑ He uses simple language.	❏ He uses the correct verb tense.	☑ His sentences are short and direct.
☑ He mispronounces a few words and sounds.	❏ He enjoys talking with adults, and sounds like one when he speaks.	❏ He misarticulates some speech sounds.
❏ He is quiet and rarely volunteers an answer.	❏ He likes to create and tell pretend stories.	❏ He may relate stories out of sequence.
2. Favorite Toys and Pastimes: When my first grader plays alone . . .		
☑ He spends hours at the computer.	❏ He likes listening to CDs and the radio.	☑ He likes sports and outdoor play.
❏ He enjoys crafts and models.	❏ He enjoys reading aloud and being read to.	☑ He enjoys bicycling, hiking, and camping.
❏ He likes to find a quiet spot and read.	❏ He likes to invent scenarios for pretend play.	❏ He loves to feed, brush, and care for pets.
3. Fine Motor Skills: When my first grader uses his hands . . .		
❏ He is precise about forming letters and staying within lines.	☑ His printing is fairly neat.	❏ He has trouble writing on lined paper.
❏ He produces neat, complete worksheets.	❏ While working at his desk, he instructs or reads to himself.	❏ He often confuses the order of letters within words.
❏ He is particular about his coloring and art projects.	❏ He frequently asks for assistance with art projects.	❏ He presses hard with pencils, paint brushes, and crayons.
4. Gross Motor Skills: When my first grader moves about . . .		
❏ He chooses board games over races or tag.	☑ He uses playground equipment to perform and pretend.	☑ He swings and climbs faster and higher than his friends.
❏ He would rather draw in the sand than use playground equipment.	❏ He likes talking games like "Mother, May I?"	☑ He loves being outdoors.

| ❏ He climbs mainly to get a better look around. | ❏ He has average coordination. | ❏ He has excellent coordination. |

5. Social Skills: When my first grader mixes with other children . . .

❏ In a group, he tends to be a loner.	❏ He is very verbal.	❏ He is most sociable on the playground.
❏ He seldom initiates conversation, but answers when spoken to.	❏ He initiates many conversations.	❏ He expresses himself through movement rather than words.
❏ He prefers individual projects to group activities.	❏ He may be reprimanded for talking too much during class.	❏ He is a leader on the playground.

6. Emotions: When it comes to my first grader's feelings . . .

| ❏ He rarely expresses his feelings in words. | ❏ He doesn't hesitate to verbalize his feelings. | ❏ He uses his whole body to express his feelings. |
| ❏ His facial expressions reflect his feelings. | ❏ He is high-strung, but calms down quickly. | ❏ He blushes and cries easily. |

7. Memory: When my first grader learns . . .

| ❏ He remembers what he sees. | ❏ He learns math facts easily. | ❏ He has difficulty recalling what he has seen and heard. |
| ❏ He reads words by memorizing them. | ❏ He reads words by sounding them out. | ❏ He requires extra help to learn to read. |

8. At School: When my first grader is in the classroom . . .

❏ He dresses neatly.	❏ His appearance is not messy, but not overly neat.	❏ He usually looks somewhat rumpled.
❏ He is easily distracted by visual images or movement.	❏ He is easily distracted by sounds and voices.	❏ He is overly active, and both sights and sounds distract him from paying attention.
❏ He insists on keeping his work area neat.	❏ He often volunteers answers and leads class discussions.	❏ He is constantly out of his seat.
❏ He demonstrates an early strength in spelling and math.	❏ He demonstrates an early strength in reading and comprehension.	❏ He has marginal skills in all academic subjects.

TOTALS: _____ LOOKER   _____ LISTENER   _____ MOVER

CHAPTER SEVEN

Learning Styles in Fourth Grade

Today's fourth graders are a sophisticated lot. During the course of a single school year, a nine-year-old, for whom parental approval has long been the driving force behind nearly every word and deed, develops greater allegiance to peers. At the same time, some of the attention previously lavished on toys and sports begins to be refocused on clothing trends, friends, the opposite sex, and the social acceptability of everything from hobbies and possessions to taste in music and TV-viewing habits. And along with all this budding social awareness, nine- and ten-year-olds must cope with new academic demands. Foreign languages and musical instruments are often introduced in the fourth grade, as is the class-changing that is part of departmentalized instruction.

Naturally, some children grow up faster than others. Sociability varies as much from child to child as do academic and physical abilities. All three traits, in fact, are direct results of the same learning patterns a child has employed since infancy. For example, an early talker usually evolves into an extremely verbal child, and this language prowess makes strong social skills almost a certainty. Similarly, the baby who sleeps only seven hours a night and walks by nine months of age will, in many cases, maintain this activity level for many years. This virtually assures difficulty with tasks that require sitting still and paying attention.

This chapter describes the effects of learning style on a child's classroom and after-school life by introducing three learners—a Looker, a Listener, and a Mover—and following their progress from September to June. A Learning Style QuickCheck for Fourth Graders (see page 191) is included to help you pinpoint your own child's learning preference.

Of course, learning style exerts a great influence on a fourth grader's academic experience. This chapter examines the different school subjects that appeal to each learner, and takes a look at typical report cards for Lookers, Listeners, and Movers. And since conference time is so valuable, suggestions are also provided for improving communication between you and your child's teachers.

A nine- or ten-year-old's after-school time is a precious commodity. The activities she chooses, the people with whom she associates, and even the degree of personal organization she brings to household tasks and homework assignments are all functions of her innate learning style. This chapter includes tips on helping your child choose extracurricular activities that will best suit her learning style, and guides you in creating the best possible at-home learning environment.

While striving for well-roundedness is still a worthwhile goal for a fourth grader, as time passes, it becomes more important and more realistic to shift parental emphasis to a child's need to master academic material. To begin with, it has been shown that the development of a child's visual, auditory, and motor skills does not automatically translate into improved class work. Many children need the additional support of special learning strategies before achieving better grades. Second, as a child matures, she is likely to become less receptive to parental attempts to introduce activities that target weak skills. Third, and perhaps most to the point, parents' time is limited. It makes sense, therefore, to focus skill-enhancement energy where it will best benefit nine- and ten-year-olds—that is, on academic achievement. With this is mind, you will find suggestions at the chapter's end to help improve performance in each of your child's school subjects.

When both parent and child acknowledge and appreciate how that child learns, the expectations of both become realistic, and the parent-child relationship is marked by understanding rather than tension. Your fourth grader is, without a doubt, on the brink of a host of social and personal changes. Help your child make the most of this exciting year.

A LOOK AT THREE LEARNERS

Daniel, Ana, and Beth are fourth-grade classmates. Each child had a birthday in the late spring. Daniel and Ana are nine years and four months of age at the start of the school year. Beth, who repeated kindergarten when it was decided that she needed an extra year to mature, is a year older.

All three children have parents who are actively involved in their schooling, and have been exposed to similar teachers, identical curricula, and comparable after-school activities. Yet the children are as different as can be. Ana's academic strengths, as you'll soon see, are Daniel's and Beth's shortcomings. Daniel is strongest in the subject areas that puzzle Ana. Beth enjoys the most success in physical education, the area in which Ana and Daniel struggle most.

It is the children's learning styles—their inborn preferences for absorbing information by visual, auditory, or tactile means—that have had such a dramatic influence on their school and home lives. Although all children do not exhibit the traits of a single learning style and may, in fact, be Looker-Listeners or Looker-Movers, each of our case-study children possesses a "pure" style. This has been done to accent the features of each sensory preference. You'll see the difference that learning style can make as we meet each child at the start of the fourth-grade year.

Nine Years of Age

Meet Daniel. Daniel, a Looker, is a logical, confident, soft-spoken child. He has two friends with whom he socializes outside of school, though he usually plans an activity with just one pal at a time. Daniel's outside time is very structured; instead of inviting his friend over to "hang out," he issues carefully considered invitations for an afternoon of creating cartoons or competing at video games. Daniel's other favorite activities include throwing darts, reading about sports records, studying astronomy, and organizing his trading card collection. As you can see, Daniel is quite comfortable with solo pursuits. He'd choose drawing over a kickball game any day.

Daniel's written work is colorful, neat, and painstakingly done. It's not unusual for him to rewrite an entire paper rather than cross out or erase an error. Daniel's artwork also reflects his fine motor skills. His projects are well planned, precisely executed, and always attractive. Most include some creative variation of the geometric shapes he finds so fascinating. He also loves to design mazes and video games of his own. Daniel's abilities don't extend to the large muscles, however. He doesn't care for gym class or team sports; in fact, he long ago traded his Little League uniform for a job as score keeper. When he does spend time outdoors, you'll usually find Daniel seated at a picnic table with a comic book, a pad and pen, or a hand-held video game.

Quiet Daniel rarely volunteers to speak in class, even though he usually knows the answer being sought. He is proud of his academic ability but does not care for the limelight. At school, as at home, he enjoys being by himself. Daniel is methodical about completing assignments, adores visual tasks like diagramming sentences, and excels at work involving maps, tables, graphs, and charts. Last year, his favorite math activity dealt with Roman numerals.

When reading, Daniel uses sentence context and educated guesswork to help him decode printed text into spoken words, for he is weak in the phonics skills that would enable him to "sound out." His reliance on visual memory also means that he remains a strong speller, while his Listener classmates are finding themselves less and less able to apply phonics rules to their fourth-grade vocabulary words. Daniel's written work is brief and to the point. He is a child of few words, anyway, and the simpler his written language, the less chance of error. It will come as no surprise that Daniel is having trouble with first-year Spanish. He is able to memorize the vocabulary, but stumbles time and again over pronunciation. It is clear that Daniel's orientation as a Looker helps him to excel in certain subject areas, but actually slows his progress in others.

Meet Ana. Friendly, talkative Ana—a Listener—has dozens of friends. She' s always the first to welcome a new child into the neighborhood, and is as well accepted by adults and older children as by her peers. In fact, Ana carefully imitates the speech, mannerisms, and dress of her teen-aged baby sitter, and is admired by her classmates for her sophisticated social behavior.

Ana loves to be the center of attention. She is always telling jokes and stories, and at home is a veritable fountain of information about her school day. Ana is active in the Girl Scouts, takes a Saturday-morning drama class, and has already played several small parts in community theater. During her free time, Ana steers clear of crafts, drawing, and other fine motor hobbies, but can usually be found entertaining friends or chitchatting via instant message or the phone.

Although Ana likes the social contact that comes with physical education and art, these two classes are still the low points of her week. She is not particularly strong or agile, and mildly resents the back-seat position she must take to her athletically or artistically gifted peers. When the results of a recent presidential physical fitness test were posted, Ana was nowhere to be found. Ana's lack of ability in art is not quite as obvious, but her efforts are neither neat nor creative, and she has trouble with assignments involving design and perspective.

In school, Ana memorizes new material easily. She loves oral presentations, and her journal writings are imaginative and peppered with descriptive phrases. Ana's book reports are long, complex, and well organized, but her shaky proofreading skills prevent her from getting the A+ she otherwise deserves. Ana also has quite a bit of trouble with other visual assignments, like those involving charts, graphs, maps, and keyboard memorization. Frequently, she loses her place, and has trouble integrating all the details to form the "big picture." In fact, because Ana lacks the visual skills so necessary in fourth-grade math, her parents have arranged weekly sessions with a math tutor. But in music, French, science, and social studies, Ana can rely on her strong auditory skills to master most of the information she needs to learn. Overall, her grades have always been very good, and fourth grade promises to elicit the same strong academic performance.

Meet Beth. Mover Beth is an athletic, highly coordinated child whose physical prowess is a function of her learning style, rather than the fact that she is a year older than many of her classmates. Beth is also an emotional soul, quick to cry in anger or frustration. It is for this reason that Beth's attempts to join in the games of neighborhood children fall flat. She is well matched physically, but is reduced to tears with a frequency that quickly becomes tiresome. In fact, the social and emotional immaturity that led Beth to repeat kindergarten is still a problem. In class, her history of academic difficulties and frequent outbursts has made her something of an outcast. In the long run, Beth's rather limited social skills result in her getting along best with children who are physically competent, but a year or two younger than she.

Beth often uses her hands to help express herself. Her vocabulary, you see, lacks color and depth, so gestures and coined terms—"measurer" for ruler, or "timesing" for multiplying—are quite useful. Beth also mispronounces many multiple-syllable words; "bisghetti" and "aksed" are two examples. She simply doesn't hear the difference between her version and the correct one.

Beth often "plays rough," but her agility guarantees her winning almost every athletic contest. She adores skateboarding, swimming, softball, soccer—all active sports, in fact. Beth sticks to gross motor play even when no opponent is available. Shooting baskets in the driveway and throwing and catching against the garage wall with her lacrosse stick are two of her favorite pastimes. Since Beth is somewhat slow to coordinate her eyes and fingers, she rarely attempts fine motor activities on her own. Her penmanship leaves something to be desired, and she is often asked to recopy assignments to make them more legible. Last year, she attempted to master the piano keyboard and recorder with the rest of her class, but soon gave up in frustration. Only in art class, where messiness can be a part of creativity, does she feel comfortable with her efforts.

At school, Beth tries hard to pay attention to her lessons rather than the goings-on around her. But it is difficult for her to keep her hands away from the science projects on a nearby table, or to resist toppling a tempting stack of books beneath her neighbor's chair. In fact, Beth's struggles with self-control are so frustrating that she eventually tunes out her surroundings altogether, preferring to amuse herself by popping the eraser off her pencil, or opening and closing the rings of her looseleaf binder. Naturally, Beth hates report card time, for in the past, her grades have led only to lost privileges.

Because Beth struggles with reading and spelling, no academic subjects come easily. She can barely manage the literature used in second-grade classes, yet her textbooks are written on a fourth-grade level. Even with simpler material, Beth's reading comprehension is poor. You see, because she has to work so hard at the process of decoding, she absorbs very little of the text. Fortunately, since first grade, Beth has visited her school's Resource Lab for some extra help, and this support has kept her abreast of written assignments and new subject matter. This year, Beth will continue to visit the Resource Lab for assistance with reading and language arts.

Timed tests and long-term assignments are torture for Beth, because she cannot plan ahead or organize her work on her own. To give Beth the best chance of completing her schoolwork, her teacher has begun shortening the child's assignments and has moved her desk closer to his. On a positive note, Beth likes the experimentation and hands-on aspects of science, and is the first to bring in items from home that relate to her social studies units. Beth's parents encourage any interests related to school and learning. They keep her supplied with magazine and newspaper articles about pollution, they've placed her in charge of the recycling center in their garage, and they've provided her with a telescope.

There is no question that among our case-study children, it is Beth whose learning style creates the greatest need for support. But with the combined efforts of her parents and teachers, Beth will enjoy both academic progress and social growth during her fourth-grade year.

Which learning style does your fourth grader possess? Is she a fussy, organized student who learns by mostly visual means? If so, she's a Looker, like Daniel. Or is she a Listener, like Ana—very social and unusually good at following directions and mastering new material? Or like our Mover, Beth, is she weak in academic subjects, remaining most attentive whenever an assignment involves her active participation? The Learning Style QuickCheck for Fourth Graders, located on page 191, will help you find out for sure. As you read the various statements contained in the QuickCheck, mark those that best describe your child. You're likely to see a heavy concentration of checks in one or two columns—a clear indication of your fourth grader's sensory preference.

HOW LOOKER, LISTENER, AND MOVER FOURTH GRADERS DEVELOP

Daniel, Ana, and Beth are clearly different students, with their striking dissimilarities also reflected in the nature of their friendships and outside interests. Listener Ana, for example, impatiently awaits recess one day because she wants to display the intricate braid her mother wove for her that morning. Mover Beth is equally impatient, but the cause of her restlessness is anticipation of the game of handball she has planned with one of her buddies. And Looker Daniel would be perfectly happy to skip recess altogether, so engrossed is he in the product map he's making for social studies class.

While each child experiences growth during fourth grade, that growth isn't necessarily a balanced affair. The academic differences between our three learners—and between real-life fourth graders who share their learning styles—remain intact. This is due to the fact that each subject utilizes particular skills—skills that are one learner's strength, but another's shortcoming. Fourth-grade math, for example, covers perimeter and area, place value, fractions, and other concepts suited to a visual learner. Science at this level is primarily a hands-on subject, and therefore best understood by Lookers and Movers. And the language arts—grammar, foreign language, writing, and literature—involve auditory exercises, making this field a natural arena for Listeners. To see how Daniel, Ana, and Beth handle fourth grade's challenges, let's look at each child at the school year's end.

Ten Years of Age

Daniel. As he reaches his tenth birthday, Looker Daniel continues to keep to himself and to seek out his own personal space in which to work and play. Daniel has always been accepted by his peers, and lately, despite his reserve, he is becoming more popular. You see, his fourth-grade classmates now place greater value on one another's achievements. So Daniel's unmatched PS-2 and Xbox skills, the gold medal he earned in the school spelling bee, and his prize-winning artistic creations have won his classmates' ongoing admiration. Lately, the girls in Daniel's class have also begun noticing his impeccable manners and flawless appearance.

At school, Daniel excels in penmanship, spelling, and math, due to his innate fine motor ability and well-developed visual memory. A lack of sounding-out skills has caused Daniel to progress more slowly in reading and in textbook-based subjects such as science and social studies. However, he leads the class when it comes to map assignments, charts, and other projects that tap his artistic skills.

The older Daniel gets, the more frustrated he becomes with the classroom antics and academic shortcomings of some of his peers. He keeps his impatience to himself, however, lest a sigh or comment lead to confrontation. Daniel continues to steer clear of activities and children with the potential for trouble, for he enjoys a pleasant relationship with his teachers and wants nothing to change that.

Daniel's current ambition is to be an architect like his uncle. Blue-prints fascinate him, as does the idea of dressing up for work each day and performing a job in relative peace and privacy. Daniel and his father frequently stop by his uncle's firm to look around. Visits to his uncle's house are a treat, as well, because Daniel gets to sit and draw at a drafting table and experiment with computer-aided design programs in the family's home office.

At school conference time, Daniel's teachers suggest that he pay closer attention during lectures, since he sometimes misses an important point or a verbal direction. Aware of Daniel's tendency to tune out when involved in a game or faced with a long-winded speaker, the boy's parents agree. In addition, because Daniel would very much like to improve his reading level, the family has asked his language arts teacher to suggest high-interest, low-level books that the boy can tackle during the summer months. Daniel's work habits and perseverance helped him greatly during fourth grade, and on the whole, his academic performance was quite satisfactory. School remains a positive experience for him, and he looks forward to entering next year's art contest and enjoying the fifth-grade privilege of working on the school newsletter.

Ana. By the end of fourth grade, Listener Ana has become the social hub around which all the activities and get-togethers of her friends revolve. Ana is seen as an authority on style and social behavior, and her friends make it a practice to run their ideas and comments by her for approval before trying them on anyone else. Like the older girls she so admires, Ana herself has helped make boy-girl pairings among her classmates something desirable by organizing outings involving classmates of both sexes, and by openly declaring her "boyfriend" of the moment.

Ana thinks she would enjoy being a teacher or an actress, but is not as serious as Daniel about looking ahead. When pressed by a well-meaning adult about her plans for the future, Ana usually casts a friendly look of amazement and responds, "I'm much too young to think about any of that." Gregarious, fun-loving Ana thinks only about the here and now, and tries to wrest the maximum enjoyment from activities that showcase her verbal talents.

Ana's classroom efforts are consistently reinforced by high grades. Her superior reading skills enable her to take the lead in many classes, because textbooks and works of literature pose no problem at all. Ana's fine motor skills are a bit weak, however, so she doesn't fare quite as well with creative projects, and continues to need a tutor's help with math computations. Fortunately, the fourth grader's verbal skills and positive attitude do much to offset any academic shortcomings. At year's end, in fact, Ana's teachers commend her for her leadership qualities and her willingness to seek assistance, and they put together a packet of schoolwork to help the child keep her skills sharp during the summer months. Ana, always eager for new privileges and higher social status within her school, can't wait to attend fifth grade. From her conversations with older friends, she is well aware of the various fifth-versus-sixth grade contests that will be available to her. Ana also looks forward to performing in the class talent show and trying out for "Brainbusters," an interscholastic team whose claim to fame is a wealth of general knowledge.

Beth. Mover Beth is a year older and, thus, larger and more physically mature than most of her female classmates. Nonetheless, as she approaches age eleven, Beth exudes a sense of confidence about her body that is lacking in many fourth-grade girls. As sure-footed and agile as ever, Beth is especially proud of her accomplishments in gymnastics—a sport that she has embraced passionately from the first. Recently, Beth has also begun to assist a neighbor by amusing her two preschool-aged sons, and this twice-weekly job has given a further boost to the fourth grader's self-image.

At the end of the school year, Beth's best friend is a nine-year-old girl from the neighborhood. Like Beth, the friend is very coordinated and prefers to be on the go at all times; but as a third grader, she makes none of the uncomfortable social demands so characteristic of Beth's classmates. You see, Beth doesn't care at all about trendy clothes or gossip. She'd much rather shoot baskets beneath the driveway lights than don a cute nightshirt and banter her way through the sleepovers that have become so popular with her peers. Yet Beth does show signs of a budding social awareness. She has been the subject of her cattier classmates' verbal jabs for a year or two now, but has only recently begun to react with shame and a left-out feeling rather than the spurt of hostility that was something of a trademark during the previous four years. Beth has also begun to be embarrassed by her emotional displays, and this new self-consciousness has occasionally helped her to think before lashing out in anger, and to consider solutions before dissolving into tears.

Last fall, Beth wanted to be a professional tennis player. She was thrilled by the prospect of earning a living at athletics, and envious of the teen-aged professionals for whom formal schooling is but a memory. However, since a recent demonstration at her school by the police department's K-9 unit, Beth has decided that a law enforcement career might be a better choice.

Beth still struggles with most aspects of her schoolwork. Her spelling and handwriting are poor because of weak visual skills, and her math computations are disorderly and sloppy. Far from memorizing multiplication facts, Beth has yet to master regrouping in addition and subtraction. She is still nearly two years behind most of her classmates in reading, and this fact makes much of her social studies, science, and language arts work exercises in frustration. Beth's teachers recommend that she continue to receive shortened, untimed assignments—ten math problems, perhaps, instead of the thirty her classmates are given—to reduce frustration and encourage more consistent effort. It is also suggested that Beth continue to be seated at the front of the classroom, and away from such high-traffic areas as the drinking fountain, pencil sharpener, and doorway. Beth's teachers see that these tactics have helped Beth tremendously during fourth grade. Even Beth, who looks forward to next year only because it brings two extra phys ed classes per week, concurs. During the summer, Beth will be taking tennis lessons, playing in a softball league, and continuing her mother's helper job, but she has agreed to see a tutor twice a week to keep her skills at their current level. (Please refer to Chapter Nine, "Learning Problems and Solutions," for more information on learning difficulties such as Beth's.)

THE RELATIONSHIP OF LEARNING STYLE TO A FOURTH GRADER'S SCHOOL PERFORMANCE

Just like the curricula of earlier grades, fourth grade's includes only one Mover subject—physical education. The rest of your child's course material can be divided into Looker and Listener subjects. What follows is a look at the visual and auditory aspects of the fourth-grade curriculum. First, each subject is categorized according to its corresponding learning style. To further illustrate the degree of challenge posed by each subject to a given learner—by math to a Looker child, for instance—sample first- and last-quarter report cards have been provided, along with a subject-by-subject look at each learner's overall academic experience.

Looker Subjects

The typical fourth-grade classroom is alive with color and detail. Chalkboards, white boards, bulletin boards, walls, and even ceilings are decorated with posters, charts, maps, and displays of students' work. It comes as no surprise, then, that Looker skills are quite valuable.

Looker fourth graders usually excel at the spelling, capitalization, and punctuation components of language arts, each of these facets being a visual exercise. You see, a Looker's ability to memorize and envision spellings is often more reliable than a Listener's habit of sounding out words. And Lookers rarely overlook the need for a punctuation mark or an upper-case letter, because they are able to view entire sentences both as single units and as combinations of independent phrases.

The need for sharp visual skills makes fourth grade math a Looker subject. Listeners may be the first in their class to memorize math vocabulary and grasp newly explained concepts. However, as computations become increasingly complex and multi-digit long division, fractions, and decimals are added to the picture, a Looker's fine motor skills and ability to form mental images are likely to boost her to the top of the class.

Art is another subject that calls upon a Looker's skills. Similarly, handwriting, which was discussed in Chapter Six (see page 131), continues to be a Looker subject because it draws upon visual and fine motor abilities. These same skills enable Lookers to excel at technology, because their innate finger dexterity, eye-hand coordination, and instant recall of the keyboard make computer assignments seem more like play than work.

Listener Subjects

Every fourth-grade subject requires that a child pay attention to some degree, and then process the information she hears. However, there are particular areas of study whose strong auditory slant makes them perfectly suited to Listeners.

Reading is perhaps the most important fourth-grade Listener subject, because literature, texts, and periodicals are used in every academic class. With their sophisticated verbal and auditory skills, Listeners are the learners best equipped to sound out unfamiliar words, remember difficult pronunciations, comprehend what is read, and recall details after the fact.

Listeners' auditory strengths also put them at an advantage in science and social studies. It's true that Lookers have the easiest time with visual aids such as charts and maps, but Listeners excel in reading and remembering textbook information. They also have little trouble remaining attentive during the lectures, projects, and note-taking that make up much of their class time, and can easily recall what they've heard.

Fourth-grade foreign language consists mainly of the memorization of simple dialogue and basic vocabulary terms. As such, much of the class work is oral in nature, with the teacher explaining, pronouncing, and then requesting recitation of words and phrases. A Listener, with her sharp ear, quickly memorizes differences in the alphabet, and has little trouble mimicking pronunciations and memorizing word lists.

The grammar portion of fourth-grade language arts is easy for most Listeners. A child with well-developed auditory skills quickly spots errors of tense, subject-predicate agreement, or sentence structure, and offers corrections that are instinctive—that is, based on what sounds right, rather than on a particular rule of grammar. For example, a Listener might correctly begin a sentence, "If I were a . . ." even though she knows that "I was" is the usual pairing, and the reason behind the use of "were" in this instance has never been explained to her. Listeners also have the edge when it come to composition, since their writing efforts are often as detailed and imaginative as their everyday speech.

Vocal music is another Listener subject. In music class, a fourth grader deals simultaneously with rhythm, tone, lyrics, and instrumentation, and is expected to understand and remember the historical background of each new composition. This calls for a discriminating ear, the ability to listen for extended periods of time, and a knack for rote memorization—in other words, Listener skills. As was explained in Chapter

Six (see page 132), it is possible for a Listener to be tone-deaf. Even so, children with this sensory preference usually learn a song and comprehend its significance more quickly than their Looker or Mover peers.

Typical Report Cards for Lookers, Listeners, and Movers

Having matched each fourth-grade subject with the type of learner who finds it most appealing, let's take another look at the classroom performances of Daniel, Ana, and Beth. As you would expect of three children with different learning styles, their report cards are not at all alike. In fact, a look at each child's first- and last-quarter grades clearly shows Daniel's preference for visually oriented subjects, and Ana's affinity for the auditory. Mover Beth, on the other hand, is hard-pressed to find any appeal at all in fourth-grade academics.

FOURTH-GRADE REPORT CARDS FOR LOOKER DANIEL

First-Quarter Report		*End-of-Year Report*	
Language Arts	B+	Language Arts	B
Social Studies	B	Social Studies	B
Science	B	Science	B+
Math	A+	Math	A
Spanish	B–	Spanish	B
Computer Technology	A	Computer Technology	A+
Art	A+	Art	A+
Music	B	Music	B
Physical Education	B	Physical Education	B
Handwriting	A+	Handwriting	A+
Attitude and Effort	A+	Attitude and Effort	A+

Daniel's grades are well above average. His lowest grade, a B– in first-quarter Spanish, reflects pronunciation difficulties rather than a lack of effort. Since neither gross motor nor auditory skills are Daniel's strong suit, he also receives B's in courses like physical education, music, and the last quarter of language arts, which focused on composition. Daniel's auditory skills also hold him back a bit in social studies and science, where his ability to envision helps him enjoy the classes' historical and categorical aspects, but his less-than-perfect grades attest to his trouble with the memorization of facts. Daniel's grades are so consistent that there is no more than a half-grade variation in any subject between September and June. This is a tribute to his self-discipline and excellent work habits.

FOURTH-GRADE REPORT CARDS FOR LISTENER ANA

First-Quarter Report		*End-of-Year Report*	
Language Arts	A	Language Arts	A+
Social Studies	A	Social Studies	A
Science	A	Science	A
Math	B–	Math	B–
French	A	French	A
Computer Technology	B	Computer Technology	B+
Art	B	Art	B–
Music	A	Music	A
Physical Education	B	Physical Education	B
Handwriting	B	Handwriting	B
Attitude and Effort	B	Attitude and Effort	B–

Ana's facility with language and listening activities is clearly reflected in her grades. Her strongest performances are in subjects with an auditory slant, like music, French, and the reading portion of language arts. Ana listens so well in class that she often masters much of the subject matter long before she reads her textbook. However, because of the visual orientation needed to grasp such concepts as place value, fractions, patterns, and perspective, both math and art pose a problem for Ana. In fact, weekly meetings with a tutor are all that has enabled Ana to keep her math grades above a C. In art, she manages by "borrowing" project ideas she remembers from past years.

The B's Ana earns in computer technology, art, physical education, and handwriting are direct reflections of motor skills that are, in her case, just average. Ana continues to labor over the computer keyboard, but puts in the extra effort needed to earn a B.

FOURTH-GRADE REPORT CARDS FOR MOVER BETH

First-Quarter Report		*End-of-Year Report*	
Language Arts	C–	Language Arts	C–
Social Studies	C–	Social Studies	C–
Science	B–	Science	C

Math	C–	Math	C–
French	n/a	French	n/a
Computer Technology	C–	Computer Technology	D
Art	C+	Art	B–
Physical Education	A	Physical Education	A
Handwriting	C–	Handwriting	C–
Attitude and Effort	C	Attitude and Effort	C

Beth's love of physical activity and difficulty with all but the hands-on aspects of learning are clearly reflected in her grades. Her strongest performance is in classes that encourage active participation and movement about the room: physical education, art, and science. Conversely, her lowest grades are in subjects that depend on sitting and listening, or worse, on written assignments. Beth's work in language arts, social studies, math, computer technology, and handwriting is actually worse than her grades indicate. Aware that she has been studying with a Resource Lab teacher, Beth's classroom teachers hesitated to defeat her by assigning grades of D. Similarly, Beth's C in Attitude and Effort was intended as reinforcement for her progress in the area of self-control. You see, with Resource Lab support, Beth brought her reading level up a full grade, and, as she gained confidence, her classroom behavior also become more acceptable. Only in French, where she was completely frustrated, did Beth revert to her former attention-getting antics. Her teachers, recognizing that foreign language is not a priority for Beth right now, scheduled her Resource Lab time in place of French class.

WORKING WITH YOUR CHILD'S TEACHER

Each of the fourth graders you met in this chapter learns by a different means. Like many visually oriented children, Daniel is organized and self-directed. Ana, who is most responsive to sound and language, is also a good student. However, both children have found that their innate skills alone cannot guarantee school success. And Beth, who is attuned to touch and movement, needs more support than her Looker and Listener classmates.

Unfortunately, school conferences and report cards cannot always paint a complete picture of your child's school life. However, you can keep abreast of changes in your fourth grader's social and academic standings by initiating more frequent contact with her teacher. Depending on your child's needs, a behavior or school-preparedness checklist, regularly scheduled notes, or brief lunch-hour phone calls to her teacher can be most informative. To avoid the omission of important points during these communications, jot down thoughts and questions ahead of time. Also consider sharing the teacher's input with your child.

The following lists have been designed to guide you in achieving more effective parent-teacher communication. Each topic relates to your child's academic or social well-being. The list directly below suggests information that you may wish to disclose to your child's teacher. The second list suggests questions that you may wish to ask during a conference.

Eight Facts to Reveal to Your Child's Teacher

- *Your child's degree of personal organization.* Tell the teacher whether your child is orderly or haphazard in her approach to school materials and personal belongings. Mention any effect your child's organizational level has had on her schoolwork. You may also wish to suggest organizational strategies that have proven helpful in the past.

- *Your child's mastery of basic facts.* Let the teacher know whether your child now uses or seems to be in need of special strategies to help her memorize subject material.

- *The employment of a tutor.* Tell the teacher if you have used or are now using a tutor, so that the teacher and tutor can coordinate their methods and goals.

- *Health-related information.* Make both the teacher and school nurse aware of any physical conditions that might affect your child's classroom performance.

- *Past evaluations and screenings.* Alert the teacher to the possibility of recurrent schoolwork problems by telling him or her of any educational or psychological testing that your child underwent in past years.

- *At-home situations.* Since even temporary upheaval can greatly affect a youngster's school performance, be sure to advise your child's teacher of any major changes in your home life.

- *A second language.* Make the teacher aware of your fourth grader's at-home use of a second language. The use of another language affects a child's acquisition of English grammar and vocabulary skills, and can have an impact on writing, as well.

- *Prior recommendations.* Advise your child's teacher of any seating or class work modifications used by previous teachers to improve school performance.

Eight Questions to Ask Your Child's Teacher

- *Is your child's homework completed and turned in on time?* Find out how you, your child, and the teacher can work together to eliminate homework problems.

- *Does your child complete the bulk of her class work?* Ask the teacher whether modifications, temporary or permanent, are needed to improve your child's ability to apply herself to tasks and assignments at school and at home.

- *Does your child pay attention in class?* Discuss strategies that might improve your child's ability to apply herself to tasks and assignments at school and at home.

- *What are your child's current reading and math levels?* Ask if the teacher feels that your child's progress accurately reflects her abilities.

- *Does the teacher recommend any sort of professional intervention?* Find out if your child might benefit from professional evaluation or additional services.

- *On what level does your child participate in class discussions?* Ask if your child voluntarily contributes to group lessons, if she expresses herself satisfactorily, and if she remains attentive when others are speaking.

- *How does your child get along socially?* Ask the teacher whether your child seems at ease among her peers, and whether her social skills seem appropriate for a fourth grader. If your child seems to be a loner, ask the teacher to recommend a youngster or two who might be appropriate playmates.

- *What can you do at home to help your child?* Find out if your child might benefit from improvement in one or more skill areas, and if there are techniques you can use at home to boost your child's growth in those areas.

LEARNING STYLE AND EXTRACURRICULAR ACTIVITIES

It should come as no surprise that a fourth grader's learning style greatly influences her selection of extracurricular pursuits. Certainly, the interests of the three children discussed in this chapter—Daniel's love of video games, Ana's fascination with the theater, and Beth's enthusiasm for sports—are all offshoots of the children's sensory preferences. And just like the special qualities of our three learners, your own child's sociability, athleticism, or creativity will be reflected in the pastimes she chooses to pursue.

By fourth grade, your child may well have tried her hand at a long list of clubs, sports, and hobbies. Or she may only be starting to display an interest in extracurricular activities. Whatever the case, don't be surprised if her interests seem to change with great frequency. By now, you see, most children need to be rewarded on some level for their participation in an activity. Those who, instead, are bored or discouraged by their own poor performance gradually leave the ranks of an organization. In fact, most nine- and ten-year-olds are well aware of what they can and cannot do successfully, and tend to make extracurricular choices accordingly. Movers gravitate toward sports; Lookers, toward artistic and, often, solitary pursuits; and Listeners, toward the clubs and activities that provide the social stimulation they adore.

As a rule, you should allow your fourth grader to take the lead in choosing outside activities. Since extracurricular pursuits exist so that children can spend their free time doing what they like and developing their hobbies, it's pointless to coerce a child into an activity in which she has no interest—no matter how great the potential benefits may be. Art club, for instance, may demand too much sitting still, or music lessons, too much practice time, to hold some children's interest for long.

Other fourth graders may be inclined to follow the lead of their friends, rather than the wishes of their parents, when selecting after-school activities. In either case, it's wise to allow your child to experiment with the clubs, teams, or lessons that she thinks she'll enjoy and that your budget will permit. Try not to express your disappointment in your fourth grader's choice of activity, your longing for her to exhibit the talents possessed by another family member, or your determination that she enjoy social or athletic opportunities lacking in your own childhood. Your child will be better served by your unconditional acceptance of her own selections and by any practical help your can offer. For instance, if your fourth grader is intrigued by a particular club, but seems hesitant about taking the first step, you can best help her by providing as much information as possible. Similarly, if your child wants to try an activity that you don't believe will hold her interest—if your Listener likes the idea of trading-card collecting, for instance—you should nevertheless encourage her experimentation.

In most cases, a fourth grader will stay with those activities that best fit her learning style. If after several weeks' trial she is not enjoying herself, there will be no harm in letting her drop out. After all, children have a right to enjoy their leisure time, and since it's sometimes difficult to anticipate whether a new activity will be a good fit, experimentation may be unavoidable.

Although it's generally not advisable to persuade a fourth grader to try an activity that seems foreign to her, every child, regardless of learning style, needs to develop herself physically for reasons of health and fitness. Competitive sports aren't a necessity, particularly for Listeners and Lookers, who are often uncomfortable with their gross motor skills. But there are plenty of noncompetitive pursuits—horseback riding, hiking, swimming, and tae kwon do, to name a few—that will help Lookers develop more physical confidence. And you'll find just as many group-oriented activities—camping, skating, and jazz dancing, for example—that will provide exercise for a Listener. Just be sure not to permit an overscheduling of your child's free time. Family activities, solitary pursuits, and unstructured visits with friends will improve your child's relationships with others and help her develop a strong sense of self.

Of course, there are times when a child seems bored and has trouble filling her after-school hours. If your fourth grader has experienced little success in choosing extracurricular pursuits, you can't go wrong by suggesting activities that fit her learning style. Following are a few ideas for each type of learner.

Activities for Fourth-Grade Lookers

Nine- and ten-year-olds who are visually oriented usually excel at fine motor pursuits, as well as any activities that call forth their ability to envision and recall. Most Lookers also love creating and organizing attractive displays. Here are some ideas that may appeal to your little learner.

- Astronomy
- Collecting coins, cards, and the like
- Computer activities
- Cooking and baking
- Crafts
- Creating a journal, scrapbook, or newspaper
- Drawing or painting
- Building model cars, planes, and boats
- Photography
- Sewing, crocheting, or needlepoint
- Simple carpentry
- Video games

Activities for Fourth-Grade Listeners

As a rule, Listeners are good conversationalists who are at ease around children and adults alike. Most Listeners exude self-confidence born of repeated social success, and are well suited to group activities and any pursuit with an auditory slant. The following list may contain some good ideas for your fourth-grade Listener.

- Acting classes
- Bowling league
- Chorus or choir
- Correspondence with a pen pal
- Day camp or recreation programs
- Reporting for a school newspaper
- Rollerblading with a friend
- Scouts or other youth groups
- Serving as a peer tutor
- Writing and staging a play

Activities for Fourth-Grade Movers

Most Movers find sports very appealing and love to spend time out-doors. At nine or ten years of age, Movers often delight in new and different pursuits, as long as the rules are simple and physical activity is a component. These ideas may interest your young Mover.

- Aerobics or fitness class
- Archery
- Bicycling
- Gymnastics and tumbling
- Hiking and camping

- Ice skating
- Long-distance running
- Martial arts classes
- Scouts or other youth groups
- Volleyball

HOMEWORK STRATEGIES FOR LOOKERS, LISTENERS, AND MOVERS

By the fourth grade, most of the responsibility for completing school-work should fall on the child. However, parents can greatly lighten the load and increase their child's chance for success by preparing a work-space appropriate to the child's learning style, providing needed resources and materials, lending support when problems arise, and assisting in the formulation of a daily plan that better organizes the child's assignments. The following are some specific ideas for helping your fourth-grade learner get the most from class and homework.

Strategies for Lookers

A Looker's preference for organization and order serves her well where schoolwork is concerned. No doubt, your child's written work has always been neat. By the fourth grade, she may have taken to person-alizing it as well by using different-colored inks, or by adding illustra-tions, a chart or graph, or an attractive cover. A Looker enjoys the process of writing as much as the end result, so don't be concerned if your child devotes more than the prescribed amount of time to written work. Her standards of acceptability are very high!

Lookers like to keep their desks and other work places as well organized as everything else in their lives. It's certainly a good idea to furnish your child with an array of art and stationery supplies, but it's better not to disrupt her sense of order by surprising her with a cleaned desk or rearranged shelves. You see, the layout of a Looker's supplies is never a random affair. Items are sorted and displayed according to their owner's carefully thought-out system.

Fourth-grade Lookers work well with flash cards. You can encourage your child to use this technique with multiplication tables, spelling words, dates of historical events, or science vocabulary. You might also suggest that your child color-code her notes. Boxing new terms and circling important names helps separate the most significant material from the surrounding text, and also provides Lookers with pleasingly attractive notebooks. If feasible, encourage your child to use a highlighting marker in her textbook to denote key names and terms. Most schools will not permit the marking of school property, but you may be able to secure an old copy from a company that specializes in used textbooks (check your Yellow Pages), or to buy a new copy directly from the publisher. Just make sure to get the correct edition. Finally, to help with long reading assignments, offer to read some of the material to your child, and teach her to note important facts on index cards.

Strategies for Listeners

Most Listeners have enjoyed so much academic success by fourth grade that their schoolwork is completed with little prodding. However, your help may be needed in selecting and enforcing the best time of day for homework. Listeners are very busy children!

Because Listeners are not visually attuned to such problems as misspellings and missing punctuation, they often need assistance with the proofreading of written work. Provide your child with guidance, and help her focus on the problem area; then allow her to find the error herself.

Your child may also need you to clarify instructions. Encourage her to read directions aloud. If this doesn't help, you might wish to offer a verbal explanation: "These math problems will all be done the same way. To figure averages, first you add the scores, then divide."

Permit your Listener to do her homework with soft music playing, but insist that the television and rock music be turned off. They are too distracting. It's a good idea to affirm your child's learning style in other ways, too. For instance, you might encourage her to make use of verbal repetition, to organize important facts into a song, or to record material on a cassette for playback at bedtime.

Strategies for Movers

A fourth-grade Mover needs a great deal of help at home; yet she is the most likely to sabotage your efforts through her natural haphazardness. Homework assignments may not be recorded, the proper materials may be left at school, notes from the teacher may be lost in transit, and the teacher's verbal directions may be missed altogether. You can help your Mover organize by encouraging her to pause before leaving the classroom or house to review a specially prepared subject checklist. This practice will jog her memory about assignments and remind her to pack the proper items. You might even ask your child's teacher to initial each day's checklist to ensure that nothing is overlooked.

At home, a Mover needs a special place to work, away from family distractions and favorite toys. The Mover's workspace may have to be set up daily, since pencils will break, paper will disappear, and workbooks may slip unnoticed between the desk and the wall. It's a good idea to provide a different-colored folder for each subject's assignments so that all work pertaining to your child's weekly spelling list, for example, is kept in one place, while her worksheets pertaining to Indian tribes remain together, as well. Ask your child to bring her folders home each day so that you can review the contents together. This will be a big help when it's time to study for a test.

Your physical presence will encourage your child to persevere with reading assignments or written work, but it's equally important to avoid getting visibly frazzled. As frustrated as you may become, saying, "Learning to add fractions is hard work. Let's find a new way to practice this," is preferable to, "We've been over this a million times! I can't believe you don't remember what to do!"

You can incorporate a Mover's preference for action into many homework assignments. When studying social studies dates, for instance, try writing each of the years or decades, as appropriate, on an index card and attaching the card to a shoebox. Then, as your child correctly recalls each date, she gets to toss a checker or coin into the box bearing the corresponding answer. When practicing multiplication tables, you can encourage your child to sway to the left when saying, "two times two," and to the right when responding, "four." You can also practice math and spelling with sets of magnetic numbers and letters.

TECHNIQUES FOR IMPROVING A FOURTH GRADER'S ACADEMIC PERFORMANCE

Our case studies have shown that by fourth grade, a child's academic strengths and weaknesses are quite obvious—just as much to the child as to her teachers and peers. Listener children, as a rule, continue their strong performance in reading and language arts, and take to foreign languages with ease. Lookers demonstrate a continued aptitude for spelling, math, the fine arts, and computers. Without intervention, Movers tend to fall further behind in academics. Even subjects like science, with its pleasing hands-on aspect, pose a problem because Movers have trouble reading their textbook.

When both parent and child appreciate the impact of learning style on a child's academic performance, it becomes easier for parents to offer understanding and support. Because academics loom so large in fourth grade—and because parents and their children are apart for so many hours each school day—at this stage, it pays to place priority on the affirmation of inborn learning style rather than on the attainment of balanced skills. By encouraging your child to use her preferred sense when absorbing and processing class material, you will help her improve her school performance even when she has no natural affinity for the subject being studied. This can best be achieved through the development of special learning strategies that capitalize on a child's strongest skills, and through the use of multisensory activities and materials—those that draw upon both a child's preferred sense *and* the sense needed for mastery of that subject matter.

On previous pages, you discovered some general learning-style based homework strategies. The following seven sections provide more specific learning strategies, as well as a wide range of multisensory techniques and materials. Each of these sections focuses on one of the various skills demanded of a fourth grader: reading, language arts, penmanship, computers, science, social studies, and math. Each one opens with a discussion of the components of the subject area, and continues with a list of tools, tactics, and learning aids that tap a child's Listener, Looker, or Mover traits, thereby improving her performance. Some strategies can be employed in the classroom, others will help with homework, and still others are intended to broaden a child's interest in the subject matter. Read through the lists carefully, and try out those suggestions that seem most appropriate for your child. You are both likely to profit from the time you spend together implementing and fine-tuning your fourth grader's newest learning tactics.

Building Reading Skills

There are several skills involved in the reading process. First, a child must learn to recognize or decode words, which involves sounding out or otherwise transforming a printed word into one that is spoken. Next, the child must possess a vocabulary sufficient to understand the words she reads, whether from memory, sentence context, or the structure of the word itself. And finally, a child must be able to read smoothly enough to be able to comprehend and recall the sequence and content of printed material.

It may well be that only one or two of these skills causes your fourth grader difficulty. You may wish to ask your child and her teacher exactly where they think the trouble lies. Once you've pinpointed the skill that needs improving, the following suggestions may prove helpful.

TECHNIQUES TO IMPROVE WORD RECOGNITION SKILLS

- Continue—or resume—the practice of reading to your child. Select a mystery, an adventure, or a story about children that your fourth grader can identify with, and read a chapter every day.

- Classic tales in video form enable a child to "see" a story before reading it. Decoding new words is often easier when the story's setting and sequence of events seem familiar.

- Make regular trips to the library, allowing enough time for your child to browse in the juvenile section. Guide your child in selecting books with enough appeal to guarantee her working through long or difficult text.

- If your child struggles to sound out words, hire a tutor. One-to-one work can clarify any basic elements of phonics that have not yet been mastered.

- Investigate the possibility of purchasing used textbooks for home use. Your child would be free to write in these, which could prove helpful for rereading and underlining before a test.

■ Encourage your child to highlight important words and phrases in her notebooks with brightly colored or fluorescent highlighters.

TECHNIQUES TO IMPROVE READING VOCABULARY

■ Buy a dictionary for home use. The *Scholastic Children's Dictionary* (Scholastic Reference) for ages eight and up is freshly updated and contains terms such as "DVD," "browser," and "rap." Colorfully illustrated, it includes an easy-to-understand pronunciation guide.

■ *The Clear and Simple Thesaurus Dictionary* (Grosset and Dunlap) is child-friendly, and provides synonyms and antonyms for almost any word your child might need.

■ The *Ultimate Visual Dictionary* (Dorling Kindersley Publishing) presents 50,000 terms illustrated with 5,000-plus color photographs and 1,000 illustrations. An amazing amount of information is packed into this small book.

■ *Brain Quest: Grade 4* by Workman Publishing has two hinged decks of boldly illustrated question-and-answer cards that explore and expand upon your fourth grader's base of knowledge.

■ *Turbo Twist Vocabulator* by Leap Frog is a hand-held device that teaches vocabulary words along with synonyms, antonyms, and root words. Thousands of new vocabulary words can be added by downloading from the Leap Frog website.

■ A fun way to expand your fourth grader's spoken and reading vocabulary is to gather the family together to play a board or card game. Excellent choices include *TriBond, Blurt, Malarky*, and *Mad Gab*, all by Patch Products.

TECHNIQUES TO IMPROVE READING COMPREHENSION

■ Choose a classic that you think will interest your child. Then borrow the book and its video version simultaneously. Your child's reading efforts will be encouraged and rewarded when she sees the story come to life.

■ If your child's reading comprehension skills are poor, consider borrowing some books on audiotape from your school or local library. Your child can follow along in the book as the text is read aloud to her.

■ Encourage your child to close her eyes after reading a passage and imagine a picture of what she has just read. With practice, the art of creating mental images will become automatic.

■ Suggest that your child sketch a picture of the action in a story or chapter.

■ Enlist your librarian's help in locating high-interest, low-reading-level books published especially for children with reading difficulties. By fourth grade, most struggling readers are offended by the idea of reading material intended for children two or more years younger.

■ Investigate the *Great Reader Series* by Leap Frog. Favorite stories come to life when your child places a book on the Quantum Pad, inserts a cartridge, and touches a page with the interactive pen. There are games, a report-writing template, a glossary of new words, and comprehension questions for each story.

Building Language Arts Skills

Language arts is a broad term that encompasses the skills a child needs to communicate through spoken or written language. At the elementary school level, most language arts programs include lessons in grammar, spelling, capitalization, punctuation, and sentence and paragraph structure. Once the basic rules are learned, language arts skills provide a foundation not only for the introduction of foreign language, but also for a lifetime of proper use of the mother tongue!

Your fourth grader may have difficulty with only one or two language arts skills, and a glance at her most recent composition may be enough to tell you where her problem lies. Are her sentences complete and properly punctuated? Are her grammar and spelling correct? If you're not sure, don't hesitate to ask her teacher which of your child's language arts skills needs strengthening. Here are some skill-development ideas that will help.

TECHNIQUES TO IMPROVE SPELLING SKILLS

■ If your own phonics background is strong, show your child how to break her spelling words into sound units, e.g., "black" into "bl-a-ck" or "thing" into "th-i-ng." Next, show her how to break words into syllables, e.g., "vacation" into "va-ca-tion." The ability to spell words by sound and syllable will increase her chance of including all the required letters.

■ Franklin's electronic SA-206 *Spelling Ace With Thesaurus,* available through Amazon, provides phonetic spelling corrections for over 100,000 words, along with definitions. Once entered into memory, spelling words can be used in games like "Hangman."

■ Encourage your child to picture a chalkboard in her mind. Then spell aloud each of her spelling words, and ask her to picture the words on her inner chalkboard. Ask about visual details such as the color of the chalk she sees and the color of the chalkboard. Attention to detail will enhance your child's ability to visualize the correct spelling.

■ Take a look at your child's list of spelling words to see whether a visual or verbal strategy might be helpful. For example, the word "together" can be envisioned as three smaller words—"to," "get," and "her." Or a saying such as "I before E except after C" may apply.

■ David Morrow's *DK Pockets: Spelling Dictionary* (Dorling Kindersley Publishing) is a miniature reference book that contains 35,000 words, with difficult plurals and parts of verbs spelled out in full.

■ *Turbo Twist Spelling* by Leap Frog allows children to create and download their weekly spelling test list. This fun-to-use interactive learning aid motivates through music, animation, and sound effects.

TECHNIQUES TO IMPROVE GRAMMAR, SENTENCE STRUCTURE, AND PUNCTUATION

■ Encourage your child to color-code the parts of speech in various sentences. Nouns can be highlighted in yellow; adjectives, in green; verbs, in blue; and so on. The same technique can be used to familiarize your child with sentence parts—subjects, predicates, prepositional phrases, and so on.

■ If your child uses grammatically incorrect speech, try rephrasing her statements as grammatically correct questions, as though you were echoing her thoughts. For example, if your child says, "My class don't have no homework," you can follow with, "Your class doesn't have any homework? That's great!" If this is done in a nonjudgmental way, you can subtly reinforce proper grammar.

■ To improve your child's punctuation skills, write a few sample sentences on a large piece of paper using two-inch upper-case letters and one-inch lower-case letters. Have your child dye elbow macaroni and glue it in the appropriate places to serve as apostrophes, quotation marks, and commas. She can then hang the finished product in her bedroom as a model for future compositions.

■ To encourage writing, buy a brightly colored notebook to serve as your child's diary or journal. Suggest that she make an entry every day, assuring her that it is completely private.

■ Reinforce the "bare bones of grammar" at Big Dog's Grammar (http://aliscot.com/bigdog). This site, designed for beginning students of grammar, contains online interactive exercises and has a sense of humor, as well!

TECHNIQUES TO IMPROVE FOREIGN LANGUAGE SKILLS

■ A paperback bilingual dictionary is a must.

■ Encourage your child to use newly learned foreign vocabulary around the house. Label household items with cards bearing their foreign names.

■ If your child is studying Spanish, take her to a Mexican restaurant and encourage her to order in Spanish.

■ Widely used by teachers of foreign languages, www.applauselearning.com offers a wide variety of products for instruction in Spanish, French, German, Italian, Russian, and Japanese.

■ Share with your child travel books and videos featuring countries whose inhabitants speak the language your child is learning.

- Browse the shelves in the Foreign Language section at a Barnes and Noble store. This bookstore contains an incredible array of foreign language books, dictionaries, and audio materials—all of which can also be viewed on www.bn.com.

Building Penmanship Skills

Some school districts place a heavier emphasis on handwriting than others. The report cards of our case-study children include penmanship grades. However, some schools cease this practice after third grade, once the cursive alphabet has been mastered. Regardless, the fourth grader who can produce legible, well-formed letters has two advantages over the student whose handwriting is poor. Cursive letters were originally designed so that the writer's pen strokes would flow smoothly and quickly across each line. This means that the student with good penmanship will complete written work with less effort than the one who's in the habit of retracing lines or lifting the pen between letters. Also, it's true that the student with good handwriting is spared the aggravations a poor writer faces when she has to proofread sloppy work, justify misunderstood spelling, or rewrite an unacceptable paper.

Granted, few fourth graders can produce the kind of wall-chart penmanship displayed in classrooms across the country. But if improved handwriting can make a difference in your fourth grader's schoolwork, surely the subject deserves some attention. Here are some ideas for improving your child's penmanship.

TECHNIQUES TO IMPROVE PENMANSHIP

- Pilot's *Dr. Grip* pens and pencils have an oversized barrel and provide a firm, comfortable hold.

- Pencil and pen grips—which can be slipped over your child's writing instruments, making them easier to hold—are available in both plastic and rubber.

- Provide your child with a beginner's book of calligraphy to promote writing as an art form, and to stimulate your child's interest in the appearance of her everyday written work.

Building Computer and Research Skills

These days, it's common for a child's computer knowledge to exceed that of her parents. We live in a high-tech age that's becoming increasingly complex. To prepare the next generation, most schools begin computer instruction in kindergarten. Regardless of your computer knowledge, there are ways in which you can help your child feel at ease with a computer. Here are some ideas.

TECHNIQUES TO IMPROVE COMPUTER AND RESEARCH SKILLS

■ If possible, give your child a guided tour of your work place to show her how computers are utilized there. This will help her understand the need to become proficient in computer skills.

■ If your fourth grader hasn't yet mastered the keyboard, Knowledge Adventure's software program *JumpStart Typing,* available through Amazon, provides thirty effective and amusing arcade-style lessons.

■ Utilize your computer to help your child with homework by visiting the www.bjpinchbeck.com website. Designed by a twelve-year-old with some help from his dad, the site provides links to more than 700 educational and entertaining sites, all of which are suitable for fourth graders and up.

■ KidsClick! at http://sunsite.berkeley.edu/kidsclick!/—a directory created by "a bunch of librarians"—contains links to sites chosen specifically for middle-schoolers.

■ Schoolwork.ugh, found on www.schoolwork.org, contains an excellent tutorial on using the Internet for research. Just click on "So . . . how do you find information on the Internet, anyway?"

Building Science Skills

By fourth grade, the science curriculum has become quite complex in most schools. Between lectures, reports, projects, and experiments, nine- and ten-year-old students are bombarded with subject material from all angles. Naturally, your child will find some units and methods of study more intriguing than others. Here are a few ideas to help improve your fourth grader's performance in science.

TECHNIQUES TO IMPROVE SCIENCE SKILLS

■ Encourage your child's interest in astronomy with a backyard telescope or a trip to a local planetarium.

■ Consider buying a microscope for home use.

■ Purchase Tom Robinson's *The Everything Kids' Science Experiment Book* (Adams Media Corporation). Here, you'll find all you need to know to create dozens of science experiments using common household items. And it's written by a high school science teacher.

■ Vicki Cobb's *See For Yourself: More Than 100 Experiments for Science Fairs and Projects* (Scholastic Reference) describes short, easy-to-do experiments. Life sciences, physical science, and technology are all addressed.

■ Seek out nearby places for fun and educational outings. A hands-on museum, a greenhouse, a nature preserve, a farm, and a zoo nursery are just a few ideas.

Building Social Studies Skills

Fourth-grade social studies is a course with many facets. For perhaps the first time, students grapple with history, geography, anthropology, global issues, and current events. Moreover, fourth-grade curriculum materials may be gleaned from such diverse sources as periodicals, television, videos, and visiting lecturers, while course work may include independent research, group work, and hands-on projects.

It's certainly safe to assume that your child will feel most at ease with social studies material when she has a bank of general knowledge on which to draw in class, and when the terminology used during the course of study sounds somewhat familiar. The following ideas can help your child approach fourth-grade social studies with interest rather than intimidation.

TECHNIQUES TO IMPROVE SOCIAL STUDIES SKILLS

■ Invest in a globe for home use. Some are available with raised terrain that will increase the globe's appeal as it improves your child's grasp of world geography.

■ Involve your child in the composition of a family history or a dated family tree.

■ Spend some time in the travel section of your local Barnes and Noble. This area is chock full of maps of many interesting locations.

■ *National Geographic Kids* is a colorful monthly magazine devoted to topics such as geography, adventure, and wildlife.

■ The monthly magazine *Kids Discover* provides an in-depth look at a different subject each month, along with excellent photographs and artwork. A recent issue was devoted to "Southwest Peoples."

■ If your child reads for fun, she may enjoy biographies, works of fiction, and history books that pertain to her current social studies unit. A children's librarian can help you locate appropriate materials.

■ *National Geographic World Atlas for Young Explorers* (National Geographic) is considered to be the best children's atlas for browsing and reference use. Included are one hundred pages of large-format world-class maps.

■ *National Geographic United States Atlas for Young Explorers* (National Geographic) is an excellent resource, with each state having its own two-page spread.

■ *I Love the USA* by Global Software Publishing allows children to view travel videos and make maps while learning facts about the fifty states.

Building Math Skills

Most fourth graders are old hands at addition, subtraction, multiplication, and division. This year, though, they are expected to put their computational skills to work on fractions, decimals, and complex equations. Students who have always enjoyed and succeeded in math will find this challenge exciting, but those who have struggled with math may become lost. Regardless of a fourth grader's math ability, though, she will be required to take the subject for several more years.

Academic concerns aside, numbers and computation are an unavoidable part of our adult lives. By working with your child to improve her grasp of math fundamentals, you will be doing her a tremendous favor. Following are some ideas to get you started.

TECHNIQUES TO IMPROVE MATH SKILLS

■ Greg Tang's clever book *The Grapes of Math: Mind Stretching Math Riddles* (Scholastic) is a collection of verses and cheerful computer-generated artwork designed to teach children problem-solving tricks and strategies.

■ Purchase a calculator with oversized keys for your child's use at home. This will encourage her to perform computations for fun.

■ Suggest that your child do her math problems on graph paper, which has both horizontal and vertical lines to help in the spacing and alignment of tabulations.

■ With *Turbo Twist Math* by Leap Frog, children play games to learn multiplication and division facts, fractions, percentages, and word problems.

■ John Kennedy's *Math Made Easy: Fourth Grade Workbook* (Dorling Kindersley Publishing) is a complete home-study program designed to help children practice essential math skills.

■ Even a fourth grader can benefit from a set of carpentry tools along with encouragement to build something along with you. Working with tools develops the ability to visualize, which is so important for math success.

As you focus on providing those at-home experiences and learning tools that will bring about improvement in your child's school performance, I urge you to be diplomatic. Nine- and ten-year-olds are well aware of, and, in many cases, quite sensitive about their academic shortcomings. An overzealous effort on your part may serve only as a blatant reminder of classroom struggles that your child would rather forget about when at home. So instead of bombarding your learner with books, toys, and activities, try to carefully select one or two techniques that seem appropriate for her, and then *suggest* rather than *insist* that she try them out.

I also caution you not to expect overnight success. Your child's proficiency—or lack thereof—in each of her school subjects has been more than four years in the making. Given the fact that a subtle approach is more effective, it may take many weeks before either of you notices heightened interest, stronger skills, and greater confidence on your child's part. Any of these gradual changes will be proof that your efforts to help your child master academic material are, indeed, paying off.

LEARNING STYLE QUICKCHECK FOR FOURTH GRADERS, NINE TO TEN YEARS OF AGE

Directions: Read the statements below, and place a check next to each characteristic that seems to describe your child. Total the checks in each column, and compare totals. You're likely to find your responses heavily concentrated in one column or evenly divided between two. These results will provide a clear picture of your fourth grader's preferred learning style.

LOOKER	LISTENER	MOVER
1. Communication: When my fourth grader wishes to express herself . . .		
❏ Her sentences are short and unelaborated.	❏ She speaks in long, complex sentences.	❏ She speaks in short sentences and mispronounces some words.
❏ She rarely volunteers answers in class.	❏ She often volunteers answers in class.	❏ She is quiet in class, but loud on the playground.
❏ Her vocabulary is about average for her age.	❏ She has a huge vocabulary.	❏ Her vocabulary is rather small, and sometimes she searches for words.
❏ She prefers to communicate face-to-face.	❏ She likes to chat on the phone.	❏ She avoids using the phone whenever possible.
2. Favorite Pastimes: When my fourth grader has free time . . .		
❏ She spends much of her time at the computer.	❏ She opens a library book from her favorite series.	❏ She enjoys attending sporting events like football games or rodeos.
❏ She excels at video games.	❏ She memorizes songs and dialogue from her favorite videos.	❏ She excels at soccer and softball.
❏ She assembles puzzles and kits with ease.	❏ She may be chosen for a role in a school program.	❏ She is expressive with her body, but is unable to memorize lines for a part in a play.
❏ She enjoys board games and is a stickler for rules.	❏ She takes charge when playing games.	❏ She prefers outdoor to indoor play, and tends to lose pieces to board games.
3. Fine Motor Skills: When my fourth grader uses her hands . . .		
❏ She produces beautiful, creative art projects.	❏ She tolerates art class, and may repeat a project from year to year.	❏ She likes the hands-on aspect of art, but is messy in her use of materials.
❏ Her schoolwork is neatly done.	❏ She turns in acceptable, though not overly neat paperwork.	❏ She writes off the line and into the margin. Her number columns drift.

4. Gross Motor Skills: When my fourth grader moves about . . .

❏ She excels at eye-hand games like horseshoes and badminton.	❏ She requires encouragement to participate in physically demanding games.	❏ She is agile, well coordinated, and good at gross motor activities.
❏ She prefers noncontact sports such as running and hiking.	❏ She likes playground games that involve word play, such as jump rope.	❏ She is usually the game leader or team captain.

5. Social Skills: When my fourth grader mixes with other children . . .

❏ She tends to be a loner within a group.	❏ She is sociable and maintains interaction by talking.	❏ She seeks out other children who enjoy noisy, active play.
❏ She prefers to work on individual rather than group projects.	❏ She prefers group projects to working alone.	❏ She doesn't work well independently, requiring frequent teacher assistance.

6. Emotions: When it comes to my fourth grader's feelings . . .

❏ She does not readily express emotion.	❏ She freely expresses her feelings by talking about them.	❏ She tends to express feelings nonverbally by shouting, hugging, jumping, or stamping her foot.
❏ Emotional displays make her uncomfortable.	❏ She is sympathetic to her friends' feelings.	❏ She tends to be moody, impatient, and easily frustrated.

7. Memory: When my fourth grader learns . . .

❏ She doodles to help herself recall information.	❏ She is good at memorizing poems, jingles, and facts.	❏ She has trouble remembering what she's seen and heard.
❏ She has a large sight word vocabulary.	❏ She remembers new vocabulary words after hearing them only once.	❏ She recalls action and movement.

8. At School: When my fourth grader is in the classroom . . .

❏ Her desk is well organized.	❏ She is fairly well organized.	❏ Her work area is messy.
❏ She is conscientious about following classroom rules.	❏ She sometimes gets in trouble for talking and passing notes.	❏ She finds many reasons to get up and out of her seat.
❏ She dresses neatly with coordinated accessories.	❏ She insists on putting together her own outfits, which may or may not match.	❏ Her clothes are often rumpled and grass-stained.
❏ She excels in math and spelling.	❏ She excels in language arts and social studies.	❏ She enjoys doing science projects, and may be receiving extra help in reading and math.

TOTALS: _____ LOOKER   _____ LISTENER   _____ MOVER

CHAPTER EIGHT

Learning Styles in Eighth Grade

Eighth grade can be a confusing time. There is no denying that early adolescence is stressful to both parent and child, for it's a period during which the child is torn between the pressures exerted by socially aware peers and the safe haven represented by the games and activities of yesteryear. Many eighth graders respond by exhibiting an odd mix of childish-versus-teen behavior. Parents quickly learn that to expect one type of behavior at any given time almost guarantees their child's display of another.

Whether a thirteen-year-old is precocious or somewhat immature, eighth grade represents a turning point in his life. The eighth grader is expected to be self-reliant about class work and homework. He also sees the future beckon, for perhaps the first time, as he learns about the role of guidance counselors and experiences the heady, almost frightening power that comes with choosing elective courses and selecting from among the array of extracurricular activities that are part of junior high and middle school life. On top of all this, popularity now become the ultimate social goal of almost every student, and boy-girl pairings are in such abundance that even the most socially resistant thirteen-year-old is likely to find himself taking a second glance in the mirror and worrying over clothing and hairstyles.

An eighth grader's social inclinations, his classroom conduct and study skills, and even his physical abilities can be traced to his learning style. Since birth, the adolescent has been attuned to particular environmental stimuli, be they visual, auditory, or tactile. A walk through the school cafeteria will confirm this. Looker students sit off to one side, perhaps with a friend, eating quietly and absorbing every detail of what is taking place around them. For Listeners, lunchtime is a social hour, and they are likely to be at the head of a table full of admiring friends. Movers find reason to leave their seat ten times in twenty minutes—for a drink of water, another straw, a redder apple, and so on.

This chapter tells the stories of three eighth-grade learners: a Looker, a Listener, and a Mover. As you follow the children's progress and development from the beginning to the end of the school year, you'll enjoy a unique view of each child's social life, classroom performance, physical abilities, and relationships with family. No doubt, you'll see your own child reflected in one of our three learners. A Learning Style QuickCheck for Eighth Graders (see page 232) is included to confirm your observations.

It comes as no surprise that learning style has a tremendous influence on a fourth grader's academic experience. This chapter describes the academic performance that typically accompanies each learning style, and looks at different ways in which you can establish positive communication with your child's teachers. A child's sensory preference affects his actions and choices outside the classroom as well as in, so this chapter also provides suggestions for parents to help their child become more socially at ease. A host of extracurricular activity ideas are provided, as well.

Hopefully, by the time their child reaches the eighth grade, parents have formed realistic expectations about his classroom performance. At this stage, it's a challenge for parents to help their child with homework mainly because of the dwindling patience that most thirteen- and fourteen-year-olds have with parental assistance of any form. Still, it can be helpful to focus some time together on academic improvement. To that end, this chapter discusses a variety of materials, techniques, and strategies that will stimulate your child's intellectual curiosity, help him with homework assignments, and improve his study skills.

Eighth grade is not too late to effect change. With patience and restraint, parents *can* help their teen-ager achieve. This chapter will help you understand your child's learning strengths and weaknesses, enabling you to set reasonable academic standards and realistic goals for the future.

A LOOK AT THREE LEARNERS

Kim, Mark, and Shawn have just begun eighth grade at a suburban middle school. The children have been classmates since kindergarten, and they all celebrated their thirteenth birthdays during the preceding Spring.

Because these three teen-agers possess different learning styles, each is drawn to different elements of his or her surroundings and responds to these surroundings in different ways. Kim has always been visually oriented; Mark is attuned to language and sounds; and Shawn learns best through movement and touch. Despite our learners' similarly supportive home environments, their frequent sharing of teachers, and some twelve years of exposure to identical resources within the community, the children have interests, talents, and work habits that are amazingly dissimilar. Not all children display the characteristics of a single learning style in this manner. Some are combination learners—Looker-Movers, say, or Looker-Listeners. However, for the sake of clarity and to highlight the features of each individual learning style, I've chosen to portray Kim, Mark, and Shawn as possessing "pure" styles. Let's visit our learners at the start of the eighth-grade year and see how sensory preference has shaped each child.

Thirteen Years of Age

Meet Kim. At first glance, Looker Kim seems quite unflappable. Quiet and serene, she has never revealed much of herself even to her family and lifelong friends. But a closer look reveals a driven thirteen-year-old who is often tense, ill at ease in social situations, and unwavering in her motivation to achieve. Every teen needs a means of self-expression. For some, it's sports; for others, it may be a club presidency. For Kim, her good grades and reputation as a hard worker are their own rewards.

Kim has three close friends, only one of whom she met through school. The other two girls are neighbors whom Kim has known for many years. All three friends are as reserved as Kim, and the time she spends with each of them is usually scheduled ahead of time for a specific purpose—completing a school project, for example—rather than being a spontaneous affair. Kim and her friends find the prospect of dating to be quite daunting, for none of them possesses the gift of small talk or the wherewithal to feel at ease at a party, much less on a date.

At the moment, Kim happens to like a certain boy, but she is much too embarrassed to admit this to her friends, and would rather die than act on her feelings. Instead, in her usual from-the-sidelines fashion, Kim becomes emotionally, rather than actively, involved in the social lives and problems of her classmates. Her long-time habit of quietly watching interactions and goings-on makes Kim privy to some fascinating details. Although she is as uncomfortable as ever with displays and declarations of affection, and though she's far from ready to test the waters herself, her careful observations have actually taught her a great deal about social behavior.

Kim is a teen of few words. People like talking to her because her intent gaze is quite flattering to any speaker, and she never forgets a face. In her spare time, Kim enjoys practicing calligraphy, writing and illustrating children's stories, and playing computer games. She has become an extremely popular baby sitter because she is vigilant, neat, and reliable. In true Looker fashion, Kim always comes prepared with a baby-sitting kit that includes crayons and paper, snap-together blocks, puzzles, and a board game or two. It's a tossup as to who enjoys the kit's contents more—Kim or her young charges.

Kim is fairly well coordinated, although in gym class, she much prefers solitary activities, like archery or the broad jump, to team sports. You see, Kim is bothered by the loose organization and unpredictability that is part of such group games as field hockey, volleyball, softball, and the like. She was approached as a candidate for eighth-grade kickline, but hastily declined such a high-profile position. Except for walks and an occasional bike ride, Kim avoids most gross motor activity at home.

Quite the opposite is true of Kim and fine motor pursuits. Always artistic, she does most of the cartoons for her school newspaper. At school and at home, she doodles and draws constantly, and has begun personalizing book covers and decorating T-shirts for her girlfriends. Kim is also quite adept at the computer, whether typing a report, creating graphics and headings for the newspaper, or instant-messaging her friends. Her parents encourage her to rent as many computer games as she likes, but strongly urge her to develop her gross motor side as well. Recently, they asked her to consider taking skating lessons.

Kim has long been aware that her attention wanders during lectures, and that she frequently forgets verbal instructions. To compensate, she jots things down in a daily planner, and does thumbnail sketches pertaining to the day's lessons in the margins of her notebooks. She reviews school notes daily, recopying, outlining, and highlighting the material to help herself better absorb it. Naturally, Looker Kim does quite well in visual subjects like math, computer technology, and art. Proud of her attractive, creative work, she tackles science and social studies projects with relish. She tends to falter, however, in auditory efforts such as the retention of material discussed in class and the taking of notes during videos. Kim is quite good at the memorization of foreign language vocabulary and spelling, but she doesn't do nearly as well with English, where study lists aren't necessarily provided for the class.

At thirteen, this Looker is well aware of her learning strengths and weaknesses. Since good grades and the opinions of her teachers are very important to her, she will, no doubt, continue to apply her visual strategies to her schoolwork. Although Kim may feel increasing social pressure as she moves through the school year, eighth grade should pose no new academic challenges for her.

Meet Mark. Socially, Listener Mark is Kim's polar opposite. Mark shows no signs of discomfort in groups or with the opposite sex; in fact, he's a great conversationalist who always seems to know the right thing to say. Introductions, apologies, advice, and even terms of endearment come easily to Mark. His teachers and parents often joke that he possesses the social graces of a cosmopolitan forty-year-old!

Mark is very much influenced by the views of older teens and by the opinions of his peers. In fact, very little that Mark buys, wears, or attempts to do is ever spontaneous. Rather, most of Mark's moves are calculated for their effect on his social status, and rehearsed for maximum appeal. That way, he can be assured of a place among the most stylish and popular boys in the school. Inevitably for a teen-ager held in such high regard, Mark has developed quite a following of his own. He so enjoys talking that he really doesn't listen to idle chatter, and frequently interrupts his friends in mid-sentence. Because Mark's personal views carry so much weight, his classmates are willing to overlook this habit.

Naturally, Mark does a great deal of socializing in his free time, as well. Joking and laughing with a group of friends and chatting on the

phone are two of his favorite pastimes. When alone, Mark reads vora-
ciously, often to the accompaniment of music. He enjoys the series of
plays and concerts his town sponsors each summer, and can't wait until
his parents allow him to attend rock concerts. It's no surprise that Mark
was voted this year's Student Council homeroom representative.
Although only one meeting has been held so far, Mark finds the concept of student government quite fascinating, and is glad to be a part
of it. His other school interests are Drama Club and French Club—both
perfect showcases for his verbal talents.

Mark tends to shy away from cooking, crafts, and other fine motor
activities, because he has long known that his eye-hand coordination is
not the best. It is for the same reason that earlier attempts at the piano
and saxophone met with failure, despite his love of music. Mark
accepts that his handwriting and school projects will never have the
visual appeal of some of his classmates' efforts; it's taken years of hard
work just to get his paperwork to its present acceptable appearance.
Mark's full-body coordination is average. Unhappy about giving less
than a stellar performance, Mark avoids team sports both at home and
at school. He does, however, enjoy those aspects of gym class that
emphasize cooperation instead of performance—spotting his classmates during tumbling, for example, or serving as squad leader.

Mark has always been a good student. His auditory skills enable
him to take notes easily, read textbooks, and glean important information from videos, lectures, and assemblies. His projects and experiments may be somewhat lacking in appearance, but Mark more
than makes up for this with creative, dynamic oral presentations and
nonstop class participation. He loves learning the vocabulary and historical aspects of foreign language, and is easily the best conversationalist in this year's French class. Mark has chosen to drop art and
computer technology—classes in which he lacks the skills needed to
excel—in favor of public speaking and vocal music. He has coped
with his ongoing math struggles by enrolling in a basic math class,
rather than beginning the algebra-geometry-trigonometry sequence
chosen by the strongest students. Even with a less-competitive curriculum and slower pace in class, Mark assumes he'll be needing help
from a tutor.

Like Kim, Mark has learned to make the most of his learning
strengths to compensate for any weaker skill areas. He studies and

reads out loud, makes frequent use of a microcassette recorder, and tries to use verbal strategies to remember visual material. To recall the order of the planets in the solar system, for example, Mark recites a sentence in which each word begins with the corresponding planet's first letter: "My Very Efficient Mother Just Sent Us New Pickles." To flourish in the eighth grade, Mark need only continue to study and interact according to the learning style he understands so well.

Meet Shawn. Mover Shawn is not a particularly sociable teen-ager. In fact, he says little, seems ill at ease around strangers and in crowds, and does whatever he can to avoid "connecting," be it by eye contact, computer, or phone. Because he is most comfortable around physical boys like himself, Shawn's chief social outlet is sports. As captain of his school's football and lacrosse teams, and as a participant in a community baseball league and various intramural sports, Shawn's after-school hours are quite full. Team sports are ideal for someone with Shawn's athleticism and social reserve. They afford a showcase for his talents, ample opportunity to interact with peers, and even an unintended sort of hero status that attracts the admiration of boys and girls alike. Shawn's penchant for physical contact—hugs, back slaps, and hair ruffling, for example—and his inclination to dress for comfort rather than style, combine to lend him an air of maturity that he doesn't really possess.

Shawn has neither time for nor interest in the clubs and service organizations that figure in the lives of many adolescents. As far as casual "hanging out" goes, Shawn would rather do this at the handball courts than in a mall or someone's basement. This Mover has always loved the outdoors, and even at thirteen, routinely ignores books, games, and the telephone in favor of backyard and street play. His passion for action carries over to foul-weather pursuits, as well. When forced to remain indoors, Shawn watches police dramas and war movies, or wrestles with his German shepherd.

Shawn's fine motor skills don't approach the level of his gross motor ability. His handwriting has always been marginal; he's never been good at video games; and his difficulty understanding design and measurement and following directions has kept him away from woodworking and other crafts. As a way of improving his written work, Shawn is trying hard to become a faster typist. For now, the hunt-and-peck method is all he can manage, so Shawn types his short assignments and relies on his older sister for help with longer papers.

Seeking help with schoolwork is nothing new to Shawn. For years, he has needed the same sort of support at home that he received in his school's Resource Lab, and has done his homework side by side with one of his parents. Lately, though, he seems to resent his parents' hovering, and has requested that they reserve their efforts for occasions when he's really stumped and asks for help. Naturally, his homework isn't as well done—or, for that matter, as frequently done—as before, but Shawn really is trying. Nowadays, Shawn is likely to appeal to his older brother or his friends for assistance with reports or big assignments. Alone, he can't manage to pull a long-term project together.

At his parents' urging, Shawn has signed up for an elective computer course, and has opted for study hall instead of a second elective. His family feels that keyboard and computer knowledge is a must for Shawn, and that he can use his study hall time for unfinished work or, when necessary, for Resource Lab. Shawn takes a remedial reading class rather than a foreign language. His science, social studies, and English classes provide him with more than enough exercise in vocabulary and spelling.

Last year, with his teachers' permission, Shawn began carrying a pocket calculator for math computations and a microcassette recorder for taping lectures. At first, he worried about the social ramifications of making his need for help so obvious, but Shawn is so admired that no one dares tease him. The availability of eighth-grade interscholastic teams, the teen's increasing popularity, and the freedom to handpick certain courses has created a potential for enjoyment that, until now, was missing from Shawn's school life.

Can you see your own eighth grader in any of our learners? It may be that Looker Kim's reticence and self-direction remind you of your own son or daughter. Or maybe Listener Mark's social and academic competence sounds more than a little familiar. If not, perhaps Shawn's athletic ability and classroom struggles strike a chord. On page 232, you will find a Learning Style QuickCheck for Eighth Graders that will erase any doubts. By marking the behaviors that are most characteristic of your child and then totaling the marks in each column, you'll obtain a vivid picture of your child's learning style.

HOW LOOKER, LISTENER, AND MOVER EIGHTH GRADERS DEVELOP

Looker Kim, Listener Mark, and Mover Shawn all follow the dictates of an inborn sensory preference. As a result of their learning style, these three adolescents have developed a unique set of social, physical, and academic skills.

As our three learners progress through their eighth-grade year, their development continues on course, influencing their grades, friendships, hobbies, and overall attitude toward school and home. While the highlight of Mark's week might be social dancing in Friday's gym class, for example, his long-time classmates Shawn and Kim dread the week's end for that very reason. And while grades and homework have long been a source of tension between Shawn and his parents, Mark and Kim receive only positive feedback at conference and report card time.

As the school year draws to a close, let's return to our three learners and see how each teen is coping with life as an eighth grader.

Fourteen Years of Age

Kim. For the first time in her life, Kim is concerned about being overlooked by her peers. Mind you, she isn't interested in being the center of attention, but it rankles a bit when her classmates garner praise and admiration for scholastic efforts that Kim easily duplicates but chooses to keep to herself. At fourteen, Kim has begun to place some value on the opinions of her peers—a sure sign of social growth.

During eighth grade, Kim became active in the Art Club. The club's handful of members are mostly loners like Kim, and she happily participated in the creation of a school gallery, feeling no social pressure whatsoever.

Kim recently sketched a collection of sportswear designs, some of which she'd like to transform into the real thing. Her parents have signed her up for a summer sewing class, which should help her realize this dream.

Kim has already been selected Art Editor of the school paper for her freshman year. Her parents, in an effort to help their daughter branch out a bit, have convinced her to play intramural tennis and volunteer at her church's Sunday School program next fall.

At school, Kim's neatness and precision help her to continue her strong performance in math, computers, and art. She remains a highly organized, self-directed student who takes great pride in her work. At year's end, Kim's lagging auditory skills still hold her back in language arts, foreign language, science, and social studies classes, all of which require a good deal of reading and note-taking. However, our Looker's beautifully executed projects and reports continue to have a positive effect on all of her grades.

Kim's teachers agree that she is a pleasure to have in class. Certainly, she is an easy student to teach, for she usually produces high-quality work on demand and requires almost no attention in the process. Despite her current yearning to become a fashion or interior designer, Kim's guidance counselor has urged the teen to continue Spanish, computer technology, and honors classes in the core subjects. Academically, high school is sure to pose few problems, and even holds some social promise now that Kim has begun to involve herself with her peers.

Mark. Now approaching the end of eighth grade, talkative, affable Mark has already had five girlfriends. He and his female pal of the moment do not date, per se, but declare their devotion by holding hands, sitting together at lunch, passing notes, and talking on the phone at least twice each evening. Mark still manages to have plenty of time for his male friends, as well as for the long list of activities in which he is involved. In fact, Mark tends to spread himself too thin, and became so busy early in the year that keeping up with schoolwork posed a bit of a problem. A disappointing first-quarter report card provided quite a jolt, and Mark has since devoted more time and attention to his course work.

Between student council meetings and functions, French Club, Drama Club, and Chorus, Mark stays after school nearly every day, and is busy many evenings, as well. He did such a fine job in a supporting role in the Drama Club's annual production that he has a shot at next year's lead. Finding himself with some free time once the play was done, Mark recently began serving as a reporter for the school paper. He enjoys this so much that, during the summer, he plans to put together a proposal for a teen column and submit it to the editor of his town's weekly paper. This summer also looks socially promising, for as incoming freshmen, Mark and his friends are finally old enough to attend the parking-lot dances held each Friday night at the high school. And even though it's only June, Mark has already received four invitations to summer parties, and has signed up as a junior counselor at a local recreation program.

Mark's command of language continues to be evident in his high-quality essays, his self-assurance during class discussions, and his ease with conversational French. Our Listener also remains a strong reader, and has such good recall of the material discussed in his classes that he rarely uses his notes or study sheets. However, at year's end, Mark's less-developed visual and fine motor skills still hold him back in math and such creative pursuits as report illustration and mapmaking.

Mark's teachers are complimentary of his ability to put his natural outspokenness to work for him. He always manages to spice up even the dullest lecture with intelligent questions, witty comments, and well-thought-out arguments. But where Mark's interjections and asides used to get him into frequent trouble, maturity has taught him to use restraint and a respectful tone. Nowadays, he's an asset to every class.

With the proper support and guidance, Mark is almost assured of maintaining his current academic standing, and is certain to thoroughly enjoy the host of new extracurricular activities to which he'll be exposed as a freshman. He has already been elected Vice President of next year's French Club, and plans to continue his involvement in the Drama Club and school paper. There's no doubt that high school will be an exciting time for a student with Mark's social and academic capabilities.

Shawn. During the school year, Mover Shawn became part of a clique of athletic boys and girls. His new friends gather regularly at school games and matches, on local fields, and in front of one another's television sets, each one comfortable with peers who share a love of sports. While one of Shawn's friends might occasionally be enamored of another, none has yet achieved the social confidence necessary to express this by spending time alone with a member of the opposite sex. Actually, though, the clique's very existence will eventually help each member reach that point. You see, Shawn and his friends feed one another's egos by focusing on athletic talent, rather than classroom performance.

Besides his involvement in sports, Shawn has become active in the school's safety patrol, a small group of students who monitor fellow classmates' hallway behavior during class changes and before and after school. Shawn is proud of having been selected from the Monday study hall roster to make classroom deliveries for the main office staff. He was recently approached by some classmates about running for freshman class treasurer, but, finding the prospect of such responsibility somewhat alarming, he firmly vetoed the idea. Instead, he looks forward to applying for membership in the Boys' Leaders' Club and trying out for junior varsity sports teams.

At the moment, Shawn believes he would be perfectly suited to an elementary physical education teaching position. He would like to coach, as well, but doesn't see how he could combine the latter with an elementary school's later dismissal time. Shawn lacks the academic confidence to consider the obvious solution—teaching in a high school—believing, like so many youngsters, that the brighter a teacher, the higher his or her grade assignment. Sooner or later, Shawn will have to face the fact that completing college, a must for every teacher, will be no small feat for him.

You see, Shawn's schoolwork remains average at best, even with the help of classroom modifications and remedial instruction. Shawn compensates for some academic limitations while resigning himself to others.

This year, Shawn's teachers have seen him progress from a disorganized, mildly disruptive classroom influence to a student who has begun to take at least some responsibility for his schoolwork and behavior. With an eye toward the future, Shawn's guidance counselor suggests that the boy add a technology class to next year's high school course load, and that he continue with computer classes. Shawn will be able to reap many social and vocational benefits from high school as long as he continues his involvement in sports, accepts the support of his parents and teachers, and maintains a realistic view of his academic capabilities. Much more so than the course of study found in grade school or middle school, high school curriculums are varied enough to hold the interest of every type of student.

THE RELATIONSHIP OF LEARNING STYLE TO AN EIGHTH GRADER'S SCHOOL PERFORMANCE

Most junior high and middle schools offer a wide variety of courses, allowing students and their families a measure of control over the formulation of class schedules. Of course, much of eighth-grade academics continues to be required work, but in many cases, there is flexibility about the level and focus of even such curricular staples as math and language arts. In addition, the existence of elective courses enables students to pursue individual interests within the framework of an ordinary school day.

Just like elementary school subjects, eighth-grade subjects can be categorized according to the different learning skills called into play by each discipline. Mover skills—body awareness and agility—are drawn upon only during physical education. In contrast, the visual and auditory skills possessed by Lookers and Listeners are exercised time and again during the school day. In the two sections that follow, typical eighth-grade courses are separated into Looker and Listener subjects. To further highlight visual and auditory aspects of the eighth-grade curriculum, sample first- and last-quarter report cards are presented for each of our case-study teens, along with a subject-by-subject look at each learner's academic experience.

Looker Subjects

In the course of a school day, eighth graders encounter posters and bulletin boards, various hallway displays, maps, graphs, and an array of other visual aids wherever they go. Lookers, naturally, are most attuned to the visual appeal of their surroundings, and are the most enamored of certain curriculum components as well.

Math, in any form, is a visual subject. Whether performing long division or working with intricate algebraic equations, a Looker's ability to envision, memorize, and compute is a tremendous classroom asset. For the same reason, spelling, capitalization, punctuation, and the use of graphic organizers—the visual components of language arts described on page 166—continue to appeal to Looker students.

Computer and art classes are often no longer requirements in junior high or middle schools, so it's likely that many of the students in these classes are Lookers, who are there by choice. After all, it is the sight-oriented teen who possesses the eye-hand coordination, fine motor dexterity, and visual skills needed to earn top grades. Handwriting, although no longer a graded subject, remains a similarly pleasurable exercise for Looker teens. Technology, a course much evolved from its roots in wood and metal shop, demands these skills, as well. And, of course, technology also requires knowledge of measurement techniques, computer savvy, and an ability to follow written directions—three additional Looker strengths.

Listener Subjects

Eighth-grade students utilize their auditory skills in every one of their classes. Certain subjects, however, have a focus on language and sound that makes them particularly appealing to those who possess the Listener learning style. An eighth-grade Listener, for instance, can be expected to shine in reading, due to the strong phonics skills that enable him to breeze through increasingly complex printed material, as well as his excellent recall and comprehension of text. Further, a Listener continues to have the edge in social studies and science, and now also enjoys an advantage in such courses as health and family/consumer science. As mentioned in Chapter Seven (see page 167), social studies and science also have certain Looker elements. However, oral presentations, class discussions, and group projects are an even larger part of each class, and are most easily handled by those with strong auditory skills. In addition, Listeners are the most comfortable with eighth-grade textbook material and are usually the best at note-taking, a process that requires a careful ongoing screening of what is heard in class.

Chapter Seven described foreign language class as an auditory exercise—a Listener subject. This continues to be the case in eighth grade, with Listeners applying their inborn verbal and phonics skills to the memorization and mastery of the vocabulary, culture, and history of another land.

Eighth-grade language arts encompasses the study of literature, grammar, composition, and spelling. Listeners retain an advantage in all but the last area of study because they are at ease with reading, have an instinctive grasp of word usage and sentence structure, and can express their thoughts clearly and accurately.

By eighth grade, vocal and instrumental music have usually been designated as elective courses, or, in some cases, have been reduced to extracurricular activities. Listener skills are very much in demand in these classes, as chorus members memorize the rhythm, tune, and lyrics of each new song, and musicians fine-tune the individual parts of each piece of music before blending those parts into a melodious whole. However, as eighth graders are introduced to increasingly sophisticated musical selections, the reading of complex written scores and the dexterity required to transform them into music becomes more and more a task for Lookers.

Typical Report Cards for Lookers, Listeners, and Movers

Now that we've grouped eighth-grade subjects according to the learning skills each commands, let's look at the grades earned by our three learners. The report cards that follow highlight the academic strengths and weaknesses that usually result from a child's inborn preference for particular types of stimulation. You'll see that subjects with a strong visual component are Kim's best, while Mark shines in classes that employ his auditory and verbal talents. Shawn gets a taste of school success, as well, by relying on outside support and by selecting his courses with care.

EIGHTH-GRADE REPORT CARDS FOR LOOKER KIM

First-Quarter Report		*End-of-Year Report*	
Language Arts	B	Language Arts	B+
Math	A+	Math	A
Social Studies	B+	Social Studies	B
Science	B	Science	B
Spanish	B	Spanish	B+
Computer Technology	A+	Computer Technology	A+
Physical Education	B	Physical Education	B
Art	A+	Art	A+

As has always been the case, Kim's report cards are something of which she can be proud. It's almost a shame that, despite her consistent effort and methodical approach to schoolwork, she receives several B's, but Kim labors over the reading of eighth-grade textbook material and has a bit of trouble with such Listener-oriented tasks as remembering new vocabulary. Fortunately, Kim's maps, timelines, charts, graphs, and other projects are so superior to those of her classmates that they offset any less-than-satisfactory test performances. And there are no troublesome texts to hinder Kim's work in art, math, and computer classes.

Despite her difficulty with pronunciation, Kim loves her Spanish class. The beautifully decorated room makes Spanish history come alive, and Kim delights in her grasp of tricky Spanish vocabulary. Her visual skills stand our Looker in good stead when it comes to the mechanics of writing in English class, as well. As Kim gradually gains control over her class schedule during the coming years, she will most certainly select those elective courses that draw upon these same excellent Looker skills. In the meantime, Kim continues to expend such consistent effort in all classes that her beginning and end-of-year grades are very similar, and overall, quite good.

EIGHTH-GRADE REPORT CARDS FOR LISTENER MARK

First-Quarter Report		*End-of-Year Report*	
Language Arts	B+	Language Arts	A
Math	C	Math	C+
Social Studies	A–	Social Studies	A+
Science	B	Science	A
French	B+	French	A
Speech and Debate	B+	Speech and Debate	A
Physical Education	B	Physical Education	B
Vocal Music	A–	Vocal Music	B+

As in Kim's case, Mark's steady grades are a reflection of his consistently high-quality schoolwork. He was somewhat disappointed with his first-quarter grades, but devoted more time to schoolwork thereafter. This year, Mark elected to take vocal music and a speech course in place of art and computer technology. Both choices reflect his enjoyment of sound and language, and both replaced classes that highlight one of his weaker areas—fine motor coordination. As always, Mark earned B's in physical education. He is not extraordinarily agile, but his leadership skills are good, and he obviously enjoys the class so much that he receives above-average grades.

Mark still sees a math tutor on Sunday evenings, and more often when the need arises. The tutor, in turn, is in weekly contact with Mark's teacher, and provides the perfect link between Mark's rather shaky skills and any puzzling new class material. Mark was fascinated by this year's American history curriculum, and his interest is reflected in his high social studies grades. In fact, Mark became so interested in the whaling industry that he made it the subject of a sophisticated twenty-page term paper, which his father typed and Mark illustrated electronically with photos from various websites. Because his parents decline to do more than assist with research and typing, Mark didn't do quite as well on his science project, a homemade anemometer. Once the projects were out of the way, however, Mark went right back to earning his usual A's in science.

EIGHTH-GRADE REPORT CARDS FOR MOVER SHAWN

First-Quarter Report		*End-of-Year Report*	
Language Arts	C–	Language Arts	C
Math	C	Math	C–
Social Studies	C	Social Studies	C–
Science	C+	Science	B–
Remedial Reading	C+	Remedial Reading	C
Computer Technology	B–	Computer Technology	B
Physical Education	A	Physical Education	A

As always, Shawn achieves his best grades in subjects that require his active participation. Physical education, naturally, poses no problem at all. And with the benefits of at-home practice and a teacher who doesn't push him beyond basic software, Shawn also does well in his computer class. For years, the experimentation aspect of science has made this one of Shawn's best academic subjects, and eighth grade has been no different, particularly since the entry of the best students into an accelerated science program has minimized classroom competition. Earlier in the year, Shawn found himself missing the art classes that had long been a part of his school life. However, when he heard from fellow students about this year's addition of art history reading assignments and papers, he knew he'd made the right choice in avoiding that program.

Remedial reading, enrollment in slower-paced classes, the extra work time afforded by study hall, and the occasional help of Shawn's older brother have combined to keep Shawn's language arts, math, and social studies grades in the "C" range. To Shawn's great relief, this has meant an end to his Resource Lab visits. Shawn has long been bothered by his need for extra academic support and is now determined to make it a thing of the past.

WORKING WITH YOUR CHILD'S TEACHERS

Most parents hope to stay as informed as possible about their child's experiences away from home. Yet even if the teen in question is among those who cheerfully share feelings and volunteer personal details, a great deal of the school experience remains unaccounted for. I don't for a moment recommend that parents try to learn every detail of their child's life, for eighth graders need their privacy. However, you will be able to help your teen through a painful social situation, a frustrating unit of study, or a prolonged lapse of effort only if you are aware of the problem's existence.

Chapters Six and Seven discussed the benefits of initiating and maintaining contact with your child's teacher, above and beyond biannual conferences and quarterly report cards. (See pages 134 to 137 and 170 to 173 for details and suggestions.) After all, grade schoolers spend many of their away-from-home hours under the watchful eye of their classroom teacher, who can often provide clues to any changes in a child's behavior, attitude, or study habits. In junior high and middle school, however, the task of staying informed is complicated by the number and variety of teachers, courses, and peer interactions to which a teen is exposed during the course of each day, as well as the increasingly social focus of extracurricular life. Gone are the days when your child and his sole teacher could understand and accept each other's quirks with an intimacy born of some twenty-five hours spent together each week.

Whereas it was recommended in Chapters Six and Seven that parents volunteer information about their child's skills, work habits, and educational history, it is unreasonable to strive for a similar rapport with six or seven different teachers, each of whom your child may see for only forty minutes a day. Most secondary schools employ counselors, crisis intervention teachers, or other support personnel to monitor major problems; but unlike grade school, there is no one to whom parents can turn for blanket information when their child faces a problem at school. Nevertheless, there are means by which you can keep abreast of the highs and lows that befall your child during his year as an eighth grader. The following suggestions may help.

- *Attend parent organization meetings.* Regardless of your level of involvement in the parent organization at your child's school, these meetings can give you an inside track on such topics as school regulations and procedures, support services, personnel changes, new programs, and scheduled events.

- *Learn as much as you can about your child's teachers.* Most school districts host a "Meet the Teacher" night. Don't miss this opportunity to view your child's school through his eyes! A brief stop at each class will give you a feel for the teacher's personality, along with valuable information about books and supplies, homework policy, upcoming projects, and expectations regarding behavior and class participation. From the start, try to get your child talking in general terms about unusual or notable classroom happenings. Each time he describes a humorous conversation, reports on disciplinary tactics, or relates a story about a teacher's personal life, more light will be shed on the teacher and class under discussion. You may also wish to turn to other parents for information about teachers to whom their children were assigned in the past. To be fair, however, you should seek second and third opinions before making any negative assumptions.

- *Make your child's teachers aware of your interest.* If you're struck by a teacher's creativity or level of commitment, send a note of commendation or thanks. If your child seems particularly enthusiastic about a project or unit of study, don't hesitate to apprise the teacher of this fact. Doing so can make the teacher more aware of your child's involvement, and may even have an effect on the format of future assignments. You should feel equally free to write, call, or e-mail when questions or problems arise. However, it's important to be tactful and open-minded. A teacher who feels that he or she is under scrutiny may minimize interaction with the student in question so as not to invite further conflict. The teen, in turn, may miss out on valuable one-to-one instruction.

- *Be aware of the fine line between concern and control.* Most eighth graders are both flattered and reassured when parents show an interest in their school life. But let that interest be misinterpreted as nosiness or interference, and the same teens are quick to bristle. As a rule, it's safe to ask your child questions that convey your interest in his friends and schoolwork provided that your tone remains nonjudgmental, your demeanor casual, and your remarks and questions relatively impersonal. Avoid prolonged discussions of subjects that make your child uncomfortable, as well as open-ended queries that require long, drawn-out replies. For example, if your teen responds to, "So, who usually sits at your cafeteria table?" by shrugging and turning his back, or greets, "What are you doing in social studies?" with a martyred sigh, it's best to change the subject. Communication may be easier when your questions focus on your child's friends, rather than your child, and when you relate stories from your own school days that parallel what you suspect your eighth grader is facing.

If your child seems to be struggling in a particular class—if his grade in the subject shows a sudden decline, for instance, or if he voices an ongoing dislike of the teacher—it's time to contact that teacher for a conference. It's a good idea to prepare your questions in advance so that you'll be sure to come away from this meeting with the clearest possible picture of your child's work and behavior. The following are some good topics for discussion.

- *What is the policy regarding homework?* Find out what the teacher's expectations are and whether your child completes assignments and turns them in on time.

- *What sort of class work can your child expect?* Ask about the usual format of each class and whether your teen pays attention during lectures. You may also wish to inquire about your child's participation in discussions, and to ask whether he takes notes when needed and prepares sufficiently for tests.

- *What sort of relationships does your child have with his classmates?* Find out how your child gets along with his peers. Ask whether he assumes the role of leader, observer, or antagonist, and whether there is anyone with whom he has a particularly close relationship. Finally, ask if his peer interactions are affecting his schoolwork.

- *Does your child work up to his academic potential?* Ask the teacher whether your child's classroom performance corresponds to his level of ability. You might also inquire about the consistency of your teen's effort and interest level. Find out whether your child might feel more challenged—or less overwhelmed—in a faster- or slower-paced class.

• *How can you help at home?* Find out if there is anything you can do to make this particular class a more positive experience for your teen. Request specific ideas that might help your child improve his grades, and ask if the teacher recommends any sort of professional intervention.

LEARNING STYLE AND EXTRACURRICULAR ACTIVITIES

Eighth graders have had several years in which to try their hand at artistic, organizational, athletic, and recreational pursuits. Most are aware of their creative, physical, and social abilities. Simply put, they've discovered which activities work for them and which do not.

By the time a child reaches thirteen or fourteen years of age, he can be spoken to honestly, albeit tactfully, about his immediate and long-term goals. With luck, your child will involve himself in the activities that will best help him to achieve those goals. If not, it isn't too late to intervene.

First, it's a good idea to limit the number of after-school organizations to which your child belongs. All too often, either an adolescent's desire to belong or his parents' goals for his future result in a jam-packed weekly schedule that is quickly coupled with irritability, stomachaches, headaches, depression, or fatigue—all signals of possible overload. Explain to your child the value of unstructured time, and help him decide which activities are most important and which should be dropped.

Second, help your child avoid disillusionment by diplomatically suggesting that he steer clear of pursuits in which he's not likely to meet with success. Guide him in examining the activity's appeal. If, for example, he has limited vocal talent but nevertheless yearns to be chosen for county-wide chorus, help him see that he's really being motivated by the group's elite status, his desire to follow the lead of a friend, or the potential for missing classes on practice days, as the case may be. Of course, if your child is realistic about his lack of talent, there's no harm in his pursuing the activity on another level—joining the school chorus, say—simply for the fun of it. On the flip side, you can guarantee a boost to your child's self-esteem by convincing him to stick with the activities he has enjoyed in the past. Remind him that even the most beloved pursuits can become boring, but that this is often temporary. Even if your teen questions the activity's social acceptability—if he is embarrassed about carrying his saxophone around the school on lesson days, for example, or if he refuses to align himself with the Theater Club's current in-group—there may be ways he can pursue his interest outside of school

Finally, even the most competent teen can benefit from a challenge. Depending on the nature of your relationship with your eighth grader, you may be able to encourage him to venture into previously untried areas. Provide all the information you can find and all the behind-the-scenes support you can muster, and stand behind any decisions to bring along a friend for moral support.

Naturally, different after-school pursuits work best for different learners. Although your teen may not always be amenable to your ideas about his free time, and will probably gravitate on his own towards pursuits that reflect his learning style, you *may* be able to help him vary his extracurricular diet. Some of the following suggestions could prove useful.

Activities for Eighth-Grade Lookers

Lookers are usually among the most confirmed homebodies. But by eighth grade, even the most reticent teens yearn to be more popular and confident. You'll have the greatest success helping your child reach this goal if the activities you suggest tap his areas of interest. For Lookers, it's wise to focus on pursuits that do not require strong people skills, but guarantee a modicum of success to the visually oriented. One of the following ideas may be right for your child.

- Art programs
- Astronomy
- Carpentry
- Collecting cards, stamps, or coins
- Computer games and design
- Library or museum work
- Math club or team
- Model-making or other crafts
- Photography or videography
- Video and board games

Activities for Eighth-Grade Listeners

Since Listeners devote much of their attention to the development of an active social life, they gravitate toward group activities. But individuality is a desirable quality, as well, so you may wish to encourage your teen to also consider hobbies and activities separate from those of his school friends. Here are some suggestions.

- Acting class
- Baby-sitting
- Bowling league
- Church group or scouting
- Community theater involvement

- Family outings
- Service clubs
- Skating lessons
- Storytelling and essay contests
- Student government

Activities for Eighth-Grade Movers

Because of their constant involvement in sports, most teen Movers are relatively at ease with same-sex peers. They may not be brilliant conversationalists, but their friendships with teammates are often comfortable. Most athletic pursuits, therefore, are good choices for Movers. You might also suggest nonsport activities that your child can enjoy without feeling academic or social pressure. The following list contains some ideas for Mover teens.

- After-school recreation programs
- Bowling league
- Ecology groups
- Group tennis lessons
- Hiking, fishing, or camping

- School decorating and cleanup committees
- Ski/snowboard club
- Town pool membership
- Track and field events
- Volleyball

THE SOCIAL IMPLICATIONS OF LEARNING STYLE

During the adolescent years, a child is hard at work carving out an identity and forming friendships with peers who either share his interests or reflect the values, behavior, and social wherewithal he'd like to possess himself. At thirteen and fourteen, a child's opinion of himself is largely based on what others think of him, and so is quite fragile. The lofty air he exhibits one minute—"I really belted that softball! Now, everyone will want me on their team!"—can just as quickly be erased— "Sara sat by Paul at lunch today. I guess she doesn't like me after all." Both in school and out of school, an adolescent's experiences, achievements, and sense of confidence have tremendous social implications. And as you might suspect, these experiences—whatever their outcome—are largely based on learning style.

Most Lookers won't actively seek feedback from friends or family, but are nonetheless well aware of others' opinions. A raised eyebrow here or a scornful glance there is all the proof a Looker needs that peer judgment is being passed. At thirteen, the Looker is as self-motivated and goal-oriented as ever, but the fruits of his labors are not held in as high regard as they were a few years back. Let's face it, good grades and manners just don't impress teens as much as friendliness, a sense of humor, athletic ability, or stylish clothes—none of which is likely to be among a Looker's strong points. Adolescent Lookers tend to have one or two close friends, though they don't share much personal information with them. And while they may appear outwardly serene, Lookers' reticence and inability to make small talk usually combine to make these teens downright uncomfortable at group social events.

Friends' opinions are a veritable driving force for adolescent Listeners. The average Listener is so group-focused that his sociability often prevents him from developing any personal interest beyond reading. The Listener will join a team or club if accompanied by his friends, but is more interested in monitoring the words and actions of its older members and having a good time than in achieving a group goal. Because Listeners are so friendly and outgoing, fitting in is not a problem, but in the classroom, a Listener's talkativeness and love of the limelight earn as much teacher disapproval as they do classmate admiration. At thirteen, however, school performance is of lower priority than social status. Looker traits may be appreciated by adults, but Listeners are popular with the group that really counts—their peers!

By eighth grade, Movers are finally able to taste the hard-won respect of their classmates. The Mover's tendency to cut up in class is suddenly seen in a new light. Although his antics probably annoyed his grade-school classmates, adolescent peers are likely to find his behavior amusing and may secretly wish to act the same way. Moreover, the thirteen- or fourteen-year-old Mover's athletic prowess and muscular physique are often the envy of his male peers, while females are thrilled by his playing performance and by the remote air that is, in actuality, a result of social unease rather than disinterest. At this age, female Movers are often worlds apart from their same-sex peers in terms of interests and skills, but are readily accepted as "pals" by boys. Movers have spent years scrambling to match the accomplishments of their Looker and Listener classmates. Suddenly—effortlessly—it is their *natural* ability that earns them peer admiration. Adolescent Movers never lack for friends, for everyone now wants to be one.

Tips for Encouraging Social Growth

Given the social implications of learning style, parents may wish to lend a discreet hand in the preservation of their teen-ager's sense of confidence. Here are some ideas to try with your Looker, Listener, or Mover.

- Quietly investigate school course listings for classes in which your child's learning style will help him shine. For example, journalism and band are possibilities for Lookers and Listeners, respectively; and aerobics and home-skills classes are well suited to most Movers. Find out as much as you can about the courses that seem best, and pass this information on to your child along with your reasons for recommending the classes.

- Keep abreast of your child's social life by appearing interested, but not inquisitive; available, but not determined to pry into his problems. It often helps to voice your own excitement and frustration with daily life. Seeing and hearing a parent "vent" can convince a teen of the emotional benefits of doing so.

- If your child is sedentary, remind him of the importance of physical activity. You can plan family activities, and can also suggest solo exercise. An added benefit to bike rides, walks, swimming lessons, and other public pursuits is that the reticent child becomes more visible to peers.

- Although the term is used loosely when applied to most young teens, opinions are sharply divided on the appropriateness of eighth-grade dating. If you or your child is hesitant about his readiness for solo outings with an opposite-sex peer, it's probably best for him to stick to boy-girl group activities or double-dates with a friend—assuming his interest extends even that far. You can be sure, however, that same-sex friends are important. If need be, you can expose your teen, without pressure, to children of families with similar values by planning two-family get-togethers, or allowing him to invite another teen to join your family outings.

- Encourage your child's feelings of independence any way you can. Allow him to manage his own money, send him shopping for his own clothes, encourage his work around the house or for hire, and allow him every possible privacy—from a separate restaurant table for him and a buddy to closed-door socializing when friends visit the house.

- When possible, focus on coeducational schools and activities. When boys and girls witness the ups and downs of one another's lives within a nonthreatening everyday environment, each develops understanding, empathy, and respect for the opposite sex. Social competence is an inevitable, if gradual, result.

- Make your teen aware of his best features, be they academic or physical. At thirteen, even the most gifted or attractive child may doubt his worth. Compliments, when genuine, can provide a much-needed lift.

- If your teen has expressed doubts about his ability to handle social situations, encourage him to anticipate awkward or embarrassing turns of events. It often helps to practice responses through role-playing. A ready answer to an intimidating bully, thoughtless friend, or teasing adult can be a real lifesaver to a momentarily panicked adolescent.

HOMEWORK STRATEGIES FOR LOOKERS, LISTENERS, AND MOVERS

By eighth grade, noting, preparing for, and completing school assignments should primarily be the responsibility of the student. You can support your teen's efforts by suggesting work strategies that capitalize on his learning strengths, and by working behind the scenes to maintain a home environment conducive to study and learning. This can be accomplished by insisting on nutritious meals and reasonable bedtimes; by creating a quiet, organized workspace; by supplying reference materials and stationery supplies; by making yourself available for assistance or advice; and—perhaps most difficult—by readily providing transportation to music lessons, cultural events, study group meetings, and the library. Here are some strategies that will make homework and learning more appealing to your eighth-grade learner.

Strategies for Lookers

From the time they can first grasp a pencil, most Looker children enjoy independent work, and this preference generally remains strong throughout the school years. Your eighth-grade Looker will appreciate a desk or other private workspace in which he can store his supplies without fear of other household members making a mess of things. You can encourage your Looker teen's creative side by supplementing ordinary desk-top items with neon markers, colored chalk, stencils, oil crayons, and gel or glitter pens. Your neat, methodical Looker will also benefit from a bulletin board and whiteboard near his work area.

As a rule, eighth-grade Lookers are quite self-reliant when it comes to recording, organizing, and completing schoolwork. You may wish to encourage your child's use of different-colored inks, thumbnail sketches, and highlighting to make note-taking more interesting. The idea of using separate notebooks and folders for each subject may be quite appealing, and at test time, you can also suggest that your child condense his notes into outline form—a technique that simplifies the memorization of facts. Although most Lookers like to study alone, your child may welcome your offer of a last-minute oral quiz. If your teen seems bogged down by a particular unit of study or a difficult piece of literature, you might search out a video or generously illustrated book that can provide missing background information.

Strategies for Listeners

Most Listener teens have little difficulty with homework. A parent's biggest problem is convincing the Listener to find time to get the work done. It is often helpful to mandate a homework time at the start of the school year. However, the Listener's extracurricular schedule often is so full that you may have to be flexible. If this is the case, frequent reminders about homework's priority status are probably in order. Fortunately, once they get started, most Listeners are responsible enough to see their assignments through, though they are likely to appreciate an offer of proofreading or typing assistance.

The presence of a friend often makes study time more palatable to the Listener. You may wish to suggest that your child tape-record material, and that he read instructions and notes aloud. As an auditory learner, your teen remembers facts and terms better when he hears them. Therefore, if your Listener is stumped by a certain mathematical process or science procedure, remind him to talk himself through the work, step by step. It may also help to furnish books or videos that relate to, and generate further interest in, any units of study that your Listener finds troublesome.

Strategies for Movers

Eighth-grade Movers are often unmotivated students, particularly when it comes to reading and written assignments. At home, it's not unusual for assignments to go undone because the Mover teen either has forgotten what the specific task was or has left the necessary books and papers at school. You can suggest that your child carry an index card in his pocket, and that he use it to note the homework assigned in each class. He can then refer to the card before leaving school to make sure he's taking home all that he needs. You may also wish to steer your child toward the use of a single five-subject notebook, complete with pockets for loose papers. This, coupled with a backpack, will help him keep track of his work.

At home, the teen-aged Mover needs a quiet workspace with plenty of room to spread out his assignments. If your child is disorganized, as many Movers are, or if he has trouble deciding where to start, it's a good idea to prepare his work area ahead of time. Then, with your child's permission, you can review his assignment list and help him set out the needed books and worksheets. It also helps to remain nearby but involved in a task of your own, so that you can answer questions and offer encouragement while still leaving the responsibility for homework completion to your child. You may well find that the sight of you, deep in concentration, will motivate your Mover to focus on his own work.

If your child has a great deal of homework, encourage him to take breaks between assignments. Ultimately, only he can control how long it takes to finish everything, but you can lend a hand by establishing set times for homework—even using before-school hours if your child seems to be at his best in the morning. When your Mover has to study for a test, he may need you to select the most important information from his textbooks and notebooks. You can offer to assist your child with reviews, but he may find that the presence of a classmate makes the task of studying more enjoyable. For long-term projects, show your teen-ager how to map out a work schedule that divides assignments into small, manageable segments, ensuring that the project will be finished on time. Your Mover may also appreciate the provision of background information. Videos and magazine photographs, for example, can improve his grasp of social studies and science material. And to help your child through literature assignments, you might wish to check bookstores for an abbreviated version of the book in question. Since handwriting is rarely a Mover's strong suit, you can also provide your child with a typewriter and the offer of your assistance with the typing of long assignments.

TECHNIQUES FOR IMPROVING AN EIGHTH GRADER'S ACADEMIC PERFORMANCE

By the age of thirteen, students are somewhat set in their classroom performance levels and their attitudes toward school. Lookers, for example, find school fairly rewarding. They particularly enjoy the process of designing and executing solo projects like reports, maps, inventions, and visual aids. Class participation and group projects, on the other hand, present uncomfortable social demands that most Lookers would rather avoid.

Listeners, who have logged in years of academic and social success, have reason to look forward to each and every school day. Many Listeners see class work as a necessary means to an end—social opportunity. So even if their immediate goal is only chatting with a certain someone outside of English class or meeting with the eighth-grade dance committee, Listeners see school as a positive force in their lives.

Movers struggle as much with eighth-grade academics as they did with the course work of earlier grades, but the introduction of elective classes finally enables them to steer clear of language, art, music, and anything with a heavy reading requirement. With support, Movers can pass most or all of their required subjects; and, though they may frequently feel discouraged, they can redeem themselves in their own eyes and the eyes of their peers once they exit the classroom. Because of their physical talents, eighth-grade Movers are often popular teens despite their social reticence.

Can an adolescent's parents play a role in their child's academic life? Will their teen accept their help—and can it really make a difference? In most cases, it's simply not realistic to expect much progress when parents and teens try to tackle homework together. Adolescents are usually too fractious, their self-esteem too fragile, and their relationship with parents too emotion-charged for parent and child to accomplish much as a team! Even the most nonjudgmental and diplomatic mom or dad is likely to meet with failure in this regard. Nevertheless, you need not stand idly by, watching your child struggle with course work. Instead, you can help by making sure your teen understands the concept of learning style and knows how his style can be tapped to assist his academic effort. You can also lend a hand with the selection of a course of study that best reflects your child's interests and abilities. School guidance counselors should be able to give you the background information you need to offer informed advice.

In the previous pages, you learned some general learning-style based homework strategies. The following five sections, which cover the courses required of most eighth graders, suggest more specific learning strategies. Included are a number of multisensory techniques and materials, which draw upon both the sense needed for the mastery of the subject matter and another sense—preferably, your child's favored sense. Review these suggestions with an eye towards selecting those that you feel would work best with your child's sensory preference. You're certain to find that use of appropriate strategies improves both your child's classroom performance and his overall confidence. As an added bonus, your child's behavior at home may be more positive and productive once you and he begin working in harmony toward a common goal.

Building Reading and Literature-Appreciation Skills

Depending on where your child attends school and the level at which he reads, he may, as an eighth grader, find himself exposed to anything from remedial techniques to literary classics. Some schools offer a single course encompassing poetry, biography, short stories, and the like; others offer a different course for each genre; and still others make literature a part of the language arts curriculum.

The skills involved in reading are no different in eighth grade than in first. The level of a student's ability to decode, or translate the printed word into one that is spoken; the size of his vocabulary; and the degree to which he comprehends what he reads are what determine his overall reading performance. Whether your eighth grader needs help with phonics or with the deciphering of Homer's *Odyssey*, you, the parent, can help. Here are some ideas.

TECHNIQUES TO IMPROVE READING SKILLS

■ Put your child in charge of reading aloud to a younger sibling.

■ Encourage the use of a bookmark so that your teen can either rest his eyes while reading or close his eyes to visualize the action—without losing his place.

■ As a visual strategy for keeping track of characters and events, teach your teen to compose a scrap-paper time line.

■ Allow your eighth grader to enjoy an interesting story line—without having to pronounce every word—by treating him to a book on tape. Amazon.com and Barnesandnoble.com both offer thousands of selections. A good choice for teens would be J.R.R. Tolkien's *The Lord of the Rings Trilogy Gift Set* (Recorded Books).

■ Rent a classic movie enjoyed by teens, such as *To Kill a Mockingbird*. Then, after your teen-ager has seen the film, provide him with the book.

■ A phonics review can improve reading skills at any age. Look for a tutor who can present beginning phonics at an interest level appropriate to teens.

■ Share the joy of literature by reading stories, poems, and novels along with your teen. Discuss the material from time to time, asking questions designed to make your child think: "Why do you suppose the heroine returned to high school?" or "What did you think of the story's ending?"

■ To build vocabulary, buy a book of crossword puzzles and work them together with your teen during car trips or rainy weekend afternoons.

■ Keep a paperback dictionary on hand for homework, or suggest that your teen take a look at www.dictionary.com to learn the meaning of new vocabulary.

■ *Roget's 21st Century Thesaurus: The Essential Reference for Home, School, or Office* (Dell Publishing) is a classic and a must-have in paperback. Also refer your teen to www.thesaurus.com and suggest he sign up for word-of-the-day e-mail.

■ *Scrabble* software by National School Products helps students build spelling skills as they play a game of Scrabble one-to-one with the computer. They can also challenge other players via the Internet.

Building Language Arts Skills

Most eighth-grade curriculums include some form of language arts—the study of spelling, grammar, research skills, and writing techniques. The presentation of language arts material varies from district to district, as does the tendency to group students by ability level. In the long run, the goal of a language arts curriculum is to improve a student's written and spoken use of English. A benefit is better research papers, and, as a result, better grades.

By eighth grade, a teen has written, and received grades on, many compositions and reports, and so should have no difficulty determining his weakest language arts skills. However, if your child is unable to pinpoint areas that need improvement, you can review samples of his work and make that determination together. Of course, his language arts teacher should also be a good source of information.

Because strong language arts skills result in better written work, the expertise your teen acquires in this class will serve him well in all studies throughout his academic career. The following are some suggestions for helping your teen get the most from his language arts course work.

TECHNIQUES TO IMPROVE LANGUAGE ARTS SKILLS

- If your child's spelling is poor, he could benefit from the support of a spelling dictionary such as David Morrow's *DK Pockets: Spelling Dictionary* (Dorling Kindersley Publishing), a miniature reference that contains 35,000 correct spellings, minus the definitions.

- Suggest that your Looker picture the word in his mind, or that your Listener pronounce it carefully to himself before putting the word on paper. Both techniques will help to avoid careless misspellings.

- After your teen has composed a rough draft of a theme or report, ask him to read it aloud to you. Doing so will make him aware of many grammatical and structural errors without your saying a word.

- Explain to your child that a rough draft is *expected* to contain mistakes. Suggest that, just like an editor, he make corrections in blue pencil before beginning his final copy.

- Keep on hand Margaret Shertzer's *The Elements of Grammar* (Longman Publishing), a concise and comprehensive reference.

- For a "bare bones grammar" review, check out Big Dog's Grammar at http://aliscot.com/bigdog.

- To improve your teen's enjoyment and skill at composition, suggest that he enroll in a creative writing class. There, ideas and feelings will carry much more weight than grammar or punctuation.

- If your child has trouble getting started on creative writing assignments, suggest that he record his story or essay on a cassette as he goes along. Then, he can revise and edit as he transfers his thoughts from tape to paper.

- Teach your teen how to "map," rather than outline, a report. By organizing material in graphic form, he can easily see the interplay among various ideas. One way to map is to place a main idea in the center of a sheet of paper, circle it, and then write secondary points on lines that branch out from the center.

■ If your teen still hasn't mastered the keyboard, check a local vocational or technical school for the availability of a typing class on weekends or in the summer.

■ Build vocabulary with *Dell Crossword Puzzles*, a monthly magazine chock full of crosswords at different levels, from easy to challenger.

■ Give your child a Franklin SA-206 *Spelling Ace With Thesaurus*. Available through Amazon, it corrects phonetic spellings of more than 100,000 words.

■ To improve your teen's grasp of a foreign language, rent a foreign film with English subtitles or plan a family excursion to an ethnic neighborhood or city in which the language spoken is the one your child is studying.

■ *The Five-Language Visual Dictionary* (Dorling Kindersley Publishing) offers 6,000 everyday vocabulary terms in English, French, Spanish, German, and Italian, along with 1,600 full-color photos.

■ If your teen is studying Spanish, he'll love Jane Wightwick's *Way-Cool Spanish Phrase Book* (McGraw-Hill/Contemporary Books), which provides useful expressions accompanied by amusing illustrations.

■ *You Be the Reporter* software from National School Products is an interactive multimedia tool that sparks the thinking-writing connection, while developing a student's ability to organize facts and write clearly.

Building Science Skills

The study of weather, rocks and minerals, matter, elements and compounds, gravity, and the solar system are all typical components of an eighth-grade science curriculum. As in language arts and math, many school districts offer similar course work on various ability levels. Others, however, use eighth-grade science to begin separate courses of study for college-bound versus vocationally oriented students.

Whatever their assigned titles, middle school and junior high science classes are pretty evenly divided in terms of visual and auditory stimuli. Course work includes a great deal of reading and note-taking, as well as the memorization of complex vocabulary, the absorption of lecture and film material, and the utilization of lab equipment. Obviously, the eighth grader with a bit of science background will be more interested in and more adept at science assignments and experiments. Here are some suggestions for improving your child's science knowledge and ability.

TECHNIQUES TO IMPROVE SCIENCE SKILLS

■ Surprise your teen with well-illustrated, easy-to-read books on any science topic that piques his interest. Ecology, astronomy, and oceanography are a few possibilities.

■ *Discover* magazine covers a broad spectrum of science news, with each issue bringing to light a new and newsworthy topic. The material is spiced with puzzles, web links, and experiments for amateur scientists.

■ Find posters of the solar system, the human body, and weather—to name just a few of the images available—at www.allposters.com. Just click on "Education" to find an array of science topics.

■ Invest in a backyard telescope to stimulate the entire family's interest in the solar system.

■ Make it a point to include a bit of eighth-grade science in family trips. Work in a visit to a cavern, a quarry, a recycling facility, or a planetarium.

■ If you live near a zoo, find out if it offers a weekend or summer program that trains teens to work with animals.

■ Encourage your teen to make his own sketches of science terms and experiments. Besides making his science notebook more visually appealing, this habit will develop your child's skills of observation.

■ Offer to help your child study for tests. As you quiz him on various topics, call the Listener's attention to his "inner voice" and the Looker's, to his "mind's eye."

■ C. Claiborne Ray's *The New York Times Second Book of Science Questions and Answers* (Anchor Books) will delight your teen with answers to questions such as "What would kill you if you fell into a black hole?" and "Why don't you sneeze when you're asleep?"

■ Written by Joyce Henderson and Heather Tomasello—a science fair judge and an international science fair winner—*Strategies for Winning Science Fair Projects* (John Wiley & Sons) is packed with tactics for putting together a winning science project.

■ Encourage your teen's interest in nature by giving him hiking gear, the materials needed to start a vegetable garden, or the components of another science-oriented activity.

■ Be on the lookout for PBS television specials on topics that might interest your teen—tornadoes, for example, or archaeological digs. A thirteen-year-old may not be eager to watch such shows during prime time (or homework time), but a tailor-made video can help fill a rainy weekend.

Building Social Studies Skills

Eighth-grade social studies can take many forms. Some districts emphasize civics, or the study of government. Others offer a separate course in American history. Still others combine the two and add a healthy sprinkling of geography. But regardless of the content of your eighth grader's social studies course, he'll be making daily use of his reading, note-taking, and class participation skills.

Just as with science, the social studies student who finds his course work appealing is likely to listen harder, read longer, and put more of himself into papers and projects. Happily, it's not too late to spark this kind of interest in your eighth grader. The following are some ideas to help you make social studies facts and figures more palatable to your teen-ager.

TECHNIQUES TO IMPROVE SOCIAL STUDIES SKILLS

■ Browse through your local videostore—or through online video selections at amazon.com and bn.com—for topics of interest as wide-ranging as the Oregon Trail and Stephen Hawking's *A Brief History of Time*.

■ An excellent reference book, Bernard Grun's *The Timetables of History: A Horizontal Linkage of People and Events* (Touchstone Books) presents a sweeping overview of history and traces major events in politics, philosophy, the arts, science, and technology from 5,000 BC to the present.

■ Your teen's room may be decorated with pop-star posters, but you can claim equal time by adorning basement or family room walls with history posters from www.allposters.com. Click first on "Education" and then on "History" to find images ranging from the Bill of Rights to world maps to the Buffalo Soldiers.

■ Provide your child with a small tape recorder to ease the listening demands of lectures and films. This device can also be used to record and play back any important facts and dates that must be memorized.

■ Browse through the travel section of your local bookstore for one of Fodor's many guidebooks to other countries. Some of the more exotic titles include *Australia* and *Ports of Call*. While you're at the store, look for maps and atlases, too.

■ Leap Frog's electronic *iQuest Handheld* offers an opportunity for middle-school students to answer questions that specifically apply to the textbooks they're using. The subjects covered include not just social studies, but also math and science, and an Internet connector allows students to download new activities.

■ Check out photo-essay books from your library. These "coffee-table" books present beautiful photographs of various peoples and places.

■ Stimulate your child's interest in other cultures by planning a family outing to an ethnic neighborhood in a nearby city—New York's Chinatown, for example.

■ Find geography coloring books at www.bn.com.

■ *National Geographic Maps* software, available from Topics Entertainment, contains 535 maps, with some going back as far as the nineteenth century. All maps were originally published in *National Geographic* magazine.

Building Math Skills

The content of the eighth-grade math curriculum varies greatly from city to city. In some parts of the country, advanced eighth graders begin a sequential course of study that encompasses all areas of math and continues throughout high school. Meanwhile, students with lesser math skills can take another year of general math before beginning the sequence as ninth graders, while the weakest students need not begin the sequence at all. But elsewhere in the country, eighth graders are assigned by ability level to different tracks of a single math course. This course covers geometric shapes, classification and measurement of angles, powers, bases, and square roots. A student's performance during the course of the year determines his math track for the following year.

Whatever your child's curriculum and level of study, math courses will probably be part of his school life for at least several more years. Here are some techniques that will improve your teen's ability to understand and apply math concepts.

TECHNIQUES TO IMPROVE MATH SKILLS

■ If your teen continues to struggle with multiplication tables, he should probably be allowed to use a calculator in class. As early in the year as possible, speak to the teacher about doing this. You may save your child months of frustration.

■ *Cuisenaire Rods* by ETA/Cuisenaire are colored rods of different lengths that stand for number values. The rods can be used to teach the decimal system, powers, roots, fractions, and introductory algebra. Find them online at www.thedowsschoolroom.com.

■ Liven up the subject with colorful motivational math posters from www.mathteacherstore.com

■ *Dell Math Puzzles and Logic Problems* is a monthly magazine that contains logic, number, and math brain teasers.

■ Enlist your teen's help with a large-scale cooking project. As you work, make a game of determining what each measurement, and the recipe's overall yield, would be if you were to halve, double, or triple it.

■ Written by David and Tom Gardner, founders of the multimedia investment company The Motley Fool, *The Motley Fool Investment Guide for Teens: Eight Steps to Having More Money Than Your Parents Ever Dreamed Of* (Fireside Publishing) shares the authors' investment strategies for adolescents and demystifies the stock market, banking practices, and IRA's.

■ Encore Software's *Math Advantage 2003,* available through Amazon, covers ten core math subjects and is packed with thousands of lessons, 3-D images, animations, and audio.

■ *Math Contests* software by National School Products allows students to build confidence in the subject through competition in over fifty challenging contests in various areas of math.

Naturally, not all of the techniques listed above will be right for every student. In some cases, my suggestions may duplicate a technique or resource you've already attempted with your teen. In others, you may read the tip and instinctively know it would not work with your child. But if the above-mentioned ideas make you more aware of the need for home support and enrichment in the various subject areas, my lists will have served their purpose!

Please remember that, despite your best efforts, it's simply not realistic to expect your thirteen-year-old's C– in science to improve to an A within the span of a marking period. When working with your child, it's important to be as concerned with personal growth as with academic achievement. An improved grade-point average may well be one of the results of your efforts to help your teen. Equally important, however, is achieving a heightened interest and greater pride in class work and projects, and a parent-child relationship free from the tension of unrealistic expectations. The knowledge of how your teen learns best will benefit you both.

LEARNING STYLE QUICKCHECK FOR EIGHTH GRADERS, THIRTEEN TO FOURTEEN YEARS OF AGE

Directions: Read the statements below, and mark each one that is characteristic of your child. When finished, total the checks in each column for a clear picture of your teen's preferred learning style.

LOOKER	LISTENER	MOVER
1. Communication: When my eighth grader wishes to express himself . . .		
❏ He carefully watches his audience for their reaction.	❏ He listens and speaks easily and effortlessly.	☑ He may sometimes feel tongue-tied.
❏ He participates in discussions when called upon, but rarely volunteers.	❏ He is uninhibited about speaking in class.	☑ He avoids eye contact with the teacher in hopes that he won't be called on.
❏ He has an average-sized vocabulary.	❏ He has a very large vocabulary.	❏ He has a small vocabulary.
2. Favorite Pastimes: When my eighth grader has free time . . .		
❏ You'll find him at the computer.	❏ He reads a great deal and often follows the works of a single author.	☑ He enjoys outdoor activities like running, camping, and fishing.
❏ He likes video games and TV sports.	❏ He loves to visit with friends and to talk on the phone.	❏ He plays a different sport each season.
3. Fine Motor Skills: When my eighth grader uses his hands . . .		
❏ He shows great dexterity, easily coordinating eyes and hands.	❏ He shies away from fine motor tasks like typing and assembling models.	❏ He feels clumsy when using his hands except when large muscles come into play, as in sports.
❏ His handwriting is excellent; his artwork, precise.	❏ His penmanship and artistic efforts are average.	❏ His penmanship and artwork are often sloppy.
4. Gross Motor Skills: When my eighth grader moves about . . .		
❏ He prefers noncontact activities, like hiking and bicycling.	❏ He prefers group activities to individual pursuits.	❏ He gravitates toward contact and competitive sports, like lacrosse and soccer.
❏ He has average coordination and is very aware of his athletic shortcomings.	❏ He avoids games and activities that might make him look foolish.	❏ He excels at nearly every sport he attempts.

5. Social Skills: When my eighth grader mixes with other teens . . .

❏ He tends to pair off with one or two close friends.	❏ He is very sociable and thrives on group activities.	☑ He's comfortable with physical closeness and may touch the person he's speaking to.
❏ He tends to be self-motivated rather than socially motivated.	❏ The opinion of friends is a strong motivator.	☑ He is more sociable on the playing field than at social get-togethers.

6. Emotions: When it comes to my eighth grader's feelings . . .

❏ He keeps his feelings in check.	❏ He doesn't hesitate to express his feelings.	❏ He tends to express his feelings with actions rather than words.
❏ He is made uncomfortable by displays of emotion.	❏ He is sympathetic and understanding when it comes to his friends' feelings.	❏ He tends to be moody, impatient, and easily frustrated.

7. Memory: When my eighth grader learns . . .

❏ He doodles and jots down notes to aid his memory.	❏ He works well with a tape recorder.	❏ He recalls actions and feelings better than spoken or written words.
❏ He makes frequent use of mental images when remembering.	❏ He talks to himself and listens to an inner voice for answers.	☑ He is aware that he has trouble memorizing, and seeks helpful strategies.

8. School: When my eighth grader is in the classroom . . .

❏ His best subjects are art, math, science, and computers.	❏ His best subjects are English, foreign language, and social studies.	❏ All academic work is a challenge. He requires a tutor to achieve mostly "C's" and some "B" grades.
❏ He is happiest working alone.	❏ He does his best work in groups.	☑ He learns best when he is an active participant in the lesson.
❏ His work and study habits are excellent.	❏ His socializing sometimes gets in the way of his school work.	☑ He requires a lot of support when studying and doing assignments.

TOTALS: _____ LOOKER _____ LISTENER __✓__ MOVER

CHAPTER NINE

Learning Problems
and Solutions

From infancy on, each child clearly displays her sensory preference for visual, auditory, or tactile information, and as a result, can be categorized as a Looker, Listener, or Mover. In preceding chapters, our case-study learners revealed their academic highs and lows to be a reflection of the way they select and absorb information from the vast amount available in their environment. Moreover, suggestions were made to help you, as a parent, modify learning style to maximize your child's learning ability.

There are, however, certain situations in which a child's learning difficulties persist despite a parent's best efforts to remedy them. This can occur for any of a number of reasons. For instance, a child may not just be a Listener by learning style, but may have such a decided preference for auditory input that she literally blocks out visual information. When children "get stuck" in one way of perceiving, they may become labeled as "learning disabled." Furthermore, what seems to be a strong learning style preference may actually be the sign of another type of problem. For example, a child who is so active that she cannot sit still long enough to process classroom instruction may appear to be a Mover, but in fact be hyperactive.

In certain cases, a child's history may reveal an organic origin to a learning disability, such as prenatal problems, an injury at birth, or a family history of learning difficulties. In almost every case, the course of educational therapy is the same whether a child's classroom problems are primarily learning-style related or organic in nature, so parents needn't despair if a specific diagnosis can't be agreed upon.

This chapter examines learning preferences that can become learning disabilities, and also provides a look at other conditions that can disrupt the academic process. Since so many learning problems surface during the elementary school years, the relationship between learning problems and the onset of academic work is clarified.

Academic problems, beginning as early as first grade, usually result in a child's being referred for evaluation. Therefore, this chapter offers some valuable information about the nature of educational and diagnostic testing. Included are descriptions of commonly used tests, definitions of diagnostic terms, and tips for highlighting strengths as well as weaknesses. And because there has been so much debate about the shortcomings of various diagnostic tests, you'll also find a look at the fallibility inherent in the testing situation, as well as the positive outcome that can result from such examinations.

Many services are available to support children who have learning disabilities. These include specific classroom modifications and school services such as individualized reading instruction, speech and language therapy, and resource support. In addition, most communities offer private services. This chapter describes various treatments and therapies, and considers the pros and cons of delayed school entry and repeating a grade. Finally, for parents of children whose self-esteem is battered by the daily challenges posed by learning problems, a list of guidelines is included to help you offer the maximum at-home support.

A generation ago, most parents bowed to the authority of school personnel when it came to the fate of the challenged learner. Times have certainly changed! The knowledge gleaned from this chapter can empower you to become actively involved in making decisions that will have a profound effect on your child's well-being not only during her school years, but throughout her life.

THE LEARNING DISABILITY PUZZLE

No hard-and-fast relationship exists between learning preferences and learning disabilities. In fact, educational professionals disagree about what constitutes a learning disability in the first place. Partly because there is no universally accepted battery of tests to confirm such a condition's existence, the definition of "learning disability" can differ not only from state to state, but even between neighboring school systems.

Some districts, for example, consider a thirty-point discrepancy between a child's scores on the visual-motor and language segments of an IQ test to be a reliable indicator of learning disability. (See page 241 for more information on intelligence testing.) Others hold that even a ten-point difference reveals a decided and potentially problematic preference for one sensory modality over another.

The employment of the learning-disabilities label itself is subject to debate. Many authorities subscribe to the idea that *all* learning problems, regardless of severity, are physiological and representative of varying degrees of brain dysfunction. Other experts believe that the majority of learning problems are learning-style related. The learning disabilities cause-and-effect war has, in fact, already spanned many years, and continues to rage on. I encourage my young clients and their families to focus on the positive—the fact that a great many learning problems, regardless of cause, can be minimized via a specific course of learning-style-modification techniques, such as those described throughout this book. How much more inspiring is this approach than the concern that a quirk of genetics has made a child's academic performance a foregone conclusion!

In my experiences with children encountering all types of academic stumbling blocks, I never lose sight of the fact that the issue of learning disabilities is complex and controversial, and that research can be cited to support almost any view of the subject. The definition of learning disability is constantly in flux, and there is no definitive measure of the existence of a learning disability or the severity of a given problem. I can think of many children who have been referred to me with a diagnosis of "severe reading disability." Yet they responded beautifully to therapy focused on improving listening skills and, as a result, caught up to their grade level. On the other hand, I've seen a number of children whose neurological tests revealed no organic cause of their learning problems, and yet failed to progress despite the use of proven approaches. Moreover, I've discovered that it may be necessary to change approaches midstream, working over time to determine what is effective and what is not with a particular child.

Planning out an individualized learning-style program for a child is my top priority. However, making appropriate referrals is also an integral part of a therapy program. When a child's history reveals that there may be an organic cause of her learning problems—an abnormally long labor, for example, or a head injury at a young age—I refer the child to a pediatric neurologist for evaluation. I would make a similar referral for a child who achieves little or no academic headway despite an intensive course of learning-style based therapy. Conversely, family doctors, pediatricians, and neurologists often refer their young patients to me to resolve academic problems.

How does a learning style become so extreme that it leads to a learning disability? Let's look at Amanda, a second grader who came to me for evaluation because she was still reading on a first-grade level. A review of Amanda's IQ testing performed by the psychometrist in her school district revealed a fifteen-point spread between Amanda's verbal and performance abilities—a difference indicative of a learning disability. Viewed from a learning-style perspective, Amanda is a Looker who has not developed the Listener skills critical to classroom success.

The same type of reliance on a single channel for learning can develop in Listeners and Movers, as well. Nine-year-old Peter, for example, wrestles with spelling and math and has very poor handwriting. In contrast to these weak academic areas, his language skills are excellent. Peter's test results show a twenty-five-point discrepancy between verbal and performance scores, in favor of the verbal, characteristic of a Listener who lacks essential visual perceptual and visual-motor skills.

Then there's Evan, an extremely active preschooler who cannot seem to follow directions, has little success with coloring and cutting, and avoids sit-down activities at all costs. Since the diagnosis of "learning disabled" is seldom used until the mastery of academics poses a problem, Evan will not receive this label until the end of his first-grade year. However, it is already evident that he is a Mover with significant delays in language and fine motor skills.

Just as I do with all my clients, I treated Amanda's, Peter's, and Evan's learning problems with educational remedies. As we've seen in earlier chapters, there are a host of strategies that can be utilized to make difficult schoolwork more palatable. Happily, most of the children in my practice show a significant improvement in their skill levels in a surprisingly short time, while enjoying a much needed boost to their self-esteem. In my experience, the positive approach almost always yields positive results.

WHEN THE INTRODUCTION OF ACADEMIC WORK REVEALS A PROBLEM

Why do so many learning problems escape notice until the grade school years? Certainly, a tremendous amount of learning takes place before this time, but usually at a child's own pace and with an attentive parent to handpick experiences that the child likes best. Preacademic work begins in preschool and kindergarten, but for the most part, the emphasis is on socialization and learning through play.

Suddenly, with the advent of first grade comes standardized testing and a curriculum jam-packed with materials to memorize, concepts to grasp, and tasks to perform on demand. Children cannot help but feel the pressure to adjust to a stranger's routine and to meet her expectations, to match the performance of classmates, and—at report-card time—to emerge shining from a subject-by-subject evaluation.

All of this is unfamiliar and stressful territory for a child, and some are better equipped to conform than others. First-grade expectations as simple as sitting through music class can be torture for some children while a delight for others. Similarly, some children master new reading vocabulary on the first try, while others wrestle with the letter-sound connection well into spring. While many children breeze through academic subjects as a result of their learning-style strengths, others find their paths slowed by a learning disability; an attention deficit disorder; or a hearing, vision, or language problem.

If you make every effort to modify your child's learning style through the toys and techniques recommended in this book, and find that she continues to struggle with course work, then, by all means, talk to your child's teacher about diagnostic testing. Most schools offer a number of services that can be a great help to your child. Resource Labs and self-contained special education classes are available in every state. The exact criteria for entry into these programs vary from state to state. However, as a general rule, a student's academic performance must be significantly lower than her intellectual ability would predict. So, for example, a third-grade child with an IQ in the average range would be expected to be reading at third-grade, not first-grade, level.

Diagnostic testing is in order if one or more of the following statements characterize your child's classroom performance. Seek assistance if your child:

- Is in first grade and cannot grasp the names of letters or the sounds they make.

- Is in first grade and cannot write or recall numbers, forgets the sequence of numbers when counting, or cannot recall the meaning of such math symbols as the "plus" (+) or "minus" (−) signs.

- Has great difficulty with one school subject while others come easily.

- Is not performing at grade level in one or more subjects despite average or above-average intelligence.

- Displays emotional distress through frequent crying episodes, school avoidance, loss of self-confidence, or the onset of bed-wetting.

THE FACTS ABOUT DIAGNOSTIC TESTING

Diagnostic testing, carried out by a school psychologist or psychometrist, is used to determine the nature and scope of a child's educational problems. While it is often performed by school district staff, some parents may elect to have it done by clinical or developmental psychologists in private practice or by those affiliated with a local college, health sciences center, or mental health facility.

Obviously, the sooner a learning problem is identified and the appropriate therapeutic services are set into motion, the better the chance that a child will be able to catch up with her classmates. Because parents know their child better than anyone, I routinely recommend that parents make teachers aware of problems they have observed or changes they have noted in their child's attitude toward school or schoolwork.

Components of Diagnostic Testing

An educational assessment covers all aspects of a student's background and classroom performance, and includes some variation of the following:

- The teacher's report
- Classroom observation
- A developmental history
- Intelligence testing

- Achievement testing
- Learning modality testing
- Criterion-referenced testing
- A portfolio of classroom work

The descriptions that follow will help you better understand the purpose and nature of each of these diagnostic tools.

The Teacher's Report

The classroom teacher is usually asked to review a list of classroom behaviors and to check off those that apply to the child being assessed. In some cases, the evaluator may confer with the teacher for additional information.

Classroom Observation

This practice gives the evaluator a firsthand look at a child's classroom behaviors and response to instruction. Of interest are a child's attentiveness, classroom participation, and peer interactions.

A Developmental History

In this component of an assessment, parents furnish information about their child's early development, including developmental milestones such as the age at which she said her first word and was toilet trained. This data paints a picture of a child's development from crib to classroom, and can bring to light early indicators of a learning problem.

Intelligence Testing

The WISC-III is the third generation of the Wechsler Intelligence Scale for Children, the most widely used instrument for intelligence or IQ (intelligence quotient) testing. It is a collection of thirteen subtests divided into two scales, a Verbal Scale and a Performance Scale. The verbal tests are language based, and correspond to Listener skills. The performance scales utilize visual-motor items—Looker skills, in other words. The two IQ scores are compared and then averaged to determine the child's Full Scale IQ.

Achievement Testing

An individual achievement test such as the Wide Range Achievement Test—Revision 3 (WRAT3) is used to determine the grade level at which a child is performing in reading, spelling, and math. The Woodcock-Johnson III (WJ III), another achievement test, allows the examiner to choose from among several subtests designed to detect underlying problems.

Learning Modality Testing

This type of testing, whether formal or informal, is used to identify a child's preferred way of learning. My own Learning Style QuickChecks are an effective means of discovering a child's learning style, and thus the best sensory channel through which to approach skill development.

Criterion-Referenced Testing

This type of testing determines the level of a child's skills. For example, an evaluator might note, "Joshua can multiply single-digit numbers, sound out two-syllable words, and use a table of contents." Such tests can be borrowed from the regular curriculum or made up as needed based on a checklist of skills expected to be mastered at a particular grade level.

A Portfolio of Classroom Work

As part of an assessment, parents are often asked to provide a file containing a sampling of recent schoolwork. A review of test papers, worksheets, artwork, compositions, and creative writing pieces reveal which assignments are most difficult for the child, how much positive and negative feedback the teacher routinely provides, and the aspects of class work in which the child excels.

Understanding a Diagnostic Report

When all tests have been administered and scored, and all observations and interviews have been completed, an evaluator prepares a written report that spells out findings and makes recommendations. As a rule, diagnostic reports are quite detailed and can run as long as ten to fifteen pages in length. It's understandable, then, that parents—stunned by the revelation of a problem and baffled by educational jargon—may leave their final meeting with the examiner confused about the exact nature of their child's problem. Keep in mind that this does not have to be the case. You can play an active role in your child's educational planning. Here are some suggestions:

1. When reviewing a diagnostic report—either in the examiner's office or at home—begin at the end, with the "Summary and Recommendations" section. The compilation of test results that precedes this

section, and can go on for pages, can be confusing, and test data, by itself, is meaningless.

2. Ask the examiner to define any unfamiliar professional jargon that was used in the diagnostic report. Jot down his or her responses, and use these notes to refresh your memory when you reread the report a few days later.

3. Ask permission to tape the session during which test results are explained and recommendations are made. The scope of the discussion and the specialized terminology used make it virtually impossible to digest all the information at once.

4. Make sure to request a copy of the report to reread and absorb at your own pace at home.

5. After you have reread the report, feel free to call the examiner with additional questions or comments.

6. Guard against feeling intimidated by the professionals. Remember that you know your child better than anyone, and that you are an important part of the assessment team. If you feel that some parts of the evaluation simply do not "fit," express your concerns before the test results and recommendations become part of your child's permanent record.

Once members of the assessment team are in agreement about recommendations, their proposals are put into writing in the form of an Individualized Education Plan, or IEP. This plan may include the use of support personnel such as a speech-language pathologist, learning disabilities teacher, occupational therapist, and/or reading specialist. Consultations with outside medical professionals such as an audiologist or developmental optometrist may be recommended, as well. (See "Who Are the Experts?" on page 251).

The "Down Side" of Educational Testing

It's important to be aware that test results can be inaccurate. To begin with, the validity of the entire test battery depends upon the experience and expertise of the examiner. Also, a child can have an "off" day and fail to display her actual potential, or may suffer from test anxiety that disrupts her performance. The following considerations should also be kept in mind:

- While intelligence testing attempts to separate innate ability from the effects of environment, most tests reward experience. This means, for example, that a child who has had frequent opportunities to work puzzles at home or school is likely to do better with a particular test puzzle than will a child who lacks this experience.

- Children from cultural and socioeconomic minority groups may show a weaker performance on individual test batteries. Intelligence tests, in particular, have been criticized as largely reflecting white middle-class values and attitudes, and, in fact, may be administered by a professional who does not understand the child's home culture and language.

- The intimidating nature of the test situation can cause an anxious child's performance to break down. The silence of the testing room along with the examiner's unfamiliar face, no-nonsense air, briefcase, and stopwatch can all be threatening to a child.

- Speed is considered a virtue in IQ testing. This means that a child who daydreams, contemplates answers carefully, or does not perform well under pressure will be penalized.

- The Verbal and Performance Scales of the WISC-III (see page 241) correspond to Listener and Looker skills, respectively. Since scores can be expected to reflect the subject's learning preference, both of these scales penalize Movers.

- By their very nature, IQ scores set up expectations in the minds of teachers, parents, and children. Too much may be demanded of high-scoring children, or too little from those who earn low scores.

Translating a Diagnostic Report With the Emphasis on Learning Style

In most cases, it's possible to translate the summary of a child's diagnostic report into learning-style terminology. Instead of a statement such as "Kristin exhibits auditory perceptual difficulties," the focus would be on her strong suit: "Kristin is a Looker by learning style, highly attuned to visual stimuli." Focusing on learning style strengths and weaknesses clarifies the type of help needed. For example, we know that Looker children need to improve Listener skills, so consulting a speech-language pathologist would be in order for a child with a diagnosed language disability. Likewise, we know that a Listener child tends to have lagging visual skills, so an examination by a developmental optometrist would be a first step in remediation.

Following is an example of a typical summary from an educational report and its learning-style-focused counterpart. This report concerns Sarah, a third-grade student who is eight years, four months of age.

Typical Summary

Sarah is a child of average intellectual ability. Her reading problem affects all academic subjects. Her auditory perceptual skills related to reading are at a beginning first-grade level; her actual reading level is second grade, second month. Sarah demonstrates short-term memory problems, and her ability to attend breaks down in the presence of noise. She has difficulty memorizing math facts. Her strengths include visual memory and eye-hand skills.

Learning-Style Summary

Sarah is a Looker by learning style. She has normal intelligence, excellent visual memory and visual-motor skills, is a good speller, and is strong in math computations. Sarah would benefit from auditory training with a school speech-language pathologist to teach her how to isolate sounds and blend them together for reading. Preferential seating near the teacher could help improve her ability to follow verbal instructions.

Clearly, when a diagnostic report focuses on learning style, the emphasis is on the positive. Recommendations naturally follow, with the goal being to build on areas of strength and to develop lagging learning-style skills.

COMMON CONDITIONS THAT CAN DISRUPT THE NORMAL LEARNING PROCESS

Some deterrents to academic progress are more common than others. The explanations provided below will help you become familiar with some of the more frequently occurring problems that disrupt the learning process. Of course, if one of these obstacles is facing your child, you'll want to increase your understanding of the problem by performing further research.

Asperger Syndrome

A neurological disorder, Asperger Syndome (AS) is characterized by a severe and sustained impairment in social interaction—in other words, a lack of social skills. In addition, children with AS often demonstrate motor delays, clumsiness, and repetitive patterns of behavior, interests, and activities. In the past, this disorder was often misdiagnosed as attention deficit disorder or autism.

Autism

Autism is a disorder originating in infancy and characterized by self-absorption, the inability to interact socially, repetitive behaviors, and severe language dysfunction. Because the onset of symptoms is often early, autism may be diagnosed in the first two years of life.

Attention Deficit Disorders

A child diagnosed with Attention Deficit Disorder (ADD) has concentration and task-completion problems. When a component of overactivity and inability to control motor behavior is also present, the diagnosis is Attention Deficit-Hyperactivity Disorder (ADHD). In either case, the child cannot focus attention sufficiently to be successful in a classroom setting.

Central Auditory Processing Disorders

Children with Central Auditory Processing (CAP) problems have no hearing loss, yet have difficulty discriminating and integrating what they hear. CAP problems often go undiagnosed until a child enters school and is exposed to intense listening tasks, such as following multiple verbal directions, learning phonics, and answering comprehension questions.

Developmental Vision Problems

A child can have 20/20 vision yet still have visual-processing or visual-perceptual problems that hamper schoolwork. A child who becomes quickly fatigued when reading, tends to skip words or sentences, or makes many errors when copying from chalkboard to paper may have a developmental vision problem.

Hearing Impairment

Even a mild hearing impairment can dramatically disrupt the learning process. Early signs of hearing loss include lack of attention, difficulty following directions, and turning or cocking the head. Children who have frequent ear infections in childhood are most at risk for hearing impairment.

Language Disorders

As a communication system, language requires the understanding and use of gestures; words; and, later, written symbols. In the first few years of a child's life, language disorders usually manifest as difficulty understanding what is said, and difficulty expressing oneself verbally. Children with language disorders are usually late in saying a first word and combining words into sentences.

Learning Disabilities

A child who has a learning disability (LD) has average or above-average intelligence, normal hearing and vision, and no primary emotional problems that could disrupt the learning process. Despite these facts, the LD child is unable to perform academically on par with her intellectual potential because of problems with attention, perception, memory, and/or thinking.

Reading Disabilities and Dyslexia

The terms *reading disability* and *dyslexia* both refer to a child's inability to read at grade level or to read at all, despite the child's normal intellectual ability. Reading is primarily a language-based skill, so children with reading disabilities have underlying language or learning disabilities that interfere with the mastery of reading. Signs of reading disability can occur as early as kindergarten, and include difficulty recalling the names of letters of the alphabet and the sounds made by these letters.

Sensory Integration Dysfunction

Children who play too rough, resist being touched, are uncoordinated, or are ultrasensitive to noise and the sensations of heat and cold may have Sensory Integration Dysfunction. This problem is considered to be the result of a poorly integrated nervous system.

Visual Impairment

The visually impaired child is one whose vision is limited to such an extent that she requires educational modifications and adaptations in order to learn. Materials are utilized to teach through sensory channels other than vision—by way of hearing and touch, in other words.

TREATMENTS THAT CAN HELP

Once the reason for a child's learning difficulties has been isolated, team members involved in her educational planning formulate a set of goals, and appropriate support services are scheduled. Such services may include classroom modifications, speech-language therapy, individualized reading instruction, time in a learning disabilities lab, and even peer tutoring. Treatments outside of the school setting can help as well. These fall into two categories: those that ready a child to learn, and those that teach specific skills and subject matter. Not all treatments work for every child. Sometimes it's necessary for parents to try out several courses of action before they discover the one or ones that are most helpful.

What follows is a look at some of the currently available treatments and the professionals who utilize them. The inset "Who Are the Experts?" on page 251 details the credentials and roles of the various experts involved.

Treatments That Ready a Child to Learn

Language Therapy

Language therapy improves a child's ability to process language and express herself verbally. Exercises and activities are designed to build vocabulary, enhance listening skills, and strengthen auditory memory. Auditory training, a component of language therapy, is used to improve a child's ability to isolate sounds, and sequence and blend them for reading. A speech-language pathologist is the professional to consult for language therapy.

Medication

When inattention; hyperactivity; a behavior problem; or a child's mood disturbance—anxiety or depression, for instance—is so severe that it interferes with school success, medication may be prescribed. Many new medications are available to treat a variety of conditions, and some older medications are being utilized in new ways. When chosen appropriately and carefully monitored, medication can mean the difference between a child's academic success and failure. Family physicians, pediatricians, and child psychiatrists and neurologists are the experts to consult when medication is being considered.

Nutritional Therapy

Some children who are referred to as "learning disabled" or "hyperactive" may actually have specific nutritional deficits—vitamin or mineral deficiencies, for example—that can interfere with learning. Other children have food allergies that result in inattention and poor classroom performance. Still others have a diet that is too heavy in refined sugar, leading to unstable blood-sugar levels and fluctuations in activity levels.

A nutritional evaluation by a nutritionist or dietician can determine a particular child's dietary needs, and a personalized diet can be designed to eliminate allergens while supplying needed nutrients in appropriate amounts.

Occupational Therapy

An occupational therapist (OT) provides services for children who have fine motor, coordination, and/or sensory integration problems. He or she teaches self-help, social, and leisure skills to promote independence. OT services require a doctor's prescription.

Physical Therapy

A physical therapist (PT) provides services for children who have gross motor, coordination, and/or sensory integration problems. A PT relies on therapeutic exercises and massage to help a child improve or regain mobility. PT services require a doctor's prescription.

Vision Therapy

Performed by a developmental optometrist, vision therapy comprises a series of optical training exercises designed to improve a child's vision. These exercises can enhance the child's ability to perform extended periods of close work, as well as to copy work from chalkboard to paper.

Treatments That Teach
Specific Academic Skills or Subject Matter

Professional Tutoring

Tutoring is usually provided after school hours by a classroom teacher, learning disabilities teacher, or reading specialist. The intent is to provide extra one-on-one academic support. Typically, a tutor reviews assignments and makes use of multisensory materials to teach and reinforce subject matter in order to keep a child on pace with classmates.

Reading Therapy

Reading therapy may be carried out by a classroom teacher, reading teacher, or speech-language pathologist. Regardless of the expert involved, the goal is to utilize special methods and techniques to teach reading basics when classroom instruction has failed. Ideally, a child's learning style is taken into consideration in planning a therapeutic approach to reading.

THE BENEFITS OF DELAYED SCHOOL ENTRY
AND GRADE REPETITION

Children who attempt to master academics without sufficiently developed auditory and/or visual skills, or without the required emotional and physical maturity, are destined to have a more difficult time than their peers. When a child is chronologically younger than most of her classmates or has lagging skills that threaten to undermine her academic efforts, there is definitely a case for granting her more time to

Who Are the Experts?

Should you wish to consult an expert for help with a problem that appears to hamper your child's ability to learn, the following professionals can be contacted directly, or you may be referred to them by either a diagnostician or your family physician or pediatrician.

Allergist. This medical doctor specializes in environmental medicine—the diagnosis and treatment of allergic reactions activated by air-borne elements, foods, and other substances.

Audiologist. This specialist holds a master's degree or doctorate in audiology. He or she tests hearing, and fits and repairs hearing aids.

Developmental optometrist. A developmental optometrist holds a doctor of optometry degree and is specially trained to work with children. This specialist tests vision as it relates to school performance, and prescribes corrective lenses and/or eye exercises.

Developmental psychologist. This specialist holds a doctorate in psychology and works specifically with children. He or she administers and interprets psychological tests with a focus on child development and learning.

Learning disabilities teacher. This specialized teacher holds a bachelor's or master's degree in special education. He or she plans individualized instructional programs and sets educational goals for children based on their specific learning disability.

Nutritionist. This health care professional specializes in nutritional sciences. Some nutritionists are also registered dieticians, holding a bachelor's degree in nutrition or a related field and having passed a national exam.

Occupational therapist. An occupational therapist possesses a bachelor's or master's degree in occupational therapy. This specialist works with the physically and mentally challenged, teaching self-help, fine motor, and social skills to promote independence.

Ophthalmologist. This medical doctor specializes in the diagnosis and treatment of diseases of the eye.

Pediatric neurologist. This medical doctor is trained to work with children, and specializes in the diagnosis and treatment of childhood disorders of the nervous system.

Physical therapist. A physical therapist holds a bachelor's or master's degree in physical therapy. He or she uses therapeutic exercises and massage to help patients improve or regain physical functioning.

Psychometrist. A psychometrist holds a master's degree in education or a related field, and is certified in psychometry by a state department of education. This specialist, found in schools and diagnostic centers, administers and interprets diagnostic tests to pinpoint learning problems.

School psychologist. A school psychologist holds a master's degree or doctorate in school psychology. He or she administers and interprets diagnostic tests to determine developmental delays, learning disabilities, and/or emotional problems; counsels students; and consults with classroom teachers.

Speech-language pathologist. This specialist holds a master's degree or doctorate in the field of communication disorders. Speech-language pathologists—who may be found in a school system, agency, or private practice—evaluate and provide therapy for disorders of language, speech, voice, articulation, and auditory processing.

mature. This can be accomplished by delaying school entry or, in some cases, repeating a grade. The subject of kindergarten readiness is controversial and emotion-charged, and the issue of grade repetition is even more so. This is largely due to a child's possible negative reaction to her classmates' being promoted when she is not. Sometimes the concern is not so much the child's reaction, but rather how the parent will feel.

In my experience, particularly with five- through eight-year-olds, when delayed school entry or repetition is handled sensitively, the potential academic gains far outweigh any social stigma attached to being "left back."

Delaying School Entry

Many school districts perform a readiness screening several months prior to the start of kindergarten to identify those four- and five-year-olds who may not yet be able to hold their own in the classroom. A typical screening might require a child to stack blocks, copy shapes, draw a person, walk a straight line, identify colors, and count to ten. Difficulty with tasks such as these can be an early indicator of physical immaturity, or of motor and/or language delays that can impede a child's progress in the first year of school.

In other districts, this same type of assessment is carried out by kindergarten teachers shortly after school begins. Based on assessment information and observations of classroom performance, teachers can usually tell by mid-year which students could benefit from an extra year to mature before beginning first grade. If parents have concerns about their kindergartener's progress, this is the time to compare notes with the teacher and to seek solutions.

Whether a child's entry into kindergarten is delayed by a year or she spends a year in an extended readiness program—sometimes referred to as a "transitional" or "developmental" first grade—the extra time can greatly improve a child's potential for academic success. First, visual and auditory abilities—Looker and Listener skills, in other words—are given an extra year to develop before the child takes on the challenge of schoolwork. Second, another year allows parents an opportunity to develop their child's strong suit and build up lagging skills via the activities recommended in this book. With time and specially chosen learning-style strategies, many children are able to "catch up" with peers before entering first grade, and thus are often able to avoid academic problems. Keep in mind, too, that it is almost always better to have your child be one of the oldest in her class than one of the youngest.

Repeating a Grade

Occasionally, physical immaturity or lagging skills simply are not identified when a child is in preschool or kindergarten. There can be many reasons for this. Perhaps the child is not far enough behind her peers for the problem to be evident, or perhaps a parent or teacher is overly optimistic about the child's ability to catch up. Whatever the reason, there are some times when a child can benefit from repeating a grade. The older the child, the more complex this solution becomes, though, and regardless of the child's age, parents should confer with the teacher, the school psychologist, an outside professional, and sometimes the child herself before any action is taken.

To be sure, grade repetition is not the answer for every struggling learner. When appropriate, and when sensitively handled, however, it can sometimes make the difference between satisfactory mainstream school progress and a child's being labeled as "learning disabled."

There are instances, of course, when a child is simply too old for grade repetition to be considered. She may have begun school a year later than her peers or have spent a year in a developmental class. Or she may be approaching adolescence with fragile self-esteem that cannot withstand any additional blows. When repeating a grade is no longer an option, there are still steps that can be taken to make your child's academic life easier. Here are a few suggestions.

- Provide as much support as possible in the form of Resource Lab or Learning Disabilities Lab assistance, after-school tutoring, and the use of multisensory materials.

- Reduce expectations for your child's academic performance. She may not be able to perform grade-level work in a particular subject even with support.

- Build self-esteem through nonacademic pursuits such as music lessons, horseback riding, or team sports.

- Pre-tutor your child by reading ahead in a problem subject to familiarize her with new vocabulary and concepts.

- Insist that your child's teacher make classroom modifications appropriate to the grade level. These can include oral testing, shortened assignments, permission to take tests without time restrictions, the assistance of a calculator, preferential seating, and/or assignment of a peer tutor.

GUIDELINES FOR SUPPORTING A CHILD WHO HAS LEARNING PROBLEMS

Whatever the cause of a child's learning problem, and regardless of the steps taken to resolve the problem, it's important to realize that classroom difficulties result in emotional repercussions. Your child will require sensitive handling both at home and at school to prevent damage to her self-esteem. Here are some suggestions to help you provide your challenged learner with a supportive, low-stress environment.

- Focus on enjoying the time you and your child spend together. Be sure to include one-to-one time that is not related to schoolwork.

- Make your child aware of her strengths, and provide opportunities for her to develop them. If she's a good runner, urge her to try soccer. If she loves animals, seek out farms or zoos to visit, consider riding lessons, or get a family pet.

- Boost self-esteem by encouraging self-reliance. As early as possible, urge your child to select her own clothes, choose what she wants to eat, and express her own ideas. Be sure to ask, "What do you think?" and "How do you feel?"

- Be aware of any negative influences at your child's school, like children who tease, a teacher who's overly critical, or homework assignments that are too time-consuming. Then act as an advocate for your child. When you become aware of a problem—say, that your child's speech therapy conflicts with her favorite music class—call for a conference with her teacher to seek a solution.

- Make your child aware of how she learns best, and stay nearby for support during homework sessions. Let your child occasionally take on the role of teacher while you play student. For example, suggest that *she* dictate her spelling words to *you* and then correct your efforts.

- Do your best to keep your own emotions in check when you take on the role of teacher at home. Exclamations such as, "Don't you listen when I explain things?" or "You're not even trying!" can be devastating to a child. If work periods together are frustrating for you both, then by all means hire a tutor. Learning specialists can be hired and replaced if need be, but the all-important role of parent is yours alone!

- Remember that patience is the key when working with a struggling learner. Try to keep your expectations realistic, accept that your child will occasionally lose ground, focus on accomplishments, and be generous with praise.

- Because children with learning problems already expend so much energy trying to keep up with their peers, they may find competition distressing. To prevent further erosion of your child's self-esteem, steer her away from situations such as competitive sports or, for an older child, the debate team.

- Provide your child with plenty of multisensory material—that is, material that stimulates more than one channel of learning. Earlier chapters of this book will guide you in identifying your child's learning style and selecting toys, games, and techniques that will develop specific skills.

- Help your child relax once school is out. Guard against tying up all of her free time with appointments, lessons, and therapies, and allow plenty of opportunities for her to play by herself or with friends, as she chooses.

As a parent, you want the very best for your child, but it really doesn't pay to agonize over your struggling learner's future. No one can accurately predict the effects of time, maturation, and therapeutic intervention on a child's academic potential, and there's nothing to be gained from worrying about your six-year-old's college or career possibilities. It's far better to stay in the present, provide support, acknowledge frustrations, and celebrate even the smallest of successes together.

Conclusion

During the course of reading this book, you have come to know Looker, Listener, and Mover children of all ages. You've noticed, no doubt, that the nine-month-old Listener in Chapter Two and the nine-*year*-old Listener in Chapter Seven are, in effect, highly similar children, differing only in the scope of their everyday activities and the particular toys to which they are attracted.

As similar as children who share a learning style are—even when they're a decade or more apart in age—children whose learning styles differ will have very *dissimilar* personalities, no matter how close their birth dates. The principal purpose of the case-study descriptions has been to highlight the innate differences between children who are born with a preference for visual stimulation (Lookers), those who favor and respond to sound and language (Listeners), and those attuned from birth to touch and movement (Movers).

When parents do not identify a child's learning style and intervene to stimulate less-favored sensory areas, that child's reliance on his inborn learning preference will continue into the school years, limiting learning options and, in some cases, resulting in a learning disability. Moreover, the child's learning style will influence more than academics, and, in fact, will affect the whole child from the time he first begins to interact with his environment. The child with the strongest self-esteem is the one who achieves not only academic success, but also social competence and confidence in his athletic ability.

Because children's perceptions and responses are dictated by learning style, very few attain developmental balance on their own. That's where parents come in. Right from the start, you can help your child by providing a made-to-order combination of toys and sensory experiences. Ideally, a child's interactions and play will first enhance his preferred learning style—as in the case of a Listener toddler whose parents form a play group to provide the access to other children that so delights their sociable son. However, as early as possible, parents must also start developing less favored ways of learning through appropriate multisensory activities. The toy, game, and software lists that appear in Chapters Two through Eight will provide you, the parents, with the learning experiences needed to round out your child's development.

It's ideal, of course, to begin guiding a child's play in the very first year of life. Yet even adolescence is not too late to effect a positive change. Just keep in mind that the focus of parents' efforts must shift somewhat according to their child's age. Until the kindergarten years, parents should aim to achieve a balance of abilities, helping their child become "well rounded" and equally comfortable with visual, auditory, and tactile stimuli. When academic work is introduced in the primary grades, though, the goal should become helping the child master reading, spelling, and math via multisensory materials that appeal to all styles of learners.

Chapter Nine revealed a number of learning problems that surface with the introduction of academics, usually during first grade. Some children so strongly favor one style of learning over the others that they become "stuck" in a preferred way of learning. When this occurs, professional intervention and specialized programming is required for academic success. But, again, learning strategies and multisensory materials will come in quite handy. In fact, even when a disability is organic in nature, the materials and tactics presented in this book can help to minimize academic problems.

A child's post-high school plans are also dictated by learning style. The child who experiences success in the classroom is certainly the most likely to consider college. Yet, even among this group, social confidence, family relationships, and specific academic strengths—all of which are offshoots of learning style—influence the choices made in twelfth grade. Will a student thrill at the prospect of a large university where lecture classes number in the hundreds, or be drawn to the more personal atmosphere of a private institution? Once enrolled, will he become involved in intercollegiate sports, or find his niche in student government? Will he declare a major as a second-semester freshman, or follow a liberal arts curriculum throughout his four years?

And what of the high school seniors who opt for vocational training or the military, or choose to forgo higher education altogether? Among this group, as well, the choices are many. The selection of physical labor over a desk job or of a high-profile trade over a behind-the-scenes position is as much a function of learning style as is the choice of leisure-time activities.

It's easy to imagine a Looker studying in his single room at a small college renowned for its fine arts programs. And we can just as easily picture a Listener quickly achieving his goal of membership in the leading fraternity of a sprawling university, or a Mover delighting in a landscaping business that enables him to spend workdays outdoors while allowing for rainy-day gym workouts and racquetball games. In each case, the individual is making choices based on likes and dislikes, strengths and weaknesses that reflect his inborn learning style.

Certainly, parents should never lose sight of the fact that their children are unique individuals who deserve unconditional love throughout life's struggles and successes. However, this book is all about *increasing* children's options for the future, and I hope I've convinced you that your child needn't be limited to typical Looker, Listener, or Mover career paths because of his innate learning style. With your help, for example, your Listener child may develop sufficient Looker skills to consider careers in medicine or banking—options that probably would not be open to him without timely learning-style-based intervention.

Can you *really* maximize your child's learning ability? Absolutely! And in doing so, you'll be giving your child one of life's greatest gifts— a loving parent's time and attention. This book has achieved its purpose if you are now in closer touch with your child and eager to have a hand in guiding his learning experiences. I wish you all the best!

Recommended Reading List

The following books, each related to personal learning styles in children, can provide you with additional information about inborn sensory preference and its effect on learning ability. Even though each author's professional perspective may differ somewhat from mine, each has documented studies and/or personal experiences that parallel my work with young Lookers, Listeners, and Movers.

Dunn, Rita. *How to Implement and Supervise a Learning Style Program.* Alexandria, VA: Association for Supervision and Curriculum Development, 1998.

Shows how to teach children in a classroom via their learning-style preference.

Gurian, Michael and Patricia Henley. *Boys and Girls Learn Differently!: A Guide for Teachers and Parents.* San Francisco: Jossey-Bass, 2001.

Discusses inherent differences in the ways boys and girls learn.

Restak, Richard and David Grubin. *The Secret Life of the Brain.* Joseph Henry Press, 2001. (Companion volume to a PBS series. Also available on DVD).

Explores the role of the brain in learning.

Silver, Harvey, Richard Strong, and Matthew Perini. *So Each May Learn: Integrating Learning Styles and Multiple Intelligences.* Association for Supervision and Curriculum Development, 2000.

Examines learning styles in the classroom at all grade levels and in all content areas.

Tobias, Cynthia Ulrich. *Every Child Can Succeed: Making the Most of Your Child's Learning Style.* Focus on the Family Publishing, 1999.

Shows how to motivate children based on learning style.

Willis, Mariaemma and Victoria Kindle-Hodson. *Discover Your Child's Learning Style: Children Learn in Unique Ways—Here's the Key to Every Child's Learning Success.* Prima Communications Inc., 1999.

Uses a workbook format to present do-it-yourself learning style assessments.

Buyer's Guide

Many of the books, toys, and games recommended in this book can be purchased in book and toy stores. But when your local merchants don't carry the desired item, you'll usually be able to order it online or over the phone. The following list will guide you in contacting the appropriate manufacturer or distributor. Whenever possible, we have included both a website and a phone number. You will note, though, that some manufacturers have provided only one means of contacting their company. Moreover, in some cases, although a website is provided, you will find that you cannot place orders online. Instead, the website will direct you to retailers from whom you can purchase the product.

Before you begin ordering recommended products for your learner, keep in mind that the Internet provides a wonderful means of "shopping around." So, especially when buying a higher-priced item, please don't hesitate to use your favorite search engine to locate the best price for the toy, game, book, or software you want for your child.

Amazon.com
Website: www.amazon.com

BabiesЯUs
Website: www.babiesrus.com

Baby Einstein
Phone: 800-793-1454
Website:
   www.babyeinstein.com

Barnes & Noble
Website: www.bn.com

Broderbund
Phone: 800-395-0277
Website: www.broderbund.com

Childcraft
Phone: 800-631-5652
Website: www.childcraft.com

Cranium
Phone: 206-652-9708
Website: www.playcranium.com

Enchanted Learning
Website:
   www.enchantedlearning.com

Encore Software
Phone: 310-768-1800
Website:
   www.encoresoftware.com

Endless Games
Phone: 201-386-9465
Website:
   www.endlessgames.com

ETA/Cuisenaire
Phone: 800-445-5985
Website: www.etacuisenaire.com

Fisher-Price
Phone: 800-432-5437
Website: www.fisherprice.com

Genius Babies
Website:
   www.geniusbabies.com

Hap Palmer
Phone: 818-885-0200
Website: www.happalmer.com

Hasbro
Phone: 800-327-8264
Websites: www.hasbro.com
   www.hasbropreschool.com

International Playthings
Website: www.cambitoys.com

JC Penney
Phone: 800-222-6161
Website: www.jcpenney.com

Kay-Bee Toys
Website: www.kbtoys.com

Lakeshore Learning Company
Phone: 800-778-4456
Website:
   www.lakeshorelearning.com

Lamaze Toy
Website: www.geniusbabies.com

Leap Frog
Phone: 800-701-5327
Website: www.leapfrog.com

Lego
Phone: 800-453-4652
Website: www.lego.com

Lincoln Logs
Website:
   http://lincolnlogs.knex.com

Little Tikes
Phone: 800-321-0183
Website: www.littletikes.com

Manhattan Baby/Manhattan Toy
Phone: 800-541-1345
Website:
   www.manhattantoy.com

National School Products
Phone: 800-627-9393
Website: www.nationalschool
  products.com

Neurosmith
Phone: 800-220-3669
Website: www.neurosmith.com

Patch Products
Website:
  www.patchproducts.com

Playskool
Phone: 800-752-9755
Website: www.playskool.com

Pressman Toy Corporation
Phone: 732-545-4000
Website: www.pressmantoy.com

Radio Flyer
Website: www.redwagons.com

Riverdeep
Phone: 415-763-4700
  or 617-778-7600
Website: www.riverdeep.net

Saddleback Educational, Inc.
Phone: 888-735-2225
Website: www.sdlback.com

Sassy
Phone: 616-243-0767
Website: www.sassybaby.com

Scholastic, Inc.
Phone: 800-733-5572
Website: www.scholastic.com

Today's Kids
Phone: 800-2588-8697
Website: www.todayskids.com

Topics Entertainment
Website: www.topics-ent.com

Toys to Grow On
Phone: 800-987-4454
Website:
  www.toystogrowon.com

Workman Publishing
Phone: 212-254-5900
Website:
  www.workmanweb.com

Index

Achievement testing, 241
ADD. *See* Attention Deficit
 Disorder.
ADHD. *See* Attention Deficit-
 Hyperactivity Disorder.
Allergists, 251
AS. *See* Asperger Syndrome.
Asperger Syndrome (AS), 246
Attention Deficit Disorder (ADD),
 246
Attention Deficit-Hyperactivity
 Disorder (ADHD), 246
Audiologists, 251
Auditory learners. *See* Listeners.
Auditory training, 248–249
Autism, 246

Babies. *See* Infants.
Brain: The Last Frontier (Restak), 11

Central Auditory Processing
 (CAP) disorders, 246
Child care, choosing. *See* Day care.
Computer skills, developing, 186
Criterion-referenced testing, 242

Day care

child's behavior during, 54–55
 for Listeners, 53
 for Lookers, 52–53
 for Movers, 53–54
 personnel, communicating
  with, 54–55
Delayed school entry, 250,
 252–253
Developmental vision problems.
 See Vision problems; Vision
 therapy.
Diagnostic testing
 components of, 240–242
 diagnostic report, 242–245
 need for, 239–240
 validity of, 243–244
Dunn, Kenneth, 11
Dunn, Rita, 11
Dyslexia, 247

Educational testing. *See* Diagnostic
 testing.
Eighth grade, 193–231
 choosing extracurricular
  activities in, 213–215
 homework strategies for,
  218–221

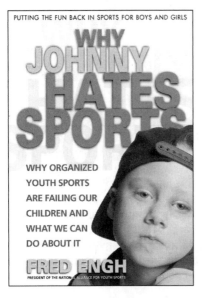

PUTTING THE FUN BACK IN SPORTS FOR BOYS AND GIRLS

WHY ORGANIZED YOUTH SPORTS ARE FAILING OUR CHILDREN AND WHAT WE CAN DO ABOUT IT

FRED ENGH

PRESIDENT OF THE NATIONAL ALLIANCE FOR YOUTH SPORTS

WHY JOHNNY HATES SPORTS

Why Organized Youth Sports Are Failing Our Children and What We Can Do About It

by Fred Engh

"Mom! Do I really have to go to the game? Can't I just stay home?" All across this country, an ever-increasing number of children are dropping out of organized sports—soccer, baseball, football, swimming, and more. Not because they don't like to play, but because the system they play in is failing them. Written by one of this country's leading advocates of children's sports, *Why Johnny Hates Sports* is the first book to look at the growing problems inherent in the way we introduce our children to sports.

In this timely book, Fred Engh examines the unsettling state of youth sports in America. He explains how and why many of the original goals of the youth leagues have been affected by today's win-at-all-costs attitude. He then documents the negative physical and psychological impact that parents, coaches, and administrators can have on children. Most important, he provides a wide variety of proven solutions to each and every one of the problems covered. Throughout the book, Engh relates stories drawn from hundreds of real life experiences.

Why Johnny Hates Sports is both an exposé of abuses and a call to arms. It clearly shows us a serious problem that has been going on too long—a problem that, until now, has been tolerated by most, with little concern for its effect on our children. It also provides practical answers that can alter the destructive course that youth sports have taken.

Fred Engh has been involved in youth sports for over thirty years—as a coach, athletic director, and sports educator. In 1981, he founded a national program dedicated to the training and certification of volunteer coaches—a program that has now trained over one million coaches. This group has evolved into the National Alliance for Youth Sports, a nonprofit organization that works to provide safe and fun sports for America's youth.

$14.95 •224 pages • 6 x 9-inch quality paperback • Parenting/Sports • ISBN 0-7570-0041-X

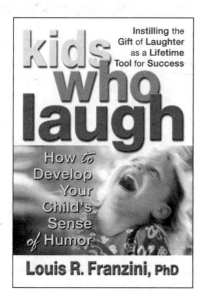

Instilling the Gift of Laughter as a Lifetime Tool for Success

How to Develop Your Child's Sense of Humor

Louis R. Franzini, PhD

KIDS WHO LAUGH

How to Develop Your Child's Sense of Humor

Louis R. Franzini, PhD

Some are born with a sense of humor—most children are not. As children grow, their use of humor is acquired through various experiences. Unfortunately, most parents never really focus on this important characteristic and have no idea how to instill this learned behavior. *Kids Who Laugh* is the first book to examine the psychology of humor in children and explore the many benefits humor has to offer, including self-confidence, coping skills, self-control, and so much more.

Most important, *Kids Who Laugh* presents the actual tools that parents can use to develop a healthy sense of humor. The author provides a wide array of easy-to-do and fun exercises designed for parents to use with their children, as well as simple strategies that parents can apply to create a customized program for their children. Throughout the book, parents will find practical suggestions, ideas, and advice on incorporating humor into their child's life—as well as a host of resources that can help them do so. Whether it's dealing with teasers or simply making new friends, laughter can make an important difference. With *Kids Who Laugh,* you can give your child a very special present that will last a lifetime—the gift of laughter.

Dr. Louis R. Franzini received his PhD in clinical psychology from the University of Pittsburgh. He is a professor of psychology at San Diego State University in California, where he has taught for over twenty-five years. For over ten years, he has focused his attention on humor research. Dr. Franzini has carefully observed stand-up comedians, has been a stand-up comedian, and has served as president of Laughmasters and Toastmasters International Club. He is the author of two books and numerous articles, and has appeared on radio and television shows throughout North America.

$14.95 • 192 pages • 6 x 9-inch paperback • Parenting / Psychology • ISBN 0-7570-0008-8